THE
VIOLE SE
OF V. MEN

In 17th & 18th Century Britain

A Dog, a Woman, a Walnut Tree;
The more they're beaten, the better they be.

Anon – Old English Proverb

Happy are you, reader, if you do not belong to this sex to which all good is
forbidden.

Égalité des hommes et des femmes – Marie de Gournay (1622)

How wretched is a woman's fate,
No happy change her fortune knows;
Subject to man in every state,
How can she then be free from woes?

Woman's Hard Fate – Anon (1733)

Woman – a pleasing but a short-lived flower, Too soft for business and too weak
for power: A wife in bondage, or neglected maid; Despised if ugly; if she's fair –
betrayed.

Essay on Woman – Mary Leapor (1722–46)

Women are not so well united as to form an Insurrection. They are for the most
part wise enough to love their Chains, and to discern how becomingly they fit.

Some Reflections upon Marriage – Mary Astell (1666–1731)

Thy husband is thy lord, thy life, thy keeper, Thy head, thy sovereign …
A woman owes her husband the same loyalty a subject owes his king.

The Taming of the Shrew – William Shakespeare (1564–1616)

… the Moon hath no Light but what it borrows from the Sun, so women have no
strength nor light of Understanding, but what is given them from Men.

The World's Olio – Margaret Cavendish, Duchess of Newcastle (circa 1624–74)

THE
VIOLENT ABUSE
OF WOMEN

In 17th & 18th Century Britain

GEOFFREY PIMM

PEN & SWORD **HISTORY**

AN IMPRINT OF PEN & SWORD BOOKS LTD
YORKSHIRE – PHILADELPHIA

First published in Great Britain in 2019 by
PEN AND SWORD HISTORY
an imprint of
Pen and Sword Books Ltd
Yorkshire - Philadelphia

HB ISBN 978 1 52673 954 4
PB ISBN 978 1 52675 162 1

Printed and bound in the UK by TJ International

Typeset in Times New Roman 10/13 by
Aura Technology and Software Services, India

Pen & Sword Books Ltd incorporates the imprints of Pen & Sword
Archaeology, Atlas, Aviation, Battleground, Discovery,
Family History, History, Maritime, Military, Naval, Politics, Railways,
Select, Social History, Transport, True Crime, Claymore Press,
Frontline Books, Leo Cooper, Praetorian Press, Remember When,
Seaforth Publishing and Wharncliffe.

For a complete list of Pen and Sword titles please contact
Pen and Sword Books Limited
47 Church Street, Barnsley, South Yorkshire, S70 2AS, England
E-mail: enquiries@pen-and-sword.co.uk
Website: www.pen-and-sword.co.uk

By the same author - *The Dark Side of Samuel Pepys* (Pen and Sword History, 2018).

Contents

Introduction

The seventeenth and eighteenth centuries are the gateway between the medieval world and the modern, centuries when western societies moved from an age governed principally by religion and superstition, to an age directed principally by reason and understanding. By the end of the eighteenth century, mankind had acquired varying degrees of awareness of logarithms, electricity, calculus, universal gravitation, and the laws governing the motion of physical objects, liquids and gasses. The telescope and the microscope had been invented, enabling the new sciences to examine the greatest and the smallest components of creation. Many of the names that are synonymous with scientific and philosophical progress are to be found there. In the seventeenth century: Galileo, Kepler, Descartes, Pascal, Boyle, Huygens, Leeuenhoek, Leibniz and of course Isaac Newton. In the eighteenth century: Franklin, Herschel, Jenner, and Volta. Messier mapped the heavens and Priestly buried the theory of 'phlogiston' by discovering oxygen. The first practical steam engine was designed by Thomas Newcomen and Edward Jenner invented vaccination against disease.

However, although the worlds of science and philosophy took giant strides away from the medieval view of the world, seventeenth- and eighteenth-century attitudes to women did not change from those that had pertained for centuries. Although many women had jobs, these were generally confined to domestic service or industries allied to catering such as brewing and baking. The professions were closed to them – women were not permitted to become doctors, lawyers or teachers for example. It would be at least 200 years before women had access to higher education; colleges and universities were barred to them, even if they came from families who could otherwise have afforded to educate their female children. Girls were rarely permitted entry to the grammar schools of the period; even the early Quakers, who claimed to believe in female education, established very few schools for girls, although from the founding of the movement in the 1650s women were at least permitted to speak during Quaker meetings. However, even a century later the uncommon nature of this privilege elicited the now infamous quip from Doctor Samuel Johnson:

> Sir, a woman's preaching is like a dog walking on his hind legs. It is not done well; but you are surprised to find it done at all.
>
> (*Life of Samuel Johnson* – James Boswell 1791)

Neither was it only men who considered women's formal education to be unnecessary; sadly many women of the period also supported the view that their gender required no further schooling in anything other than that which concerned itself with religion or domestic duties:

> I desire (if the child be a daughter) her bringing up may be learning the Bible, as my sisters do, good housewifery, writing and good works: other learning a woman needs not.
>
> *(The Mother's Legacie to her Unborne Child* – Elizabeth Jocelyn 1624)

Women who did have sufficient education and literacy to become authors invariably found themselves abused and ridiculed. Eliza Haywood (c. 1693–1756), was a writer, actress and publisher with more than seventy published works to her credit and now acknowledged to be an important founder of the modern novel. In her own time however, she was described by Jonathan Swift (1667–1745) as a 'stupid, infamous, scribbling woman', and by Colley Cibbler (1671–1757) actor–manager, playwright and Poet Laureate as one of 'those shameless scribblers'.

John Strype (1643–1737) clergyman, historian and biographer was very specific about what he considered it was seemly for girls for be taught:

> There be also in and about the City, schools for the education of young Gentlewomen in good and graceful Carriage, Dancing, Singing, playing on Instruments of Musick [*sic*] Reading Writing French, raising paste [i.e. making bread and pastry] etc., which render Women, that have these commendable Qualifications, so much beyond others in their Behaviour, Conversation, and good Housewifery.

Around 1721, the tutor of Charlotte Clarke (who would one day become a famous actress), had to obtain her mother's permission to teach his clever pupil Latin, a subject not thought appropriate for young girls to study. Even as the end of the eighteenth century approached, some women's negative attitudes to female education had not changed and schooling in anything beyond a rudimentary level thought to be unnecessary:

> It is necessary for you to be perfect in the first four rules of arithmetic – more you can never have occasion for, and the mind should not be burthen'd with needless application
>
> *(An Unfortunate Mother's Advice to Her Absent Daughters* – Lady Sarah Pennington 1770)

INTRODUCTION

By the end of the seventeenth century, only around fourteen per cent of women could read and write and this had still only risen to forty per cent by the middle of the eighteenth century. This lack of education meant that women in the seventeenth and eighteenth centuries were automatically excluded from fulfilling political, professional or civil service roles and were therefore regarded as second-class citizens and inferior beings, a view implied in some patronising advice from James Boswell that should be followed when flattering women: 'Be sure always to make a woman better than her sex' (*James Boswell's London Journal* 1762–63).

Women, whatever their station in life, remained subservient to whichever man was considered to be their superior: in youth – their fathers, if married – their husbands, if a servant – their employer. This subservient position, together with lesser physical strength than men, meant that women could readily be subjected to physical and mental abuse and they were – in every aspect of their lives both private and public, secular and religious. As victims of abuse, neither had they any recourse to protection from the law; the Lord Chief Justice of England, Sir Matthew Hale (1609–76) wrote that the common law permitted the physical disciplining of wives, servants, apprentices and children all of whom could be subject to 'moderate correction' even if the application of such discipline resulted in death.

In the higher echelons of society, young women were not only subservient to their fathers, but commonly had little or no say in the choice of a husband, and should they object to the arrangement made for them, they were unlikely to receive much sympathy or support, even from their mothers. When the diarist John Evelyn's daughter eloped in 1685, he wrote to Samuel Pepys:

> What shall I say? I would support this disgrace with the best remedies to allay the passion and Indignation of an injur'd parent and a Man; but confess it harder to me, than had been her Death, which we should have less regretted: and you will by this imagine and with some pity, the overwhelming sorrows under which my poore wife is labouring afresh[1]

In 1617, Frances Coke, the 14-year-old daughter of the jurist Sir Edward Coke, refused to be betrothed to the 26-year-old Sir John Villiers, who, by-the-by, was subject to occasional bouts of insanity. Her mother, Lady Elizabeth Hatton (she had retained her title from her first marriage) had her daughter tied to the bedposts and whipped until she consented to the match.

If the common law provided no avenue of recourse for women, neither did the established Christian religion offer any protection. St Peter himself had described women as being 'the weaker vessel', and this relative frailty was seen as rendering women not only inferior but made them easy prey for the devil, as described by the theologian William Perkins writing in 1608: 'the woman, being the weaker sex, is soon entangled by the devil's illusions'.

The view of women as inherently weaker and therefore susceptible to evil influence was by no means exclusively a British trait, but followed a long tradition in almost all societies from time immemorial (a view still current in some countries of the world), resulting in an acceptance of the necessity of male rule, man-made laws, the superiority of male intellectual contributions, and consequently, by extension, the advocacy of male dominance as natural and inherent in the nature of things. Woman's affairs should be confined to matters relating to procreation and domestic arrangements, contributions generally considered of far lesser value than those of men. In her preface to *The World's Olio*, Margaret Cavendish, Duchess of Newcastle (circa 1624–74) was able to write:

> so man is made to Govern Commonwealths, and Women their private families … and if it be as Philosophers hold, that the Moon hath no Light but what it borrows from the Sun, so women have no strength nor light of Understanding, but what is given them from Men.

The all embracing male-domination of society become even more pronounced during the seventeenth and eighteenth centuries, when a combination of secular and religious influences forced women into even greater subservience, their acceptance of which was violently enforced both domestically and legally:

> Already designated inferior to men in intellect and virtue in the seventeenth century and enjoined by the Scriptures and subsequent Christian teachings to humble obedience to their betters, women were subjected to increased domination as the century advanced. A massive body of contemporary political theory and Puritan theology encouraged men to take their authority as husbands and fathers more seriously. Under common-law practice, moreover – a married woman was subject to the concept of the femme couverte: the total dependence upon her husband, in whom all legal rights were vested, so that she could not administer her own property, make a contract, sue or be sued in tort. Nor had she any legal right over her own children.[2]

The first work to provide a definition of women's legal rights such as they were was published in 1632 by John More. Entitled *The Lawes Resolutions of Women's Rights of The Lawe's Provision for Women,* the work attempted to 'comprehend all our Lawes concerning Women, either Children in government or nurture of their Parents or Gardians, Mayds, Wives, and Widowes, and their goods, inheritances, and other estates'. Not surprisingly, the author came to the conclusion that

INTRODUCTION

'Women have nothing to do in constituting Lawes, or consenting to them, in interpreting of Lawes, or in hearing them interpreted at lectures, leets or charges, and yet they stand strictly tyed to mens establishments, little or nothing excused by ignorance.'

To dispel any lingering doubt about women's position in society, they are to be found at the end of a list of people to whom a man is entitled by law to administer corporal punishment: 'If a man beat an outlaw, a traitor, a pagan, his villein, or his wife, it is dispunishable [sic], because by the Law Common, these persons can have no action.'

Furthermore, the work seems to go on to suggest (perhaps with tongue firmly in cheek) that the woman is not disadvantaged if she chooses by way of retribution to beat her husband in return, he likewise has no recourse in law!

> The sex feminine is at no very great disadvantage ... because the poor wench can sue no other action for it, I pray, why may not the wife beat the husband again? What action can he have, if she do ... the actionless woman beaten by her husband hath retaliation left – to beat him again, if she dare.

Occasionally, some lone voices questioned the logic of the subservient and disenfranchised position in which women found themselves, views that found little or no sympathy:

> Who gave men the authority to deprive them of their birthright, and set them aside as unfit to meddle with Government; when Histories teach us that they have wielded Sceptres as well as Men, and Experience shews [sic] that there is no natural difference between their understandings and ours, nor any defect in their knowledge of things, but what Education makes.[3]

Numbers of scholars have seen the seventeenth and eighteenth centuries as a period when a crisis occurred in the relationship between men and women, and the new atmosphere of liberty and discovery fomented an attempt to enforce a traditional patriarchy on society. In a traditionally male-dominated society, women were not only seen as weaker, but had also been regarded as standing lower in the order of creation, something which the pious poet John Milton struggled to understand, but even then describes women as a defect of nature:

> O! Why did God,
> Creator wise, that peopled highest heaven
> With spirits masculine, create at last

THE VIOLENT ABUSE OF WOMEN

> This novelty on earth, this fair defect
> Of nature, and not fill the world at once
> With men, as angels, without feminine,
> Or find some other way to generate
> Mankind?
>
> *(Paradise Lost – Book X* John Milton)

This misogyny found even more overt expressions in the poetry of John Wilmot, 2nd Earl of Rochester (1647–80):

> Trust not that thing called woman: she is worse
> Than all ingredients crammed into a curse ...

... and in an even more acerbic vein:

> Love a woman? You're an ass!
> 'Tis a most insipid passion
> To choose out for your happiness
> The silliest part of God's creation.

The greatest misogynist of all was perhaps the fencing master who in his day was also a well known pamphleteer, Joseph Swetnam (died 1621). In 1615 he published a pamphlet entitled *The Araignmant of Lewde, Idle, Froward and Unconstant Women*, which proved immensely popular, running to thirteen reprints in the seventeenth century and another five in the eighteenth, and which contained the following description:

> They lay out the folds of their hair to entangle men into their love; betwixt their breasts is the vale of destruction, and in their beds there is hell, sorrow and repentance. Eagles eat not men until they are dead but women devour them alive. For a woman will pick thy pocket and empty thy purse, laugh in thy face and cut thy throat. They are ungrateful, perjured, full of fraud, flouting and deceit, unconstant, waspish, toyish, light, sullen, proud, discourteous and cruel.

It's difficult to avoid the conclusion that Master Swetnam had had a bad experience with women! The roots of this misogyny can be found in the preceding Elizabethan age; as early as 1541, women were being maligned in a popular work that ran to four editions over thirty years, and which expressed itself in chillingly similar tones to those of the later pamphleteer, described as being 'impossible to please, untrustworthy, crabbed, talkative, shrill-voiced, loose in morals and froward'.[4]

INTRODUCTION

Nevertheless, that same age had given rise to a new 'middle class' with their own cultural and social attitudes, and had released women from their medieval bonds, so that Frederick, Duke of Wurttemberg visiting England in 1602 was able to write, 'the women have perhaps more liberty than in any other place'. A proverb of the time ran thus: 'England is a paradise for women, a prison for servants and a purgatory for horses.'[5]

The social turbulence of the first half of the seventeenth century had afforded middle-class women new opportunities. The Civil War had deprived many of their husbands and fathers, and as a result, they found themselves unexpectedly managing family estates or businesses. New religious freedoms had attracted women into the many new sects like the Quakers or the Ranters, where they were afforded a voice in preaching and teaching. In a time of unprecedented and unbridled political discussion, many better educated women saw no reason why they should not enter the debate and voice their opinions alongside those of men and began publishing their own books and pamphlets.

These new liberties, and the prominence thus gained by women, were perceived as a threat by the leaders of society; a political satire of the restoration period regarded the change as a temporary diversion from the norm and asked 'canst thou divine when things shall be mended?' The answer was never – the genie was out of the bottle and if it could not be wholly reversed it must therefore be strictly and severely regulated. For society to be ordered correctly, the 'fair defect' thus named by Milton must be kept in subjection. Thus arose an unlikely masculine alliance against the new feminine assertions, across all sections of society from Puritan preachers to court judges, from husbands to court rakes. This reaction often found expression in the violent and brutal treatment of women who were seen to have stepped out of line, whether legally, socially or domestically and from which their sex had no recourse to protection, justice or restitution. In this climate, the routine punishment, humiliation and abuse heaped upon women through judicial cruelty or domestic violence became the norm and from which three centuries later, western society has barely escaped and in some parts of the world, hardly at all.

This work records the many kinds of violent physical and verbal abuse perpetrated against women in Britain and her colonies, both domestically and under the law, during two centuries when huge strides in human knowledge and civilisation were being made in every other sphere of human activity, but male attitudes to and the treatment of women remained firmly embedded in the medieval.

Footnote: Although the work concerns itself with the seventeenth and eighteenth centuries, it extends in some areas into the nineteenth century where, in the colonies in particular, similar physical abuse continued to be perpetrated against women, despite changing attitudes in the mother country.

Chapter 1

Domestic Violence

Thereupon she giving me some cross answer I did strike her over her left eye such a blow as the poor wretch did cry out and was in great pain.

(The Diary of Samuel Pepys 19 December 1664)

home myself, where I find my wife dressed as if she had been abroad, but I think she was not, but she answering me some way that I did not like I pulled her by the nose, indeed to offend her, though afterwards to appease her I denied it, but only it was done in haste. The poor wretch took it mighty ill, and I believe besides wringing her nose she did feel pain, and so cried a great while.

(The Diary of Samuel Pepys 5 April 1664)

These casually violent responses of Samuel Pepys to a petulant wife would have been the usual reaction of many husbands in the seventeenth and eighteenth centuries and Elizabeth's suffering would have been the common experience of many women:

Thy husband is thy lord, thy life, thy keeper,
Thy head, thy sovereign; one that cares for thee …

Thus Shakespeare's Kate, who, in the last act of *The Taming of the Shrew*, articulates her inferiority as a wife to the patriarchal rule of her husband. Logic dictated that since the man's role in society was to rule in the public sphere as well as in his private household, he, as the ruler, needed to have the power to impose discipline:

The position of a woman in the seventeenth-century English marriage was dictated by the patriarchal nature of family relationships, with an emphasis on the subordination of women. Common law was strongly biased in favour of the husband/father. It was still a fact that a married woman had no financial rights independent of her

1

husband. The man also had a right to beat his wife, which was, sadly, a rather common practice.[1]

The perception that a man had the right to beat his disobedient wife persisted well into the twentieth century. The vicar and poet the Reverend George Bird (1858– 1941) wrote 'It is a man's duty to rule his own household; and if his wife refuse to obey his orders, he is justified, according to the law of God, in beating her in order to enforce obedience.'

In exercising his 'rights' to physically discipline the women in his household, a man would not have had any need to conceal or otherwise disavow his behaviour. Both religious teaching and their feminine characteristics conspired together to convince women that their subordinate nature was divinely ordained and that their part in the biblical account of man's fall from grace demonstrated their weaker moral character, in need of male governance. Some small benefit accrued to the wife in as much as should she and her husband jointly commit a crime, she could not be found guilty as she would be deemed to be following her husband's instructions.

Physical chastisement of his wife, children and servants was regarded as a necessary duty and obligation and, most importantly, within reasonable limits was regarded as socially acceptable. Others might be well aware that a man was habitually abusing his wife and daughters by the application of physical chastisement, but would say nothing to mitigate or prevent such abuse.

The legal status of a wife in relation to her husband and her total reliance upon him for her financial security placed an abused woman in an invidious position. Typical of such a case is that of Thomasin Wheeler, who appeared five times before Hackney Justice of the Peace Henry Norris between 1731 and 1735 to complain of her husband's cruelty and neglect. On 12 June 1732, Justice Norris recorded in his notebook:

> Thomasin Wheeler complains against her husband John Wheeler for assaulting her & beating her in an unmerciful manner & threatening her life & neglecting to provide for the Support of his wife & 2 children.

Twice, Henry Norris remanded John Wheeler on a charge of common assault, the only charge available to cover domestic violence, first to Newgate Prison in 1732 and again in May 1735 to the Clerkenwell Bridewell. On both occasions Thomasin had sworn on oath that he had beaten her barbarously and threatened her life, and neither could he produce sureties for his appearance in court. Had John Wheeler been found guilty, he would in all probability have been fined 12*d* [equivalent to approximately 5p today] before returning to the matrimonial home. However,

Thomasin appeared at Hackney Petty Sessions pleading for his release, as in his absence, she had been forced to rely on poor relief to support her children. No matter that she was in danger of her life if her husband returned home, she could not afford to have him locked up.

In 1624, in the alleged poisoning of Elizabeth Samways by her husband, the court was told by both neighbours and family that 'he beat his wife and [did] give her many blows with a cudgell'. Elizabeth's mother described how her son-in-law punished his wife 'beatinge her often with ropes and cudgels and lodging her in the lower part of his howse [*sic*] adjoining to his barne, upon straw with a bolster of dust under her head'.

Indeed, there were legitimate reasons to claim a long-standing legal basis for domestic chastisement by the husband:

> Blackstone, the eminent legal authority, says there was an old common law which authorised the husband to give his wife moderate correction. As he was made to answer for her misbehaviour, it was held right and proper that he should be entrusted with the power of restraining her by domestic chastisement, in the same moderation that a man is allowed to correct his apprentices or children.[2]
>
> In Wales, the ancient law gave the husband specific rights in punishing his wife, but did impose limits; he was permitted to give her three blows with a broom handle![3]

In Georgian England, husbands were still legally entitled to 'correct' the behaviour of their wives so long as moderation was employed. Judge Francis Buller (1630–82) even went so far as to specify that a husband could beat his wife with a stick so long as it was no thicker than his thumb, earning himself the nickname 'Judge Thumb' in satirical prints of the day. These guidelines followed what were the generally accepted criteria throughout most of Europe in the seventeenth and eighteenth centuries. Even in far away Moldovia the law stated that:

> a husband was expected to beat his wife in a mild, rational way, and for a justified and serious reason … a violent husband was immune to the judge's punishment if two postulates were met; the wife was beaten by her fault and with a mild violence.[4]

Violent abuse of children was undoubtedly commonplace and girls as well as boys often came under the lash. Little evidence remains of lower-class children's experience, but for aristocratic children history has sometimes reported examples of such abuse. Frances Coke was 14 years old when her father, the lawyer Sir Edward Coke (1552–1634) wanted her to marry 26-year-old John Villiers, a self-harming depressive and the brother of the Duke of Buckingham, the king's favourite. Frances's mother, Lady Hatton, wanted her to marry the Earl of Oxford (as did Frances herself). King James 1 (1566–1625) became involved and ordered that Frances should marry John Villiers, and after much intrigue involving kidnap and forged love letters, the upshot found Lady Hatton imprisoned and Frances tied to the posts of her bed and whipped until she consented to the match!

Sometimes the abuses heaped upon the wife by her husband exceeded that which even in their time would have been socially acceptable. In a pamphlet dating from 1684, a woman named Mary Hampson described the appalling abuse she suffered at the hands of her violent husband, including starvation, beatings and eventual eviction from the marital home. Mrs Hampson's story began in 1656 when she married solicitor Robert Hampson under pressure from her family. Her husband's behaviour soon became violent, with beatings that were sometimes administered in front of Mr Hampson's friends and associates. Mary describes how starvation was added to the beatings:

> He went out of town, and left me in a sad and weak condition with very little money …. next morning [he] came to my bed-side, and told me if I would not arise and be gone I should starve there. For he had given strict order to my maid, his clark [*sic*] and laundress, not to let me have anything to eat. And all that day I could get nothing to eat. He came to me at twelve a clock, and seeing my maid had brought me some broth to drink, did threaten her. About eleven a clock at night I went into his study to speak with him, hoping his fury was abated. He drew a pistol out of his pocket and set it to my throat saying, that if I would not be gone out of his lodgings he would kill me.

Later, Mary describes how two of her husband's friends were invited to watch her being beaten, before he threw her out into the street:

> So soon as they were in the chamber, Mr Hampson shut the door, and said that I came to molest him, and did strike me upon the head to the ground; then threw me against a glass-door. Feeling myself hurt in the arm with the glass (although much ashamed) I cryed out. The two men Edwards and Robinson stood as applauders of Mr Hampson. When I cryed out Mr Hampson opened his inward chamber door, and there was his cleark [*sic*] and another man, ready at Mr Hampson's order to drag me into the street … and at the

Temple Gate, the cleark said I was mad, and that they had order to bring me to Bedlam.[5]

Extreme violence visited upon their wives by men who have failed utterly to control their tempers remains a common theme in court cases throughout the seventeenth and eighteenth centuries. A few consecutive entries from the casebook of Justice Henry Norris in 1733 demonstrate how common domestic violence was in that period and also, how many battered wives sought the protection of the court:

Monday, 18 June 1733 Thomas Dotchell complains agt: Thomas Williams for beating Anne Dotchell his wife in a barbarous manner made out by ye Oath of Mary Mattison done last Saterday in [ye *deleted*] Hackney Marsh, Stamped upon her Stomach & beat her about most grievously. Granted a warrt for him.

Same day On his being brot: by [*blank*] Griffith Headbo: ye matter was heard & Mary Mattison made Oath yt Tho: Williams did assault her Anne Dotchell and Stamped on her Stomach without her having Stricken him. Tho: Dotchell Swears yt She is now extream [*sic*] ill & as he is told inwardly bruised being big wth Child & cannot attend.

Sunday, 24 June 1733 Thomas Dotchell [and] Elisabeth Fletcher Sworn. Both say yt they apprehend Anne Dotchell is in great danger of her life lying now extremely ill by the hurts She received as they are informed in her quarrel wth Thomas Williams.

Friday, 13 July 1733 Mary Kingsland complains agt: Jno: Jones for assaulting her last night & throwing her violently on ye ground & kicking her whereby She was very much bruised & hurt at ye Wtt Hart on Camb: heath. On hearing ye matter Mary Kingsland Swore to the assault as above & Abigail Johnson as witness on oath confirmed the Same.

Saturday, 29 September 1733 Hannah Preston complains agt: her husband Edward Preston for beating her last Wednesday & especially for neglecting to make any provision for his family She having 3 children by him to keep ye eldest 9 years, ye 2d 3y: ye [other *deleted*] 3d under 1 year – to wch She made oath.

Tuesday, 2 October 1733 Thomasin Wheeler complains agt: her Husband John Wheeler for beating & abusing her last night & threatening her life last night. On oath made granted a warrt: agt him.[6]

The murder in 1737 of Mary Totterdale by her violent husband is typical of many such cases. John Totterdale, a victualler, was indicted for assaulting and murdering his wife,

> with both his Hands, in and upon the Stairs of his Dwelling-house, the said Mary did cast and throw down, and she on the Stairs, so lying, he, the said John, did drag and pull down to the Bottom, and her the said Mary, from the Bottom of the said Stairs, into a certain Room in the said House, did cast and drag, and the said Mary so lying on the Floor, he, with both his Hands and Feet, her Head, Neck, Breast, Shoulders, Back, Sides, Belle, and Thighs, did strike, kick and stamp upon; giving her, as well by throwing and dragging her down the said Stairs, as by stricking [*sic*], kicking and stamping upon her, several mortal Bruises, of which she instantly died.

The facts of the case are related in extraordinary detail by the Ordinary (the chaplain) of Newgate and are worth recounting in full:

> John Totterdale, 32 Years of Age, of honest Parents, about three Miles from Taunton, in Somersetshire, who sent him to School to read and write, and to be instructed in the Principles of Religion. When of Age he was not put to any Trade, but his Father being a Husbandman, bred him the same Way. He lived by serving Gentlemen or Farmers in the Country some Years, and was looked upon as an honest good-natur'd Fellow. About sixteen or seventeen Years ago he came to Town thinking to better his Fortune in or about London; all the Masters he served were two Gentlemen, one an eminent Brewer at Knightsbridge, another of the same Business at the Horse-Ferry, Westminster, nigh to which Place he took a House after he had married, and both these Gentlemen were civil and kind to him. He had been married to this Mary (his unfortunate Wife) about twelve or thirteen Years; she was born in King-street, Westminster, and by her has had six Children, two of whom are now living, one a Boy about eleven, another a Girl about eight Years old. He for some Time lived tollerably with his Wife, but they both being given to Drinking, it occasioned many Janglings and Disputes,

and he frequently abused her, and often beat her in a barbarous unmerciful Manner; the Disagreement at last grew so great between them, that the poor Wife would often make Elopements from him, and sometimes would stay away two, three, or six Weeks, generally carrying off a Guinea or two, and once six; this he complained of as a Fault in his Wife; I told him the Reason of this might be his beating and abusing her in such a barbarous Manner, and the Truth of this he could not deny, but lamented grievously over his passionate and hasty Temper. He kept a Victualling House nigh to the Horse-Ferry, had pretty good Business, and might have lived very well, if he and his Wife could have agreed, and have lived peaceably together, but Prudence and the Grace of God was wanting ('tis to be feared) in them both, and this occasioned all their Misfortunes. The barbarous Murder for which he is to suffer, was committed upon the following Occasion.

August the 1st he sent out his Wife to get a small Debt of five Shillings, which he looked upon as lost Money; she received it, but meeting a Neighbour as she was coming Home, she told her the Success of her Errand, and that he would give her a Judas Kiss for getting the Money, though she expected no Good to follow, but cruel Treatment according to his ordinary Custom; all this he verrified upon their meeting together, for as soon as she got Home, she gave the Crown to her Husband, and he kiss'd and embrac'd her in a very loving Manner, pretending to be very much pleased with her. This seeming Kindness did not last long, for the poor Woman being a little in Drink, went up Stairs to lie down upon a Bed; upon this the Devil entered Totterdale, and in a violent Fit of Passion he ran up Stairs after her, dragg'd her out of Bed by the Heels, and beat her and stamped upon her in a most barbarous and cruel Manner; upon somebody's speaking to him and upbraiding him with Cruelty, he left her and went down Stairs; they hid her at the Foot of a Bed; but his violent Passion and cruel Disposition still continuing, he went up Stairs again, and opened the Chamber Door which a Lodger had locked upon her, and found her; with great Fury he threw her upon the Floor, and a Man laying hold on him to hinder him, he sprang from him, and threw her down the Stairs, himself following, kicking and stamping upon her Belly, Breast, Legs, Head, and other Parts of the Body, till he had kick'd and spurn'd her to the Bottom; then he dragged her into a little Room which was their Bedchamber, shut the Door upon them, and continued beating her in this unmerciful Manner till she died; all this was done in less than the Space of one Hour, and without any the least Provocation, she not having been heard to say any Thing that might provoke him thus barbarously to treat her, only she at first cried out two or three Times Murder, and when her Strength was quite spent, she was heard speaking faintly twice or thrice. Johnny, Johnny, don't kill me; for God's Sake don't murder me, or to that Purpose. Nine of her Ribs were broken, some of them into three, four, or six Pieces, one of them was all shatter'd into small Pieces and beat upon her Kidneys. When this was done, he lock'd his dead Wife up in the Room, and for two Hours nobody offered to lay hold on him; during which Time, though he might have made his Escape, he was in such Confusion, and his Conscience so perplexed, that he could not move out of the Place, till a Soldier and a Constable came and carried him, without any Disturbance, before a Justice, who committed him to the Gatehouse till he was removed to Newgate, to take his Trial at the Old-Bailey, where he deservedly met with his Doom. He was an irreligious profane Fellow, unu'sd to Duty and Religion, and kept Company with lewd Women; he pretended that his Wife was guilty in this Respect, with other Men in the Neighbourhood, on which Account there were mutual Jealousies between them; but yet he said he could not entertain any Thoughts of her having wronged him that Way. He pretended to be sick, and kept the Cell most of the Time he was under Sentence, but his Indisposition proceeded more from Fear and Trouble, and Sulliness of Mind, than any Sickness of Body, for when the Dead-Warrant came down, he attended regularly in Chapel, and was attentive to Prayers and Exhortations, though indeed he did not seem so deeply affected as he ought to have been, yet when I spoke to him, he sometimes would cry and weep a little. He was an obdurate hard-hearted Wretch, but profess'd a deep Repentance for all the Sins of his Life, especially the great Crime of murdering his own Wife; that he believed in Christ, and was in Peace with all Men.

THE ORDINARY of NEWGATE, His ACCOUNT of the Behaviour, Confession, and Dying Words, OF THE MALEFACTORS, Who were Executed at TYBURN On WEDNESDAY the 5th of OCTOBER 1737

Printed and Sold by JOHN APPLEBEE, in Bolt-Court, near the Leg-Tavern, Fleet-street. M,DCC, XXXVII. (Price Six-pence.) [2½p today]

A similarly brutal fate awaited the wife of Robert Hallam who was executed for her murder at Tyburn on 14 February 1732. Her confessed infidelity tempted him to equal indulgence of his lust and he had affairs with several women, including the wife of a waterman, who killed himself as a result.

On one particular night Hallam came home drunk and went straight to bed, instructing his wife to get undressed and come to bed likewise. Having removed her outer garments she sat on the edge of the bed partially clothed, as if afraid to get in while her husband became increasingly enraged at her reluctance to accede to his request. Becoming increasingly afraid she ran downstairs, closely followed by her husband who locked the front door to prevent her going out. Still pursued by her husband she ran up into the dining-room, where he dealt her several blows before going to an adjoining room to seek his cane with which to administer a thrashing. Seizing her opportunity, she locked him in, whereupon he became so enraged that he broke down the door, seized her and dragged her to the window. Witnesses said they heard her calling out 'Murder! for God's sake! for Christ's sake! for our family's sake! for our children's sake, don't murder me, don't throw me out of the window!' Ignoring her pleas, he threw her out of the window head first, breaking her back and fracturing her skull so that she died instantly. In spite of his claims at the trial that his wife had thrown herself to the ground, the jury were not convinced and Hallam was hanged.

In the twenty-first century, acts of cruelty by a husband would undoubtedly result in prosecution and marital divorce. However, before the mid-nineteenth century the only way of obtaining a full divorce was by a Private Act of Parliament. Between 1700 and 1857 there were 314 such Acts, almost all of them initiated by husbands and moreover, husbands who were wealthy and privileged. Even then divorce was granted by Parliament in this manner only for adultery. Wives, if they could independently afford to, could only initiate a divorce Bill if the adultery was compounded by life-threatening cruelty.

In 1670 a case arose which not only exhibited domestic cruelty on an epic scale and scandalous adulterous relationships, but drew in the involvement of Parliament, the church and even King Charles II. John Lord Roos, the younger son of the Earl of Rutland, had married Anne Pierrepoint, the daughter of the Marquis of Dorchester and benefited from an enormous dowry of £10,000. All appears to have been well with the marriage until Anne became pregnant, when there was a significant falling out between her, her husband and her mother-in-law, when Anne refused to wear tight-fitting corsets during her pregnancy. The row seems to have escalated, as Anne was left alone with a staff of just four maids and a footman in the huge fortified manor house of Haddon for a month, while the rest of the family and most of the servants moved to Belvoir Castle to celebrate Christmas without her.

Once reunited, the marriage seems to have deteriorated still further, with John drinking to excess with his male friends, to the extent that the sexual relationship of husband and wife became almost non-existent and they took to sleeping in separate chambers. Anne discovered however that she could excite her husband sexually by dressing up as a boy. The improvement in their relationship was short-lived as another serious row developed when she performed this transvestite transformation on an occasion (for whatever reason) during his absence.

In June 1659, ten months after their wedding, Anne gave birth to a daughter, who died shortly after. Although soon pregnant again, her marriage continued to deteriorate and led to her returning to her father, taking with her all her jewellery and plate, later alleged to be worth £5,000, an enormous sum of money in the day when a servant earned but a few pounds a year. Following yet another reconciliation, Anne returned to Haddon, but left her valuable possessions in the care of her father. This led to yet another serious falling out, with John swearing that he would never sleep with his wife 'between the sheets' again. Sometime before January 1661, Anne's father sold the jewellery in order to recoup her dowry.

Later, John would claim to never having slept with his wife after January 1659, but Anne claimed that he came to her covertly and that he could 'perform the actions of a husband as well out of the bed as in it', indicating that he had observed the letter of the oath rather than the spirit! This initially seems to have been borne out by Anne becoming visibly pregnant again some two months later, although she rather cast doubts on the efficacy of her case by informing her husband during another row that 'a better man than you got it' and singing a risqué ditty entitled 'Cuckolds all in a row'. In later evidence she was alleged to have told her maid that her husband's excessive drinking rendered him incapable of performing his marital duties: 'one may as soon raise a house as raise him'.

Whether true or not, John unsurprisingly alleged that his wife had committed adultery and locked her in her room for the remaining seven months of her pregnancy. When her confinement came in September 1661, the midwife was ordered to withhold assistance until Anne confessed the identity of the father. She refused to comply with this demand and after much pain, gave birth to a healthy son, which John had removed from her after two days. It was later alleged that he had tried to get a local shepherd to put a brand on the child as a mark of shame; whether or not this is true, he certainly had the boy baptised 'Ignotus' to indicate that the child's father was unknown.

In December 1661, Anne's father, the Marquis of Dorchester, managed to get his daughter released from captivity and sent to London, where the Privy Council attended by the king himself, heard evidence from both sides. The conclusion was that Anne had probably committed adultery, but as it could not be proved, John Lord Roos should make a private separation agreement. No such agreement was reached, but in the meantime, Anne gave birth again in April 1663. This time John produced a wealth of evidence that his wife had numbers of illicit sexual partners and secured a separation order from the Court of Arches. This still left the danger, however, that unless he could prove that Ignotus was illegitimate, the child would one day inherit the title and estates of Earl of Rutland.

In order to circumvent this possibility, a private Bill was introduced in the House of Lords for the 'illegitimating of a child called Ignotus born of the body of Anne Lady Roos'. Before the Bill could complete its passage however, Anne gave birth yet again, so a new Bill was introduced bastardising all children born to her since 1659. Even this was not an end of the matter. Years later in 1670, John Lord Roos petitioned Parliament for an enabling Act to allow him to remarry. King Charles is alleged to have supported the Bill, for if successful he saw a similar route thus opened to him for a divorce from his queen, Catherine of Braganza, thus freeing him to beget a son and heir elsewhere. In the meantime, it is said that he attended incognito the sessions in the House of Lords when evidence was being presented, revelling in the salubrious details of Lady Roos's sexual exploits, which he commented was 'better than a play'.

Wife-beating was both widely tolerated and sanctioned by law in eighteenth-century England. Yet the ordeal suffered by Mary Eleanor Bowes, Countess of Strathmore, at the hands of her husband so shocked Georgian genteel sensibilities that she not only won landmark legal battles, but her husband was committed to prison. A wealthy young widow, Mary was tricked in 1777 into marrying an Irish fortune-hunter named Andrew Robinson Stoney, who faked a duel to win her hand. Squandering her wealth, Stoney – who changed his name to Bowes – beat Mary with sticks, whips and candlesticks, tore out her hair, burned her face and threatened to slash her with knives. Terrified for her life, after eight years of physical and mental torture, Mary fled the marital home and embarked on what were then audacious legal suits to win a divorce, reclaim her fortune and regain custody of her children. Her divorce case in the church courts on grounds of adultery and cruelty, backed by courageously given eye-witness accounts from servants, was one of only a handful of successful divorce cases initiated by women when it was first resolved in 1786.

But her ordeal was far from over. Horrified that he might lose his fortune, her husband kidnapped Mary from a London street in a desperate bid to force her to rescind the divorce proceedings. Dragging her across snow-covered moors, Bowes threatened to shoot Mary with a pistol and with rape. Eventually rescued after eight days, Mary went on to win her divorce through two appeal stages as well as reclaiming her property and her children, while Bowes spent the rest of his life in jail for what *The Times* newspaper described as 'a detail of barbarity that shocks humanity and outrages civilisation'. When Mary died in 1800, she asked for the blindfolded figure of Justice to stand guard at her tomb. But it would be almost another century before women earned even minimal protection against abusive husbands.

Wives might have suffered at the hands of their husbands, but they could also suffer physical abuse at the hands of other women. In 1638 a pamphlet appeared in London entitled *Stripping, Whipping and Pumping, Or, the Five Mad Shavers of Drury Lane*. It recounted how a Drury Lane barber named Evans was observed drinking with a young woman named Joan Ilsley, allegedly the nurse who had attended upon his wife during child birth. Evans's wife came to hear of this and suspecting the woman had designs upon her husband, sent Joan an invitation to a roast pig supper, which the unsuspecting nurse duly attended. Upon arrival however, she finds Mrs Evans and four of her female friends lying in wait for her. She is seized and held as the women strip off her clothes, gag her and then flog her with a birch rod so severely that her flesh is rendered red raw. A razor is sent for and the struggling woman is cut during what might be supposed is an obscene shaving operation. Dragged downstairs, she is held first under one pump and then another, held under the water and in the words of the pamphlet, 'shamefully used'.[7]

The pamphlet's title page carried a woodcut of the nurse being stripped naked while a boy is seen arriving carrying a razor. Similar treatment of women by others obviously occurred, if not frequently, then often enough to allow a later pamphlet on a different subject, *A Discovery of Six Women Preachers* (London 1641), to reuse the woodcut with the dialogue removed. This publication attacks female preachers, associating them with disorderly, lawless women, guilty of whoredom or carrying out unnecessary violence.

Domestic violence was not only inflicted upon wives, but female servants might also find themselves subjected to physical abuse if their work failed to satisfy their employer:

> Saturday. This morning, observing some things to be laid up not as they should be by the girl, I took a broom [i.e. probably a birch rod] and basted her till she cried extremely, which made me vexed, but before I went out I left her appeased.
>
> (*Diary of Samuel Pepys* 1 December 1660)

On rare occasions, maids who had been subjected to physical abuse managed to petition the courts for relief. The Reverend Zachary Crofton (1626–72) was an Anglo-Irish Nonconformist minister and controversialist, one-time Rector of St Botolphs, Aldgate, London. He was prosecuted in 1657 for severely punishing his servant girl, Mary Cadman to whom: 'he gave the correction of a schoolboy [i.e. birched] to his servant-maid ... who later sued him in Westminster Hall.' (*History of the Flagellants* Jean Louis Lolme, 1780)

The case became notorious, and the theme of a play in 1661 entitled *The Presbyterian Lash*, by Francis Kirkman. Unusually in the period, the reverend gentleman went to gaol.

In the case of Katherine Auker in 1690, relief granted by the court was only temporary and the implication of the judgement is that the unfortunate victim would ultimately be returned to her abuser:

> Order upon the petition of Katherine Auker, a black, Shows she was servant to one Robert Rich, a planter in Barbadoes, and that about six years since she came to England with her master and mistress; she was baptised in the parish Church of St Katherine's, near the Tower, after which her said master and mistress tortures and turned her out: her said master refusing to give her a discharge, she could not be 'entertained in service elsewhere'. The said Rich caused her to be arrested and imprisoned in the 'Pulletry Cemter', London. Prays to be discharged from her said master, he being in Barbadoes. Ordered that the said Katherine shall be at liberty to serve any person until such time as the said Rich shall return from Barbadoes.[8]

On rare occasions, the court not only found for the unfortunate woman, but saw fit to grant permanent relief from their suffering, although how Frances Woodward made her living without completing her apprenticeship from which she was released is not recorded:

> Order for discharging Frances Woodward from her apprenticehood with Stephen Dodd, victualler, of Ratcliff. She had been originally apprenticed to Katherine Attwood by the parish authorities of St Paul, Shadwell, and by her was assigned to Stephen Dodd. By Dodd and his wife she had been much beaten and bruised, and whipped from the shoulders to the waist until her body was bloody and raw.[9]

Mistresses too might use physical chastisement to punish their servants. On 30 January 1760, Lady Frances Pennoyer of Bullingham Court, Hertfordshire, recorded in her diary that her maidservant had been overheard speaking in the housekeeper's room about a matter that was not to the family's credit. This was not her place to speak and her ladyship resolved to make her know and keep her place:

> she hath a pretty face … and should not be too ready to speak ill of those above her in station. I should be very sorry to turn her adrift upon the world, and she hath but a poor home. Sent for her to my

room and gave her choice; either to be well whipped or to leave the house instantly. She chose wisely, I think, and, with many tears, said I might do as I liked. I bade her attend at my chamber to-morrow at twelve.

The diary entry for the following day takes up the story;

Dearlove, my maid, came to my room as I bade her. I bade her fetch the rod from what was my mother-in-law's rod closet, and kneel and ask pardon, which she did with tears. I made her prepare and I whipped her well. The girl's flesh is plump and firm – and she is a cleanly person, such a one, not excepting my own daughters, who are thin, and one of them, Charlotte, rather sallow, as I have not whipped for a long time. She hath never been whipped before, she says, since she was a child (what can her mother and her late lady have been about, I wonder) and she cried out a great deal.[10]

It is interesting to note that Lady Frances's mother-in-law apparently kept a stock of whipping implements in the house and the diary details concerning the maid's physical appearance and reaction hint at more than a trace of sadism.

By far the most extreme case of domestic violence against domestic servants in the period seems to have been that of Mrs Elizabeth Brownrigg, who was hanged for murder at Tyburn in September 1767. Elizabeth Brownrigg was married to a plumber near Fleet Street in London, with a small house in Islington. She had given birth to sixteen children, and as a midwife, was appointed by the overseers of St Dunstan's parish to take care of the poor and pregnant women in the workhouse. The story of her treatment of girls under her care scandalised the general public of the day.

The young Mary Mitchell was apprenticed to Mrs Brownrigg in the year 1765, and at about the same time Mary Jones, a child of the Foundling Hospital, was likewise placed with her in the same capacity among a number of other female apprentices, taken on in order to save money on hiring servants. Whenever their work was deemed to be unsatisfactory by Brownrigg the apprentice girls were punished with almost unimaginable cruelty. They were laid across two kitchen chairs and whipped or caned until the mistress was exhausted. If they fainted under the lash, their heads were place in a bucket of cold water to revive them. Unable to withstand this cruelty, Mary Jones managed to escape and found her way back to the Foundling Hospital where her injuries caused the hospital's solicitor, Mr Plumbtree, to write to the Brownriggs threatening prosecution. Despite the Brownriggs disregarding this threat, no further action appears to have been taken and the unfortunate girl was eventually returned to the Brownriggs' care.

On the other hand, Mary Mitchell continued with her mistress for a further year during time which she was treated with increasing cruelty. She also managed to escape but unfortunately was met with the Brownrigg's younger son, who returned her to the house. There she was stripped naked, tied, and beaten with a broom, a horsewhip and a cane until she became unconscious. Forced to sleep in a freezing cellar on a diet of bread and water, she was often denied even these essentials and when she broke open a cupboard to supply herself, she was again stripped and horsewhipped. In order to prevent further escapes, Mary was chained at night with the links drawn tightly around her neck and her hands tied behind her back.

On occasion, Mrs Brownrigg deemed the offence to be deserving of even more severe punishment and the offending girl would be stripped naked and suspended by her wrists from a water pipe which ran across the kitchen ceiling. In this position the girls would be horsewhipped until the blood flowed from their wounds. Mary Clifford managed to complain of her harsh treatment to a French lady who lodged in the house, and who in turn took up her case with Mrs Brownrigg. The only outcome of this encounter was that Mary had her tongue cut twice with a pair of scissors. Further beatings followed until the girl's untreated injuries began to show signs of mortification.

At this point, fate took a hand. Mary Clifford's mother-in-law came to town, and enquired after the girl, being told by the workhouse that that she was apprenticed at the Brownriggs. However, upon arriving at that establishment she was refused entry and turned away in a threatening and abusive manner. Fate was not to be denied however and Mrs Deacon, the wife of the baker next door, overheard the conversation and called her in. There she was told of the cries and groans that could be heard coming from the Brownrigg house, which led the Deacons to believe that the apprentice girls were being cruelly treated.

In the meantime, Mr Brownrigg had bought a hog in Hampstead, which was put into a covered yard at the property, the skylight being removed to give ventilation to the animal's quarters. This gave the Deacons the opportunity to set their servants to spy upon events in the house and their reports shortly bought Mr Grundy, an overseer of the workhouse, to arrive and demand to see Mary Clifford. Mrs Brownrigg denied knowing any girl of that name, but their only 'Mary' was Mary Mitchell whom they could see if they wished. The Deacon's servants declared that Mary Mitchell was not the girl they had seen being abused upon; Mr Grundy sent for a constable to search the house, which was done, but no discovery of Mary Clifford was made.

Grundy, the overseer, took Mary Mitchell with him to the workhouse, where, on removing her bodice, it was found to be stuck so fast to her wounds that she shrieked with the pain. Upon being assured that she should not be sent back to the Brownriggs, she gave an account of the brutal treatment that she and Mary Clifford had sustained; and confessed that she had met the latter on the stairs just before they came to the house. This initiated a further search of the house, whereupon Mary Clifford was discovered in a cupboard in the dining room. She was in an awful condition and an apothecary sent for to treat her wounds declared her life to be in danger.

James Brownrigg was promptly arrested but his wife and son made their escape. The girls were taken to St Bartolomew's hospital where sadly Mary Clifford died a few days later. Apprehended, and sent for trial at the Old Bailey, father and son were acquitted of the higher charge and sentenced to six months in prison. Mrs Brownrigg however, in a trail which lasted only eleven hours, was convicted of wilful murder and sentenced to death. After being publicly hanged at Tyburn (now the site of Marble Arch in London) her body was put into a hackney-coach and taken to be dissected and anatomised as was the custom of the day. Stripped of all flesh, her skeleton was exhibited by being hung up in Surgeons' Hall.

Black people in seventeenth and eighteenth century Britain (of which there were about 5,000 in 1700) were almost entirely to be found in domestic service of one sort or another. Unfortunately, they were in an even worse position than white domestic servants in that they could be, and were, bought and sold as slaves. Legal cases in 1677 decided that 'blacks' were non-Christians and as such not entitled to the rights of other citizens. In 1680, the Bishop of London stated that baptism of 'blacks' into the Christian faith did not enable the person to be emancipated from slavery, thus blocking the only legal exit from that condition.

Black boys and girls were often kept as fashionable decoration – Charles II's mistress, the Duchess of Portsmouth, was painted with her arm around the shoulders of a small, immaculately attired, black maid and in another portrait, holding the hand of a richly dressed black page boy. Adult maids, however, were subject to many more risks in addition to those that threaten their white sisters: those of sexual harassment and unwanted pregnancy. The sad case of Katherine Auker, a black woman imported from Barbados around 1684, was still condemned to her master's ownership, even after torture, abandonment and wrongful imprisonment. Her petition to the court for release tells her tragic tale:

> Order upon the petition of Katherine Auker, a black. Shows she was servant to one Robert Rich, a planter in Barbadoes, and that about six years since she came to England with her master and mistress; she was baptized in the parish Church of St Katherine's, near the Tower, after which her said master and mistress tortured and turned her out: her said master refusing to give her a discharge, she could not be 'entertained in service elsewhere.' The said Rich caused her to be

arrested and imprisoned in the 'Pulletry Cempter', London. Prays to be discharged from her said master, he being in Barbadoes. Ordered that the said Katherine shall be at liberty to serve any person until such time as the said Rich shall return from Barbadoes.[11]

A decision by the Solicitor General stated that 'Negroes' ought to be 'esteemed goods and commodities within the Trade and Navigation Acts'. The ruling permitted slave owners to use property law with regard to their slaves 'to recover goods wrongfully detained, lost or damaged' as they would any other type of property, thus Katherine is only 'free' until her erstwhile master reclaims his property.

Chapter 2

Sexual Abuse

'I should have mentioned last night that I met with a monstrous big whore in the Strand...I went into a tavern with her, where she displayed to me all the parts of her enormous carcass; but I found that her avarice was as large as her arse, for she would by no means take what I offered her.'

'In the Strand I picked up a profligate wretch and gave her sixpence. She allowed me entrance. But the miscreant refused me performance. I was much stronger than her and *volens nolens* pushed her up against the wall.'

(James Boswell *London Journal* 1762-1763)

The sort of physical or verbal abuse indulged in by Boswell is relatively minor compared with the perpetration of rape, in modern times defined by the Sexual Offences Act 2003, is the penetration with a penis of a vagina, anus or the mouth of another person when consent has not been given. In the seventeenth century the situation for women who had been the victims of such an assault was muddied by a number of misconceptions that had been enshrined in law. First, it was believed that a woman could only conceive following sexual intercourse if she had given her consent:

Rape is the carnal abusing of a woman against her will. But if the woman conceive upon any carnal abusing of her, that is no rape, for she cannot conceive unless she consent.

(*Law or Discourse Thereof* Sir Henry Finch 1627)

Second, because she was her husband's property, in law a woman could not be raped by her husband:

But the husband cannot be guilty of rape committed by himself upon his lawful wife, for by their mutual matrimonial consent and contract the wife hath given up herself in this kind unto her husband, which she cannot retract.

(High Court Judge Sir Matthew Hale 1609–76)

Finally, women who had been raped faced the very same difficulty in the seventeenth and eighteenth centuries that they have faced ever since, as clearly described by Justice Hale:

> It is true that rape is a most detestable crime, and therefore ought severely and impartially to be punished with death; but it must be remembered, that it is an accusation easily to be made, hard to be proved, but harder to be defended by the party accused, tho' innocent.

In the seventeenth century, a woman who brought a charge of rape against a man was automatically regarded with suspicion. A woman's sexuality was controlled first by her father until she was married, after which that power was passed to her husband. To allege that she had had sexual intercourse with a man outside marriage, even against her will, was to impugn the authority of her male keeper and to bring an accusation down upon her head that she was at best unchaste, or worse, that she was promiscuous.

Additionally, women in the seventeenth and eighteenth centuries were adjudged to be weak, irrational and a slave to their emotions, so that their testimony was at best regarded as unreliable and that they had in some way connived with their attacker. Even in modern times, young women alleging that they have been sexually assaulted risk the accusation that by the nature of their manner or dress, or their perceived character, that they were 'asking for it'. Things were no different in the eighteenth century; at the Middlesex Sessions in 1739, Sarah Main claimed to have been raped by seven men while she 'screamed out and the fiddler play'd all the time'. She lost the case after a witness testified that 'people give the girl a bad character'.

The complainant in a seventeenth-century rape case was invariably female and the jurors judging the case exclusively male – at that time not a conjunction likely to result in a successful outcome for the plaintiff. Furthermore, contemporary law books stated the necessity in cases of rape of firstly proving penetration, then also proving that she had resisted, cried out for help, or if not, that this was because she had been gagged. As if this didn't render the chance of success minimal to say the least, any previous consensual relationship with the assailant ruled out a charge of rape completely.

Yet another complication was added by the widely held belief that women were possessed of a much greater sexual appetite than men. Indeed, some went further and alleged that women were sexually insatiable;` a seventeenth-century Chapbook[1] entitled 'Nine Times a Night' claimed that: 'Nine times a night is too much for a man, I can't do it myself, but my sister Nan can.'

This apparent insatiability was sometimes alleged to find relief in masturbation, thought to be punishable by God, as any sexual activity not intended for procreation was a mortal sin:

> The anonymously published *The Ladies Dispensary* (1739) gave an account of a woman who, having between the ages of fourteen and nineteen masturbated, fell into fits where she would scream out, throw off her clothes, 'endeavouring to lay hold of any man she saw, that he might lie with her', and finally died in a 'sudden raving fit' aged twenty-three. The author concluded that 'We see then what, and how many, are the diseases and inconveniences which the fair sex are capable of bringing on themselves by an unnatural abuse of their own bodies.[2]

Other risks attended the sexually abused woman; not only was there the possibility of an unwanted pregnancy as a result of the assault, but should she allege that her condition was a result of her rape, then she was automatically assumed to have participated willingly in the act. Samuel Pepys was terrified on one occasion that the pregnancy of a woman with whom he had had sex was caused by the fact that he had made her experience orgasm:

> je l'ay foutee sous de la chaise deux times [I fucked her twice under the chair], and the last to my great pleasure: mais j'ai grand peur que je l'ay fait faire aussi elle meme [but I greatly fear that I made her do it to herself as well, i.e. orgasm]
> (*Diary of Samuel Pepys* 16 January 1664)

These beliefs survived well into modern times; for most of the nineteenth century it was believed that it was impossible to rape an unwilling woman – that somehow her thighs would have got in the way, or that her subconscious was willing, whatever her voice might say. Until the late 1970s the police in the United Kingdom routinely asked women who were reporting that they had been raped whether or not they had experienced orgasm.

Pepys might have been frightened that he had made the woman pregnant, but his concern would have been nothing to that felt by the woman. For a woman to hide the fact that she was pregnant was a crime in law during this period, yet women routinely did so and thereby risked prosecution in the courts. Unmarried women might have been terrified of becoming pregnant but even married women could be distraught at the prospect of an unwanted or unaffordable child.

SEXUAL ABUSE

To be unmarried and to become pregnant during this period virtually guaranteed that a woman's life was completely and utterly ruined. Unless the father was free to do so and was prepared to marry her, she was doomed to a life of impoverished single parenthood, as no one else would take her on together with an illegitimate baby. She could try and force the man to support the child if she could prove it was his, but in an age before DNA testing that might prove extremely difficult. Going through a legal process was both expensive and unlikely to succeed; the jury would be entirely male and most probably biased against her, given their likely perception of her character. In any event, none of the potential solutions were likely to be successful if she had been raped, even if the identity of the assailant was known.

If, as was sometimes the case, that the woman refused to name the father, there was a belief that if interrogated by the midwife, the pregnant woman might name the true father during her labour, on the basis that in her agony, she would be incapable of lying, a principle often used to justify the use of torture. In reality, it was so obviously unreliable and open to abuse that it was rarely used. Without a husband to support her and her child, a woman would be forced to provide for herself. However, in a time without childcare and with her reputation ruined, employment would most likely have been out of the question. Neither would she have been able to rely on the support of her parents, who would probably have disowned her – the diarist John Evelyn wrote that he would rather have wished his daughter dead than she bring dishonour on the family:

> but confess it harder to me, than had been her Death, which we should have less regretted: and you will by this imagine and with some pity the overwhelming sorrows under which my poore wife is labouring afresh.[3]

As a result, the care of most bastard children was thrown upon the public funds of the parish, a very cogent reason for the law taking a very serious view of illegitimacy: 'Mary Clark of Aylesbury, widow, to be paid £1.13s 9d [£1.69] for nursing and for burying the bastard child of Alice Heritage.' (Buckinghamshire Session Records – Epiphany Session 1697–98)

Of all the various social classes of women in the period, female servants were often the most vulnerable to sexual abuse. Most 'lived in' with their employers and even where they were provided with segregated accommodation, they were still generally considered to be sexually available to the males of the family. Samuel Pepys regularly and systematically assaulted his maidservants and his wife's female companions:

> The virtue of Pepys' female servants, if good-looking, was usually attacked by him.
>
> (*Pepysiana* Henry B.Wheatly 1899)

I have lately played the fool much with our Nell, in playing with her breasts.

(Diary of Samuel Pepys 17 June 1667)

Up, and did this morning dally with Nell and touch her thing, which I was afterward troubled for.

(Diary of Samuel Pepys 18 June 1667)

away home and to bed – apres ayant tocado les mamelles de Mercer, que eran ouverts, con grand plaisir. [after having touched Mercer's breasts, which were uncovered, with great pleasure.]

(Diary of Samuel Pepys 18 April 1666)

Late seventeenth-century houses were crowded with rooms used for multiple purposes. Privacy was limited and servants often ended up moving from room to room, sleeping in truckle beds alongside their employers ... the closeness of family life raised suspician and dangers for single-women servants ... Samuel's apparent assumption of a right to touch and kiss female servants was not uncommon.[4]

If Pepys wasn't groping his maidservants, he might well have been thrashing them:

This morning, observing some things to be laid up not as they should be by the girl, I took a broom [probably a birch rod] and basted [thrashed] her till she cried extremely, which made me vexed, but before I went out I left her appeased.

(Diary of Samuel Pepys 1 December 1660)

Upper-class men in particular saw servant girls as legitimate sexual targets and having both relative wealth and influence, were often able to escape prosecution or censure, even when their dishonourable behaviour was discovered. In a case from 1684, Elizabeth Vesey sought separation from her husband on the grounds that he had been unfaithful with another woman, infected her with venereal disease and had tried to rape the maidservants. The MP Sir Nicholas Le Strange (1509–58) is recorded as saying that 'chambermaids are commonly the master's whore', and the politician Sir Ralph Verney (1613–96) requested a friend to find him a maidservant who would 'fit him as a whore', as his former maidservant had done.[5]

Masters and (or) their sons were often thought to be the guilty agents of their female servants' unwanted pregnancies, precisely because they had both opportunity and inclination. However, it was usually the maid who suffered the consequences, whether pregnant or not. When Samuel Pepys was discovered in flagrante by his wife, with his hands under the skirts of her maidservant Deb Willett, it was Deb who was thrown out onto the street. Pregnant maids were usually dismissed from service, often forcing them to become either prostitutes or homeless vagrants, for whom little or no charitable relief was forthcoming; St Thomas's hospital in London was declared to be for the relief of 'honest persons and not of harlots'.

If the man in the case was sufficiently wealthy, powerful and therefore influential, he could simply deny the accusation and arrange matters so that the woman and another innocent man took the blame. In seventeenth-century Somerset, Ann Bishop, having been impregnated by the wealthy Robert Cribb, named a different man as the father. She had been told by Arthur Pulman, the Constable of Martock, that if she did not deny that it was Robert Cribb's child, he would 'have her whipped to the bone [and] have her laid in the gaol until she would rot'.

In a similar early eighteenth-century case in Lancashire, a local constable named James Cash made his maidservant Ellen Greenhalgh pregnant. He persuaded her to name Thomas Houghton, the local unmarried blacksmith, as the father. The truth emerged when master and maid were discovered in bed together. At the following Quarter Sessions court, the charges against both the men were dropped, but Ellen was found guilty and ordered to be whipped!

Other than turning to prostitution, the alternative for a pregnant maid was to terminate the pregnancy. The practical ways in which a pregnancy could be terminated and the fact that women of all social classes were prepared to take them demonstrates how desperate they considered their plight. They could risk incredibly dangerous abortions, usually effected through taking violent purgatives or by internally puncturing themselves – methods that often proved just as fatal to the woman as to the baby. Some would give birth to the infant naturally but kill it immediately afterwards, then claiming that it had been stillborn. Numbers of women were executed, rightly or wrongly, in the period for failing to convince the jury that they had not murdered their new-born child.

It is not clear how many men became involved in the termination of unwanted pregnancies, but the 1644 case of Elizabeth Linton is one such violent example:

> In 1644 Elizabeth lived as a servant with Miles Read and his wife, who had noted Elizabeth's pregnancy, and said to her: 'I fear thou art with child.' Her servant answered again 'if I be God feared it will.' Stephen Maultas, who was probably the father of the child, later appeared at the house and threatened that 'I will be thy midwife'. Shortly after, Maultas met with her 'on the backside of the town' and beat her severely, announcing his intent to make her miscarry and

23

'spew it out of her mouth'. Elizabeth Linton 'was delivered of two children' before going 'threescore yards', but the deposition does not relate whether the babies survived ... As a result of the many various factors litigating against a successful outcome, prosecution of rapes in these centuries are sparse; for example less than one per cent of all indictments from the Home Assize Circuit for the years 1558 to 1700 are for rape.[6]

Similarly, during the hundred years between 1730 to 1830 prosecutions are equally sparse; there were only two hundred and ninety-four prosecutions for heterosexual rape in the Old Bailey; a guilty verdict was given in only fifty-one of these cases (17%), and twenty-eight of the offenders were executed; fifty-seven of the cases involved girls under the age of 10 years, and 10 of these offenders were found guilty.[7]

However, the statistics belie the suspicion that, given the lack of effective policing and what to modern eyes would be almost pitch darkness during the night in many streets, there can be little doubt that such assaults were more commonplace than as rare as the statistics seem to indicate. Thanks to Samuel Pepys' diary, we know of several such occurrences and as a result of his characteristic frankness, also gain an insight into what was probably a typical male reaction of the period:

> This night late coming in my coach, coming up Ludgate Hill, I saw two gallants and their footmen taking a pretty wench, which I have much eyed, lately set up shop upon the hill, a seller of riband [sic] and gloves. They seek to drag her by some force, but the wench went, and I believe had her turn served, but, God forgive me! what thoughts and wishes I had of being in their place.
>
> (*Diary of Samuel Pepys* 3 February 1663)

Pepys' reaction, far from thinking of going to the women's assistance (probably unwise given the odds), his first thought is a fantasy about being in the rapists' place! Being assaulted in the street was clearly a common hazard for women in Pepys' day, as he later describes a very similar situation;

> Among others, there were two pretty women alone, that walked a great while, which being discovered by some idle gentlemen, they would needs take them up; but to see the poor ladies how they were put to it to run from them, and they after them, and sometimes the ladies put themselves along with other company, then the other drew back; at last, the last did get off out of the house, and took boat and

away. I was troubled to see them abused so; and could have found in my heart, as little desire of fighting as I have, to have protected the ladies.

(ibid Pepys 28 May 1667)

A third instance involves one of his regular mistresses and despite the assailant being known to the victim, rather than seeking retribution on her behalf, Pepys' immediate reaction is to slander the woman's character:

My joy in this made me send for wine, and thither come her sister and Mrs Cragg, and I staid a good while there. But here happened the best instance of a woman's falseness in the world, that her sister Doll, who went for a bottle of wine, did come home all blubbering and swearing against one Captain Vandener, a Dutchman of the Rhenish Wine House, that pulled her into a stable by the Dog tavern, and there did tumble her and toss her, calling him all the rogues and toads in the world, when she knows that elle [she] hath suffered me to do anything with her a hundred times.

(ibid Pepys 6 July 1667)

Samuel Pepys himself was by no means reluctant to use physical force against women who proved reluctant to give their consent:

Up and walked to Deptford, where after doing something at the yard I walked, without being observed, with Bagwell home to his house, and there was very kindly used, and the poor people did get a dinner for me in their fashion, of which I also eat very well. After dinner I found occasion of sending him abroad, and then alone 'avec elle je tentais a faire ce que je voudrais et contre sa force je le faisais biens que passe a mon contentment' [overcoming her resistance I did what I wanted to my contentment]. By and by he coming back again I took leave and walked home, and then there to dinner.

(ibid 20 December 1664)

Thence to the office, and there found Bagwell's wife, whom I directed to go home, and I would do her business, which was to write a letter to my Lord Sandwich for her husband's advance into a better ship as there should be occasion. Which I did, and by and by did go down by water to Deptford, and then down further, and so landed at the lower end of the town, and it being dark 'entrer en la maison de la femme de Bagwell' [entered the house of Bagwell's

25

wife] and there had 'sa compagnie' [her company], though with
a great deal of difficulty, 'neanmoins en fin j'avais ma volont
d'elle' [nevertheless in the end I had my way with her] and being
sated therewith, I walked home to Redriffe, it being now near nine
o'clock, and there I did drink some strong waters and eat some
bread and cheese, and so home

(ibid 20 February 1665)

Did Pepys feel any shame or remorse for his adulterous and illicit relationships?
He certainly had a completely different set of values when it came to judging the
behaviour of others. When in 1666 he heard tell of an attempted rape by his colleague
at the Admiralty, the staunch puritan John Creed, he was (slightly) outraged:

an odde story lately told of him for a great truth, of his endeavouring
to lie with a woman at Oxford, and her crying out saved her; and this
being publicly known, doth a little make me hate him.

(ibid 18 February 1666)

Pepys lived through the English Civil War (1642–1649) and as in all such conflicts,
soldiers on both sides committing rape was a commonplace occurrence, despite
the offence carrying a mandatory death penalty in both the Royalist and the
Parliamentarian armies. The Earl of Essex's military articles drafted in 1645 for the
'New Model Army' specified capital punishment for all 'unnatural abuses' which
included 'rapes and ravishments'. However, this did not apparently deter troops
inflamed by recent action, as at Birmingham in 1643, where the soldiers:

beastly assaulted many women's chastity, and impudently made
their brags of it afterwards, how many they had ravished; glorying
in their shame, especially the French among them were outrageously
lascivious and lecherous.

(*War in England 1642–1649* Barbara Donagan, OUP 2008)

Not satisfied with just raping women, Cromwell's troops are alleged to have
perpetrated the most revolting and brutal assaults on female royalist supporters
that they happened upon. Near Rugby, they captured one Agnes Griffin, whom they
crucified by nailing her hand and foot to a tree, before crippling her with cuts to her
head and body, forcing her to drink her own blood. She was later awarded 4s (20p)
in damages and granted the right to beg for alms.[8]

(Comparisons of pre-decimalised British currency amounts and their modern
equivalents occur throughout this work. For an explanation of comparative values
see Appendix J)

SEXUAL ABUSE

Both at the time and subsequently, popular opinion has largely blamed foreign mercenaries for much of the raping and pillage that commonly followed English civil war actions:

> In the early years of the war, Parliament lost popular support through employing brutal foreign mercenaries and soldiers of fortune. Heavy resentment against the high level of pillage, looting and rape by foreign mercenaries – the worst offenders were probably the Germanic and Bohemian buccaneers who fought for the Puritans.[9]

The French and German troops were not the only nationalities to indulge their base instincts. the case of Elizabeth Frollbit, a young unmarried servant from York, was probably typical of the kind of opportunistic assault by soldiers experienced by many women. In 1737 Elizabeth claimed to have been raped by William Hunt 'a soldier in Major Churchill's regiment of dragoons quartering in and about this said city'. She had been milking a cow in the late afternoon in a stable, when Hunt 'came to this informant, and turned her said master's cow out of the said stable and assaulted this informant in a violent manner and threw this informant on the ground and had carnal knowledge of this informant's body and ravished this informant'.[10]

Some rapes seem to have been planned in cold blood rather than executed in the heat of the moment. One James Graham, a soldier in the occupying force in Dundee, broke into a house at midnight and, stripping off his clothes, attempted to force one of the two women occupants, Elizabeth Michelson, to have sex with him. When she rebuffed his advances, he beat both her and her child 'black and blue' before turning on the other woman, Margaret Patterson, whom he also beat severely before threatening to burn down the house. In spite of the severity of the offence, rather than being hanged, Graham was sentenced by court martial to be given sixty lashes at the cart's tail and imprisoned at the general's pleasure.[11]

> In spite of there being relatively few individually documented cases during the English civil war, rape clearly formed part and parcel of the conduct by soldiers of both sides; Sir Marmaduke Langdale's men reportedly pillaged and raped their way across Northamptonshire in 1645, binding men and forcing them to watch as soldiers assaulted the women of their families. The royalist capture of Burton-on-Trent produced claims of rape by pillaging soldiers, who allegedly assaulted the women and forced them into the river, where many drowned. Despite the horror of rape, courts-martial for the offence

27

are vanishingly rare in the surviving records of both royalist and parliamentary forces. In ninety-two cases, only two were for rape. One convicted soldier received sixty lashes, while another received a lash from every carter in the baggage train[12]

In the days before the current '18' movies, the graphic portrayal of rape as an entertainment proved just as popular with the general public as it does now. In December 1680, the play *Lucius Juniuous Brutus* by Nathanial Lee was presented by the Duke's Company at the Dorset Garden theatre. The play, which graphically portrayed the legendary rape of Lucrece by the soldier Tarquin and her subsequent suicide, was an immediate success but was closed down by the Lord Chamberlain, not because of the portrayal of violent sexual assault upon a woman, but because of its 'very Scandalous Expressions & Reflections upon ye Government'.[13]

However, nothing excited the eighteenth-century public imagination more than a true-life case involving innocent young maidens and lecherous priests, especially if the story was claimed to be factual. In 1732, J. Millan published a book entitled *A Compleat Translation of the Whole Case of Mary Catherine Cadiere*, a case which had recently scandalised the whole of France. Mary Catherine Cadiere was a beautiful 20-year-old who had been brought up in a deeply devout family in Toulon and had ambitions to be beatified; she was receiving religious instruction from a 50-year-old Jesuit priest named Father Girard. In the story, Catherine relates how the priest progressively seduced her, kissing her and placing her hands under his cassock until:

> One day, I remember among others, as I was coming out of a severe fainting spell, I found myself stretched out on the floor with Father Girard behind me, running his hands over my breasts, which he had uncovered.

The priest explained his behaviour by informing the bewildered young woman that it was God's will that she experience humiliation as a route to perfection and that one day God would wish him to put his belly to hers. On another occasion, Father Girard arrived to find Catherine lying on the bed. He climbed in beside her and undressed her, while 'his hands explored every nook of my body. As I was subject to fainting spells I could not answer for what he did when I was in that state.'

Matters escalated, with Father Girard making her remove her clothes before caning her on the buttocks, telling her that she must be punished for not freeing herself of her scruples. On later occasions, he made her strip naked and lie face down on the bed 'with a pillow under her elbows' while he applied a whip to her buttocks, kissing the places where the whip had fallen and then gently scratched her until she felt 'mouille' [wet] and 'chatouille' [ticklish] in her private parts.

SEXUAL ABUSE

Despite a subsequent trial, conducted in a welter of accusations including sorcery, an alleged pregnancy and an abortion, Father Girard was acquitted and retired to his native Dole, where he died in 1733. Catherine dropped out of the public eye and went back to live quietly with her mother. The book recounting her experiences was a bestseller in both France and England.

Sadly, it would appear that the sexual assault of children by paedophile males was as common in the period as it is alleged to be in our own time. Reports of the sexual assault of female children by adult men has become horribly familiar to the public in the twenty-first century, but was equally well known in the eighteenth, although it gave rise to scant reporting in the journals of the day:

27 June 1730 On Monday last, one Jones was committed to Newgate, for committing rapes on the bodies of two children near Cow-Cross, one deaf and dumb, the other blind; the eldest not 12 years old.

(London Journal July 1730)

On 4th June 1726 the landlord of the King's Head tavern in Hog Lane was sent to Newgate prison in London by Justice Ellis for 'ravishing' his own daughter aged between eleven and twelve years of age.

(London Journal June 1730)

Francis Hayes was tried on two indictments, the first for violently assaulting Anne Lemman, an infant aged seven years with an intent to commit rape and thereby giving her the foul disease; and the second indictment was for violently assaulting and abusing Mary Swan, an infant aged eight years, with an intent also to commit rape, and thereby giving her the foul disease. On the first, he was sentenced to imprisonment for six months, to stand in the pillory and to give £100 security for his good behaviour for three years; and on the second he was sentenced to six months imprisonment after the former time was expired, to stand once in the pillory and to give £100 security for his good behaviour for three years.

(Public Ledger or The Daily Register of Commerce and Intelligence, 8 January 1761)

28 February 1719: On Thursday Sir John M [urra]y, Bart. was try'd at the Old-Bailey, for a rape on a girl of 11 years of age; as was also, Gulliford, the silver smith's man, for a rape on his masters daughter of 10 years of age, and were both acquitted; upon which, the women in court clapp'd their hands, and gave other testimonies of their joy and satisfaction.

(The Historical Register Volume 1 – 1724)

> *6 August 1726:* Daniel Curtis, about eighty years of age, was indicted for carnally knowing his own daughter, and getting her with child. The daughter gave evidence … that her father had lain with her for several years, and that she had two children by him, viz. one about 3 years ago, and the other in March last; the first of which, she said, being born alive, was carried into the garden, and buried by her father; and that she heard it cry, but did not see it, her father doing the office of a midwife. But she appearing to the Court to be little better than a natural [a simpleton], the prisoner was acquitted.
>
> (*The British Gazetteer* 1726)

Even when the case was proved, the sentence of the court seems outrageously light to modern eyes:

> James Bell was tried, being charged on oath, on suspicion of having forced and carnally known Susanna Man, a child not 10 years old, and being found guilty of the assault, was sentenced to be two years imprisoned, to pay a fine of 20 marks, and to remain in gaol till the said fine is paid.
>
> (*Daily Journal* 3 August 1730)

Comparisons regarding the nature of sexual offences in that period with those of modern times are also complicated by the fact that in the seventeenth and eighteenth centuries (and indeed into the nineteenth) the age of consent for girls was (with some relatively small variations) 10 years of age, thus sexual intercourse with a girl was only deemed automatically to be rape if she was below that age.[14]

Chapter 3

Libel & Slander

Sexual abuse occurs in times of both peace and armed conflict, and appears widespread in all its forms throughout Britain during the seventeenth and eighteenth centuries. Then, as now, sexually motivated abuse covered a wide spectrum of human behaviour. In extreme cases it could be defined as any act leading to sexual gratification, obtained by violence, coercion or threat, and often directed against women as their physical strength is relatively weaker compared to that of men.

At the lower end of the spectrum, it took the form of a verbal assault, very commonly employed against women in the period, either slandering an individual woman's character or, like Joseph Swetnam mentioned in the introduction, demeaning the female gender generally. Verbal abuse, when a man forcefully criticises, insults, or denounces a woman, is always characterised by underlying anger and hostility. When used face to face, it is intended to harm the self respect and confidence of the recipient, when used in a descriptive manner, it is intended to damage the character of the recipient or demean their social or economic worth.[1]

Pervading negative attitudes towards female sexuality and morals were, as is still the case today, often indicated by the abusive language used to describe them. Samuel Pepys habitually used insulting language to describe the moral characters of ladies of his acquaintance, though presumably not to their faces:

> Lady Bennett (a famous strumpet)
> > (*Diary of Samuel Pepys* 22 September 1660)

> Lady Shrewsbury, who is a whore and is at this time, and hath for a great while been, a whore to the Duke of Buckingham
> > (ibid 17 January 1668)

And of his wife's companion Deb Willett, with whom he had an infamous affair:

> I am apt to believe, by what my wife hath of late told me, [she] is a Cunning girl, if not a slut.
> > (ibid 12 November 1668)

However, Pepys sometimes muddies the waters by using abusive terms in a complimentary context, or simply implying a kitchen maid; thus his description of a servant girl as:

> our little girl Susan is a most admirable Slut and pleases us mightily, doing more service than both the others and deserves wages better.
>
> (ibid 21 February 1664)

Even the normally restrained John Evelyn cannot help but import abusive descriptions of women into his descriptions of the poor air quality in London. Butchers produce 'horrid stinks, nidorous [*sic*] and unwholesome smells … ', but Londoners 'would rather dwell ne'er Ten Bawds, [i.e. a women given to fornication] than One Butcher'.[2]

Perhaps one of the worst literary misogynists of all time was the author Jonathan Swift (1667–1745), describing a woman in his seminal novel *Gulliver's Travels* as an 'ugly, evil-smelling animal', and in a work entitled *Polite Conversation* written in 1738 stated that 'a dead wife under the table is the best goods in a man's house'. Some of his comments are less offensively comprehensible, but there is a suspicion that they are nevertheless intended to be unflattering: 'last week I saw a woman flayed [severely whipped] and you will hardly believe, how much it altered her person for the worst.'

Swift was following a long tradition of libelling women in literature. Authors in the seventeenth century had been obsessed with the falseness of women's emotions; the Elizabethan dramatist and pamphleteer, Thomas Dekker (1572–1632) wrote:

> Trust not a woman when she cries
> For she'll pump water from her eyes
> With a wet finger, and in faster showers
> Than April when he rains down flowers.

Even Shakespeare was cynical about the same subject when he has Othello say: 'If that the earth could teem with woman's tears, each drop she falls would prove a crocodile' (*Othello* 1604) and likewise the Jacobean dramatist John Webster (1580?–1634?) 'There's nothing sooner dries than woman's tears' (*The White Devil* 1604).

James Boswell was living in London when he met Samuel Johnson, the man with whose name he was to become forever synonymous; the journal that he kept during the year 1762–63 records their first and subsequent meetings and their conversations concerning art, literature and life in general. The same journal also records Boswell's sex life, not only with ladies of fashion, but also his various assignations with the professional ladies of the town, with whom he regularly consorted in order to satisfy his not inconsiderable feelings of lust. Despite using these women, who in all probability had no other means of support, he not only describes them in his journal using the most insulting language, but is not above employing physical violence towards them as well as subjecting them to verbal abuse.

On the night of the king's birthday, Saturday 6 June 1763, in order to avoid being recognised as a gentleman he dresses in his oldest soiled clothes, including a hat belonging to a disbanded officer of the Royal Volunteers, and sallies abroad 'resolved to be a blackguard and to see all that was to be seen'. It is not long before he has his first adventure of the night:

> I went to the Park, picked up a low brimstone [harridan, shrew, virago], called myself a barber and agreed with her for sixpence, went to the bottom of the park arm in arm, dipped my machine in the Canal and performed most manfully. I then went as far as St Paul's Church-yard, roaring along, and then came to Ashley's Punch-house and drank three three-penny bowls. In the Strand I picked up a little profligate wretch and gave her sixpence. She allowed me entrance. But the miscreant refused me performance. I was much stronger than her and volens nolens [willing or unwilling] pushed her up against the wall. She however gave a sudden spring from me; and screaming out, a parcel of more whores and soldiers came to her relief. 'Brother soldiers,' said I, 'should not a half-pay officer roger for sixpence? And here has she used me so and so'. I got them on my side, and I abused her in blackguard style, and then left them.[3]

Not satisfied with physically and verbally abusing the woman and impersonating an army officer, Boswell continues on his night-time perambulation of the town, and attempts to pick up a third woman:

> At Whitehall I picked up another girl to whom I called myself a highwayman and told her I had no money and begged she would trust me. But she would not. My vanity was somewhat gratified tonight that, notwithstanding of my dress, I was always taken for a gentleman in disguise.

Boswell regularly employed prostitutes in order to slake his lustful appetites, usually going 'armoured', that is to say wearing a condom, for the eighteenth-century gentlemen were well aware of how venereal diseases were transmitted and pregnancy brought about, even if they were ignorant of the cause. Although he

33

is happy to satiate his sexual desires with these women, he is unfailingly abusive about them in his journals:

> I should have mentioned last night that I met with a monstrous big whore in the Strand, whom I had a great curiosity to lubricate, as the saying is. I went into a tavern with her, where she displayed to me all the parts of her enormous carcass; but I found that her avarice was as large as her arse, for she would by no means take what I offered her.

Like Samuel Pepys a century before, he is not only abusive to and about prostitutes, but is forever swearing to cease any further connection with them, a resolution which, like Pepys, he consistently fails to honour;

> At night I took a streetwalker into Privy Garden and indulged sensuality. The wretch picked my pocket of my handkerchief, and then swore that she had not. I was shocked to think that I had been intimately united with a low, abandoned, perjured, pilfering creature. I determined to do so no more; but if the Cyprian fury should seize me, to participate my amorous flame with a genteel girl.

It was not only prostitutes and poor women who suffered verbal abuse. Some of the most acerbic attacks were made on women of wealth and class. John Wilmot, 2nd Earl of Rochester was particularly abusive about various women at the court of Charles II. Wilmot was renowned for composing short lampoons on the sexual mores of those of his acquaintance. Cary Frazier, the daughter of the king's physician and a maid of honour was one who felt the sharp edge of his sarcasm:

> Her father gave her dildoes six,
> Her mother made 'em up a score,
> But she loves nought but living pricks
> And swears by God she frig no more.

Further up the social scale, female aristocrats felt the bite of his vitriolic pen. Barbara Palmer, Lady Castlemain, the Duchess of Cleveland and the king's favourite mistress, had already been called a 'vile whore' to her face by courtiers in St James's park, but Wilmot's libels were even more colourful:

> Castlemain is much to be admir'd
> Although she ne'er was satisfied or tired
> Full forty men a day provided for this whore,
> Yet like a bitch she wags her tail for more.

And in a similar vein …

> That pattern of virtue Her Grace of Cleveland
> Has swallowed more pricks than the ocean has sand …

Jonathan Swift (1667–1745) wrote much scatological verse concerning women's natural bodily functions, none more overtly misogynistic than a poem entitled 'The Lady's Dressing Room' (1732). This poem describes how Strephon explores his mistress's dressing room and beginning with an ideal image of his lover, he looks through the contents of her room, but encounters only objects that repulse him: sweaty smocks, dirt-filled combs, oily cloths, grimy towels, snot-encrusted handkerchiefs, jars of spit, cosmetics derived from dog intestines, and a mucky, rancid clothes chest and culminating in the discovery of her (not empty) chamber pot. After his discovery of Celia's nauseating dressing room he can never look at women the same way again:

> The stockings why should I expose,
> Stained with the marks of stinking toes;
> Or greasy coifs and pinners reeking,
> Which Celia slept at least a week in?

The appendix at the end of this book lists nearly 140 slang words from the seventeenth and eighteenth centuries alluding to women's persons and their occupations, almost all of them derogatory and misogynistic in nature.

Chapter 4

Abduction & Clandestine Marriage

In the twenty-first century the very word 'clandestine' suggests something which is at best secretive and at worst illegal, but in the seventeenth and eighteenth centuries many couples preferred to have a such a marriage, to the extent that tens of thousands of couples of all social classes were legally and respectably married in 'clandestine' ceremonies.

A 'clandestine marriage' was entirely legal as long as the ceremony was performed by an ordained clergyman. It had a number of advantages over an official marriage: it was cheaper and quicker and it did away with the need for publishing banns and buying a licence. Moreover, the betrothed couple were not restricted to marrying in their own parish, and if needs be the date of the ceremony could be backdated to cover an unplanned pregnancy; such desperate couples could be married away from the public eye as well as interfering or furious relatives. It was also an attractive option for foreign couples not registered as resident in a parish or serving soldiers and sailors on time-constrained leave.

A number of places in London became well-known centres for clandestine marriages including All Hallows Church in Honey Lane, St Pancras in Soper Lane, the Mayfair Chapel (which tried to encourage business by having as a centrepiece the supposedly embalmed corpse of the wife of the parson) and the most popular of all, the chapel in the notorious Fleet prison, which also offered as part of the wedding package a dining room, coffee shop, and sleeping facilities.

In common with all prisons at the time, bribery and corruption in the Fleet prison ensured that anyone willing and able to pay could do more or less as they pleased. This guaranteed that for the right fee governors, wardens and clergy would obligingly look the other way if the marriage was in any manner suspect or one or other of the two parties (but most commonly the female participant) appeared to be less than willing.

Fleet marriages, as they became known, were always regarded with suspicion and were eventually banned and the clandestine marriage business simply moved outside its walls to an area which for some inexplicable reason fell outside the jurisdiction of the church but was still classed as being under 'the Rules of the Fleet'. This unsavoury neighbourhood amazingly allowed prisoners to live in lodgings outside the prison as long as they paid the gaoler a fee to compensate him for loss of income. Taverns and coffee houses such as the 'Bull and Garter', 'The Great Hand and Pen' and 'The Star' recognised a good business opportunity and turned themselves into extremely profitable 'marriage houses', some even maintaining an in-house clergyman.[1]

It takes little imagination to realise that such a complete lack of legal safeguards quickly and easily led to abuse and criminal activity, where unscrupulous men might satisfy their carnal lusts with little or no risk to themselves, and others made money from facilitating such an opportunity. The writer, journalist, pamphleteer and spy Daniel Defoe observed that 'a gentleman might have the satisfaction of hanging a thief that stole and old horse from him, but could have no justice against a rogue for stealing his daughter', and who had to confine his daughters to their rooms to prevent them from being abducted by 'rogues, cheats, gamesters and such like starving crew'. Defoe's anxieties were well-founded as the sad case of a young woman by the name of Sibble Morris clearly illustrates.

On 5 March 1728, 16-year-old Miss Sibble Morris and her maid Anne Holiday were paying a second visit to a Mrs Hendron, whom they had visited on one previous occasion. On the way they met two acquaintances, Kitty Pendergrass and Peggy Johnson, who informed them that Mrs Hendron was out on a visit to a house in New Round Court in the Strand and that Sibble and her maid could accompany them to that address. Upon arrival they were ushered into a darkened room, the windows shuttered against the light and the only illumination being from a few candles. The dimly lit room already contained a number of people, including one Richard Russell, an allegedly wealthy merchant previously introduced to Sibble by Mrs Pendergrass, a Mrs Rigy and an unknown clergyman.

Sensing that all was not well, Sibble and her maid tried to leave, whereupon both were seized and dragged forcibly into the room, the door slamming behind them. Preparations were made as if for a marriage ceremony, the bride being in a state of panic and having to be restrained throughout the ceremony. Mrs Pendergrass had informed the terrified girls that calling for help was useless as no one would her them and even though the bride was unable to speak throughout the proceedings the clergyman claimed at the subsequent trial that he had noticed nothing amiss and was under the impression that a gentleman was clandestinely marrying a servant girl, who was overcome by the whole situation.

The ceremony over, Sibble was dragged upstairs to a candle-lit bed chamber where Mrs Hendron held her spread-eagled and pinioned to the bed while Kitty Pendergrass and Peggy Johnson stripped off her clothes. Once naked, she continued to be held down on the bed until Richard Russell joined them.

It was only on the following Thursday that Sibble's father heard about the marriage from a man who had pretended to be a friend of Russel. On hearing the devastating news Mr Morris confronted his daughter, who in her distress admitted that it was due to fear and shame that she had not told him what had happened. Mr Morris refused to speak to Russel who on hearing that a warrant for his arrest had been issued, fled. Throughout the trial, Sibble maintained that she had never at any point agreed to the marriage. Russel's female accomplices were found guilty of aiding and abetting a kidnap and rape and sentenced to death but the incompetent, oblivious and brainless clergyman (if you can believe he really did not know what was going on) was let off.[2]

The incidence of abduction of wealthy women in Ireland during the seventeenth and early eighteenth centuries appears to have been endemic. The Irish antiquary Thomas Crofton Croker (1798–1854) wrote that:

Any farmer's daughter [who] was supposed to possess a dowry was likely to be immediately seized and taken forcibly away from her father's house by a young man at the head of a gang of twenty or thirty associates.

In 1634 the situation resulted in the Irish parliament passing an act which provided for the punishment of those who 'take away … and deflower … maydens that be inheritors', a measure which directed that those found guilty of such infractions should be imprisoned for two to five years and their next of kin disinherited.

Members of the aristocracy who had fallen on hard times often saw the abduction of a wealthy woman as a way out of their predicament and one such was Patrick Sarsfield, 1st Earl of Lucan (1650?–1693). Sarsfield's first recorded involvement in the abduction of a woman took place in London in May 1682 when he, one Captain Robert Clifford and a James Purcell, all reputed to be gentlemen and of good family, abducted Ann Siderlin, a recently bereaved widow whose wealth and property was coveted by Captain Clifford. When the matter came to court, Sarsfield was lucky to escape prosecution for his role in this incident, but his good fortune did persuade him persuade him to mend his ways. Less than a year later, he abducted Elizabeth Herbert, the widowed second daughter of Lord Chandos. Elizabeth was not impressed by his declarations of love, and refused absolutely his offer of marriage.

Faced with an unwilling abductee, Sarsfield undertook to release her if she promised not to initiate his prosecution. Realising that her freedom depended on her compliance, she agreed.

ABDUCTION & CLANDESTINE MARRIAGE

As the case of the 1st Earl Lucan demonstrates, abduction of a woman for illicit or immoral purposes was not confined to the criminal or poorer classes in society. The English aristocracy were also known to fall back on the stratagem, as the diarist Samuel Pepys recounts:

> Thence to my Lady Sandwich's, where, to my shame, I had not been a great while before. Here, upon my telling her a story of my Lord Rochester's running away on Friday night last with Mrs [Elizabeth] Mallett, the great beauty and fortune of the North, who had supped at White Hall with Mrs Stewart, and was going home to her lodgings with her grandfather, my Lord Haly, by coach; and was at Charing Cross seized on by both horse and foot men, and forcibly taken from him, and put into a coach with six horses, and two women provided to receive her, and carried away. Upon immediate pursuit, my Lord of Rochester (for whom the King had spoke to the lady often, but with no success) was taken at Uxbridge; but the lady is not yet heard of, and the King mighty angry, and the Lord sent to the Tower.
>
> (*Diary of Samuel Pepys,* Sunday 28 May 1665)

In spite of infuriating the king and being sent to the Tower, it seems that Rochester had not abandoned his matrimonial plans, as in January 1667 he again ran off with Elizabeth and they were married in a clandestine ceremony at Knightsbridge Chapel, contrary to the wishes of her father, John Mallett.

When the lady was unwilling to go quietly, it comes as no surprise that threats of physical violence and/or blackmail were commonly used as ways of persuading a reluctant woman to cooperate with her abductors. In 1701, the 17-year-old heiress, Pleasant Rawlins was arrested for an imaginary unpaid debt of £200 trumped up by one Haagen Swendsen, a German adventurer who had previously made advances to the young woman, but who had been decisively rejected. The suitor was not to be denied his consummation however, and very soon physical force was added to the lies already employed.

Seized under false pretences, Pleasant was taken first to the Star and Garter in Drury Lane but then moved to The Vine in Holborn where Swendsen's accomplice, a Mrs Baynton, convinced the girl that she would be incarcerated in Newgate for debt if she refused to go through with the marriage. Now more afraid of being murdered by her captors than worried about imprisonment, a terrified Pleasant reluctantly agreed to the union and was married to Swendsen in the Fleet Prison. When Pleasant's horrified family finally found out what had happened to her, Swendsen and Mrs Baynton were arrested and the marriage ruled illegal. Swendsen was found guilty and hanged but Mrs Baynton 'pleaded her belly' [i.e. claimed that she was pregnant] and escaped the death penalty.

THE VIOLENT ABUSE OF WOMEN

The passing of the Marriage Act as proposed in 1753 by Lord Chancellor Hardwicke and implemented the following year put an end to clandestine marriages of all descriptions. From then on it was illegal to get married without publishing banns or obtaining a licence. Girls under the age of 21 were required to obtain the permission of their parents or guardians and the marriage itself had to take place in an Anglican church (although Jews and Quakers were exempt). Verbal and written contracts without any of the foregoing were no longer accepted as legal evidence of a marriage. Couples had to register their marriages in the parish register and the signatures of the bride and groom had to be witnessed by two independent witnesses, a requirement still applicable to this day.

Chapter 5

The Smart of the Lash

Throughout history, the female criminal has always been regarded by society as doubly deviant; firstly, because she had violated the criminal and moral law and secondly (and in some eyes perhaps more importantly), because she had violated the close strictures governing the female role within society.

In December 1678 a number people accused of theft appeared for trial at the Old Bailey, including six women. The court records reveal that not only did the judge sentence them to a brutal physical punishment typical of the time, but first saw fit to subject the women to a litany of threats and a vitriolic verbal assault, describing them among other things as being 'a parcel of sluts':

> Then the Prisoners Convict for Petty Larceny, who were these … Mary Read, Mary Hipkins, Margaret Smith, Mary Hutchins, Judith Smith, and Anne Harris: whose Sentence was delivered thus:
>
> 'You the Prisoners at the Bar, I have observed in the time that I have attended here, that your Pick-pockets, Shop-lifters, and you other Artists, which I am not so well acquainted with, which fill up this place, throng it most with Women, and generally such as she there, Mary Hipkins, with whom no admonitions will prevail. They are such, whose happiness is placed in being thought able to teach others to be cunning in their wickedness, and their Pride is to be thought more flie than the rest: A parcel of Sluts, who make it their continual study to know how far they may steal, and yet save their necks from the Halter, and are as perfect in that, as if they had never been doing anything else. But take notice of it, you that will take no warning, I pass my word for it, if e'er I catch you here again, I will take care you shall not easily escape.
>
> And the rest of those Women, that have the impudence to smoke Tobacco, and gussle in All [ale] houses; pretend to buy Hoods and Scarfs, only to have an opportunity to steal them, turning Thieves to maintain your luxury and pride: So far shall you be from any hope of mercy, if we meet with you here for the future, that you shall be

sure to have the very rigour of the Law inflicted on you. And I charge him that puts the Sentence in Execution, to do it effectually, and particularly to take care of Mrs Hipkins, scourge her soundly; and the other Woman that us'd to steal Gold Rings in a Country Dress; and since they may have a mind to it this cold-weather, let them be well heated.

Your Sentence is this, that you be carried from hence to the place from hence you came, and from thence be dragged tied to a Carts-rail through the streets, your Bodies being stript from the Girdle upwards, and be Whipt till your Bodies bleed.[1]

Lower courts commonly sentenced women to be sent to the 'house of correction' or Bridewell. The name 'Bridewell' as a designation for a prison was first applied to an institution founded near St Bride's well in the city of London. In 1553 King Edward VI gave the palace of the same name (built 1515–20 for Henry VIII) to the City of London as a penal workhouse for the reception of vagrants, homeless children and disorderly women:

This Edward of fair memory the Sixt,
In whom with greatness goodness was commixt,
Gave this Bridewell, a palace in olden times,
For a chastening house of vagrant crimes[2]

The individuals who qualified to be incarcerated in this 'chastening house' were defined by Bishop Ridley, interestingly with women of loose morals at the top of the list: 'The strumpet and idle person, for the rioter that consumeth all, and for the vagabond that will abide in no place [i.e. one who might currently be recognised as homeless].'

As late as 1775, John Howard[3] the Sheriff of Bedfordshire (1726–90), undertook a tour of British and European prisons and was appalled at what he found. His report 'The State of the Prisons' published in 1777 stated that 'they were badly maintained, inadequately cleaned and disgracefully supervised and managed to extort excessive fees from the prisoners for the slightest privilege'. In visiting Wymondham Bridewell in Norfolk, he found the women prisoners to be 'dirty and ficky [sic] objects at work with padlocks on their legs'.

At the Bridewell in Abingdon, Oxfordshire, he found eight women confined in two rooms, one 9ft by 8 (2.7 x 2.4 meters) and the other 4½ft square (1.4 meters). The straw on the floor had been worn to dust and was swarming with vermin. The prisoners were in irons and had no water available. Fresh air and exercise were permitted in the yard once a week on Sundays.

The reality was a long way from the originally declared intention of being about reform rather than punishment, with inmates required to earn their keep. In all Bridewells the disobedient were beaten in turn, twenty-four to forty strokes being the usual sentence depending on the severity of the offence. Over two-thirds of the prisoners were female, and although information about prisoners' backgrounds is limited, most appear to have been poor and single, and many were only recent migrants to London. Virtually all the prisoners were put to hard labour during their term of imprisonment, typically beating hemp.

In addition, over half of those incarcerated were also sentenced to be whipped, often several times, either upon reception and before release (known as 'welcome' and 'farewell') or at pre-determined intervals throughout their imprisonment. The instrument of punishment was commonly a cat o' nine tails, with a whalebone handle to which were attached nine cords, 36in long [91cm], each knotted seven times to ensure that the skin of the victim was broken, as prisoners were often sentenced to be whipped until their bodies were 'bloody'.

Particularly punished in this way were those deemed guilty of petty theft, lewd conduct and night-walking (prostitution). Anyone who could show no permanent abode was deemed a vagrant and publicly whipped out of the town. 'Travellers' were even more severely dealt with; when a band of gypsies were rounded up at Haddington in 1636, the men and women without children were hanged or drowned. The women with children were accorded the 'merciful' penalty of being flogged through the town, branded on both cheeks and thrown out onto the road again.

Additionally, women who had simply been found to have given birth out of wedlock or who were discovered in an adulterous relationship were punished for sexual deviancy or 'wantonness'. Prison in this period is not seen as a punishment in itself, merely a place where physical chastisement is administered, or a place in which to await the convicted individual's public punishment:

> Mary Williams for going away and leaving her Children to be Chargeable to the Parish of Kingsbury is ordered to be sent to the said parish on Wednesday the first day of July and there to be publickly [sic] whipped at the whipping Post at six o'clock in the afternoon and referred to Thomas Niccoll Esqr to Continue or discharge as he shall think fit.[4]

More than half of offenders were released within a week of their commitment, and two-thirds within two weeks. For the most part, punishment in houses of correction took the form of what would now be described as a short, sharp shock. Bridewells quickly obtained a reputation for the regularity and severity of the corporal punishments administered to its unfortunate inmates. The expression 'whipping cheer' meaning a good flogging, occurs often in the literature of the period and was well understood at the time:

> Hell is the place where whipping-cheer abounds
> But no one jailor there to wash the wounds.[5]

Shakespeare was well acquainted with the expression, knowing full well what awaited women unfortunate enough to find themselves incarcerated in such an institution; Mistress Quickly and Mistress Doll are taken to prison by a most unsavoury beadle who promises Doll that 'she shall have whipping cheer I warrant her' (*Henry IV Part 2*).

The twice-weekly floggings of women in these institutions was notoriously carried out in a chamber adjacent to the courtroom in front of the president, the assembled governors and the members of the general public at a pre-ordained time:

> as morning prayers and flagellation ends. It is between 11.00 and 12.00 in the morning, after church service, that criminals are whipped in the Bridewell.
>
> (*The Dunciad* Alexander Pope 1688–1744)

The procedure for punishing the convicted women is described by Edward Ward in his publication *The London Spy*, a periodical published between 1660 and 1667 (and later as a book in 1703). It concerns an innocent country gentleman visiting his friend in London, and the adventures they fall into. He gives vivid descriptions of the lower classes of the day and the methods they employed to make ends meet – including prostitution, robbery, burglary and other felonious activities:

> Women to be punished were stripped bare to the waist and whipped on their naked backs before the court of governors. The President sat with his hammer in his hand, and the flogging ceased and the culprit taken down from the whipping-post only when he deemed the punishment to be sufficient and the hammer fell. The call from the friends or relations of the miscreant 'Oh, good Sir Robert, knock! Pray, good Sir Robert, knock!' became at length a common insult among the lower orders intonating [*sic*] that a woman had been whipped in the Bridewell.
>
> (*The London Spy* Edward Ward 1660)

In addition to undergoing severe corporal punishment, the convicted women were unwittingly the object of erotic entertainment for both sexes. The author Sir Walter Besant tells us that 'the flogging of women in the Bridewell was one of the sights of London to which anyone could go'. Members of the general public were admitted to the court to witness the execution of these whippings, a day out that became immensely popular – especially among fashionable women who made up parties to witness the spectacle. This was obviously an erotic attraction universally patronised by society ladies throughout Europe – their enthusiasm is mentioned several times in Wilhelm Reinhard's work 'Lenchen im Zuchthause' (first published in Germany in 1840, the English version appeared as 'Nell in Bridewell') which although fictional, undoubtedly reflects what was a common public attraction at the time:

> But oh, you should have seen, how the great ladies, who never fail to be present at 'Welcomes' and 'Farewells', how they rush into the hall …. The high-born ladies came first; everybody else had to give way before them and make room … where places had been specially reserved for them … the spectators, nearly all of them of the female sex, strictly ordered according to rank, now crowded closely round, almost all of them manifesting the utmost delight at being able to assist at such a pleasant spectacle … accompanied by experienced prognostics of the effect of the strokes and of the pain caused thereby, so soon to be visible.

The terms 'welcome; and 'farewell' relate to the practice, common in Germany and sometimes ordered in England that the woman be flogged upon arrival in the Bridewell and then again immediately before being discharged.

The West End dainties paid a visit daily
To see the strumpets whipped at the Old Bailey
(*The Rodiad* attributed to George
Coleman 1762–1836)

Such was the popularity of the spectacle in London that a special gallery had to be built to accommodate them. Before the construction of the gallery, the governors sat behind the public in the court and therefore could not get an uninterrupted view of the women being stripped and whipped without making the spectators stoop down. This caused disturbance and disruption in the court, so in order that everyone should get a good view of the spectacle, the whipping post and the platform upon which it stood had to be raised:

> Also this Court by dayly Observacon [*sic*] finding That by reason of the *Whipping* post standing Soe low the Governrs Cannot Soe the Correccon [*sic*] given without causing the Spectators to Stoop downe wth [which] Occasions a great Noise and disturbance in this Court. It is therefore Ordered That the workemen belonging to this Hospll.

45

doe raise the same Soe that it maybe more Usefull & Convenient for the future If it may be done without Disfiguring the Forme of this Court roome.[6]

In his journal, Edward Ward graphically describes his visit to the London Bridewell, where the court was in session:

From thence my friend conducted me to the Bridewell, being Court Day, to give me the diversion of seeing the lechery of some town ladies cooled by a cat o' nine tails … my friend led me up a pair of stairs into a spacious chamber, where the court was sitting in great grandeur and order. A grave gentleman whose awful looks bespoke him some honourable citizen, was mounted in the judgement seat, armed with a hammer, like a change broker at Lloyd's Coffee House, and a woman squirming under the lash was in the next room where folding doors were open so that the whole Court might see the punishment inflicted. At last down went the hammer, and the scourging ceased. The honourable Court, I observed, were chiefly attended by men in blue coats and women in blue aprons.

Another accusation being then delivered by a flat-cap against a poor wench, who having no friend to speak on her behalf, proclamation was made, viz: 'All you who are willing E—th T—ll shall have present punishment? Pray hold up your hands'. This was done accordingly, and then she was ordered with the civility of the house, and was forced to show her tender back and tempting bubbies to the grave sages of the august assembly, who were moved by her modest mien, together with the whiteness of her skin, to give her but a gentle correction.

(*The London Spy* Edward Ward 1660)

Having satiated themselves with watching the women undergoing corporal punishment, Ward and his friend took a look at the prison where they were confined:

We followed our noses and walked up to take a view of these ladies who, we found, were shut up as close as nuns. But like many other slaves, they were under the care of an overseer who walked about with a very flexible weapon of offence to correct such women as were troubled by idleness.

(ibid)

Not surprisingly, these sights have been described as the pornography of the age, with much erotic appeal and especially popular it seems with those who were responsible for its imposition, a fact that did not go unnoticed in the day. The author John Leanerd makes it clear that many enjoyed sexual satisfaction from the spectacle, thus saving themselves the cost of hiring a prostitute. In a play published in 1678, a girl declares to the Justice of the Peace who is courting her: 'I could love you could you forebear that hard-hearted trick of seeing women whipped at the House of Correction'. The Justice replies 'I never use it, but I know some of your London justices do, it is a kind of pleasure to 'em and I dare say, saves 'em many a crown in the year'. (*The Rambling Justice* John Leanerd 1678)

> You must yourself recognize that there exists in some minds a certain morbid love of the lash which may yet be so modified that although abuses exist in all systems of punishment, the act itself can be quite regular and conformable to law, while the feelings, and indeed the accessory motives, of judge, spectators and executors may be in themselves sinful and blameworthy.[7]

There is no doubt that many individuals of both genders obtained sexual gratification from watching the suffering of the unfortunate women who found themselves under the lash. Some publications described the attachment to this form of titillation in even greater detail, frankly acknowledging their masturbatory potential. A lampoon entitled the *City Painter* published in the 1680s describes how a well-known knight of the time regularly attended the Bridewell, where he was usually to be observed,

> peeping at the wenches backs and calling for their petticoats to be pulled yet lower [in order] that he may see the buttocks of the whore. Often at the sight of a milkye skin under the lash he hath been groping in his codpiece, frigging while she's whipt.

Surely there is more than a hint of licentious glee in the voice of Henry Fielding's Justice, who explains why he has sentenced a young man and woman to be sent to the Bridewell:

> Aye, [says the justice] a kind of felonious, larcenous thing, I believe I must order them a little correction too, a little stripping and whipping.
> (*Joseph Andrews* Henry Fielding 1742)

The corporal punishment of domestic servants also had erotic appeal for some employers. A work entitled *Memoirs of a Domestic Servant* published in London in 1797 recounts how the narrator John is compelled by his mistress to whip a page-boy while she watches. This accomplished, she then orders him to strip and whip her two nieces in turn, which he does.

Town councils were particularly concerned with controlling women's public behaviour and, especially their sexuality, in order to create an orderly society and eliminate the creation of bastard children. In 1650, the Commonwealth government had introduced an act of parliament for 'The Suppression of the Detestable Sins on Inceste, Adulterie and Fornication', which ordered that all bawds 'had to be whipped openlie and branded with an AB on the fore-head'. The act was obviously less than successful in inhibiting licentious behaviour, for by 1690 the Society for the Reformation of Manners was calling for all prostitutes to be whipped, as indeed many had already been:

> Jennie and Betty do the Lash defie
> And swear they'll use the Trade until they die
> Bridewell afflicts their backs, but let me tell ye
> They are not tormented below their belly
>
> *('The Bridewell Whores' Resolution'* –
> Jacobean ballad)

Couples arrested for keeping a bawdy-house (brothel) would be subject to the same penalties as the whores for whom they provided. However, it was not uncommon for the man in the case to escape scot-free while the woman often suffered a multiple penalty:

> John Sissell and Margery Sissell for keeping a bawdy-house. The said John is at large; the said Margery has judgment to be carted and *whipped* and to find sureties for good behaviour, after imprisonment for one month.[8]

However, any behaviour thought to be unworthy of a woman and likely to cause a disturbance was soon brought into the legal net. This attitude meant that residents often complained to their council about women whose behaviour was considered inappropriate and the council then took action. For example, on 5 September 1757, Aberdonian Fanny Hall was 'complained upon several times for haunting loose and disorderly company [and for] disturbing the neighbourhood where she resided at unreasonable hours in the night-time'. At the court session in the spring of 1758, she was first publicly whipped at the post and then banished from the town.

As is the case in modern times, British courts took a dim view of crimes involving the theft of money by deception, and for a woman the penalty could be both humiliating and painful:

Order for Jane Smyth and Elizabeth Boyle, convicted of cheating and defrauding Isabel, wife of William Scales, of £9, to be stripped naked from the middle upwards and publicly *whipped* at a cart's tail round Red Lion Square, in the parish of St Andrew's, Holborn, and to be remanded to Newgate gaol until they undergo their punishment and pay their fees.

Order for Elizabeth Boyle and Alice Jones, convicted of defrauding Katherine Shute, widow, of £9, to be fined 6/8, and for Elizabeth Boyle to be put upon the pillory before Grays Inn Foregate, in the parish of St Andrew, Holborn, for the space of one hour, with a paper over her head describing her said offence. Alice Jones is to be stripped from the middle upwards and publicly *whipped* at a cart's tail from Gray's Inn Foregate to Southampton Street, in the parish of St Giles'-in-the-Fields. The said Elizabeth and Alice are both remanded to Newgate gaol until they pay their fines, undergo their punishment and pay their fees.[9]

Alice Jones was obviously a serial offender – having been whipped at the cart's tail from Gray's Inn to Southampton Street, she was to be similarly whipped, this time with a different accomplice, from Holborn Bar to St Giles in the Fields:

Itt [*sic*] is ordered by this Court that Alice Jones & Jane Cheese who now stand convicted upon an Indictment against them for a notorious Cheat & Misdemeanour be and they are severally fined for the said Offence One Shilling and that they be stripped naked from the middle upwards and openly whipped at a Carts Tayler upon such day at the Sheriffe of this County shall forthwith appoint from a certaine place called Holborne Barrt in the parish of St Andrew Holborne in this County through the publick Street to & against the parish Church of the parish of St Giles in the Feilds in the said County untill their Bodies be bloody and the Said Alice Jones & Jane Cheese are remanded to his Maties Gaole of Newgate there to remaine untill they pay the Said Fine & undergoe the Said punishment then to be delived (... if detained for no other cause) paying their Fees Severally 16s: 03d[10]

The severity of a flogging at 'a cart's tail' depended almost entirely upon the length of the route specified by the court and thereby the number of lashes the miscreant could expect to receive. In the first order, Jane Smyth and Elizabeth Boyle are to be 'carted' round Red Lion Square in London, which still exists today. The square is approximately 350 meters in circumference, a distance that would take perhaps up to fifteen minutes or more behind a slowly lumbering cart. Assuming the beadle applied the lash to the women's naked backs four or five times a minute, Jane and Elizabeth could expect to receive at least three or four dozen lashes.

The second order is of a much greater magnitude – Gray's Inn in London is around one 1,500 meters from Southampton Street by the shortest possible route (ignoring modern one-way street systems), which might take the cart half an hour or more. Elizabeth and Alice might therefore to expect at least 120 strokes of the 'cat', perhaps more if the beadle felt particularly vindictive.

An appearance in court was not always necessary. Local mayors wielded considerable powers and quite often dispensed summary justice without bothering with the inconvenience of a trial. Thomas Powell, mayor of Deal in Kent in 1703, pursued a personal campaign against vice, offenders against common decency and those who broke the sanctity of the Sabbath. He recorded in his diary how he had taken the law into his own hands:

> took up a common prostitute, whose conduct was very offensive, and brought her to the whipping-post – being about mid market, where was present some hundreds of people. I caused her to have twelve lashes, and at every third lash I parlayed with her and bid her tell all the women of her like calling wheresoever she came, that the Mayor of Deal would serve them as he had served her if they came to Deal and committed such wicked deeds as she had done.

Disturbance of the peace or immorality were not the only things that could lead a woman to the whipping-post. Over indulgence in alcohol, as poorly regarded then as now, might have the same outcome. On 30 April 1690 at Durham, Eleanor Wilson, a married woman, was found to be drunk during the Sunday church service and as a result she was publicly whipped on the following market day between 11 a.m. and 12.00 noon.

However, it was offences of the flesh that often carried the greatest severity of punishment, such penalties administered not just once but over and over again. In 1754, Sarah Deacon was unfortunate (or unwise) enough to bear an illegitimate child. For this 'crime', she was sentenced to be confined to the House of Correction for a full month and taken out every Friday afternoon to be whipped at the post between 2 p.m. and 3 p.m. in the market place at Thatcham in Berkshire.

Conversely, becoming pregnant might be the only chance a woman had of being let off from a flogging to which she had been sentenced:

> Wednesday 8th May 1799. Sarah Liscombe a woman two months gone with child (by own declaration & the observation of our Apothecary Mr Haslam) having been ordered to be whipped, the whipping is to be omitted in that account.[11]

The definition of immorality in women was broadly based and its punishment had a long history. Even a woman who had been faithful to the same man for a long period of time – what now would be described as a 'common-law wife' – was not immune from punishment for sexual impropriety. At the beginning of the fourteenth century, the register of the Bishop of Worcester recorded that a sub-deacon had cohabited with a woman for many years and she had born him no less than five children. When it was discovered that they were not legally married, she was sentenced to publicly receive nine strokes of the birch on nine consecutive Sundays and nine market days, a total of 162 lashes. The sub-deacon got off significantly more lightly, being sentenced to fasting and to stand in front of the church font for seven Sundays, while thirteen poor people prayed for him. Such double standards in the punishment of men and women who had offended against public morality are common throughout history and with few exceptions it seems to be the female half of the offending pair that suffers under the lash. In 1669 in Hastings, a servant girl named Anne Park had an illegitimate child by her employer, George Laby. She was sentenced to be stripped to the waist and publicly flogged at the whipping-post, while he was sentenced to pay half-a-crown (12p equal to more than two weeks wages for a domestic servant) per week maintenance for the child.

Quite often, the father of an illegitimate child had to pay the expenses arising from his misdemeanour, but it was the woman who had her character blackened and suffered judicial corporal punishment:

> Confirmation of an order by which Thomas Edge of Lee Grainge, butcher, who was found the father of the bastard child of Elizabeth Francklyn of Lee Grainge in Quainton, single-woman, was ordered to pay all expenses to which the churchwardens and overseers of Lee Grainge had been put, and hereafter to indemnify the parish of the cost of maintenance. On the finding that Elizabeth Franklyn was a 'very lewd woman' she was committed to the bridewell of Aylesbury to be kept at hard labour until by further order she was discharged.[12]

The father of an illegitimate child might get himself off the hook by various means, without ever having to appear in court or pay maintenance, while the woman in the case suffered imprisonment and quite possibly a whipping:

> Jane Hawkins of Denham for a bastard child[13]
>
> Henry Turner of Denham, labourer, having confessed himself to be the father of the bastard child of Jane Hawkins of the same, spinster, and having refused to give security for the maintenance of the child, voluntarily enlisted as a soldier under Captain John Busby, and was discharged from the Bridewell at Chepping Wiccombe.[14]

Often, the punishment for moral offences was inflicted outside the church on a Sunday, in order that the assembled worshippers could witness retribution visited upon those who broke the appropriate commandments. Thus Agnes Bourman was sentenced at Glastonbury in 1621 to be 'openly whipped' in full view of her entire local congregation. Edith Pool of Norton Fitzwarren must, for once, have wished for a longer sermon, as she was sentenced to be 'whipped severely through the streets of the parish immediately after evening prayer'. As long ago as 1369, the Bishop of Carlisle sentenced two women for immoral behaviour to be beaten after church on Sunday mornings, ordering that each was to receive twelve separate floggings with a bull's pizzle (a whip fashioned from the animals' dried and stretched penis), an instrument capable of inflicting extreme pain and considerable injury.

Flogging was not the only form of abuse to which women were subjected while incarcerated in the Bridewell. Ironically, women convicted of sexual misconduct for which they had been imprisoned and whipped often found that their prison had been turned into a brothel. The prison's matron employed at the turn of the seventeenth century, Alice Millet, would end up as a defendant in the Bridewell court herself, charged for being 'false to her trust'. According to the court record, Millet was 'responsible for the reform of her prisoners', yet she 'encouraged them in wickedness, allowing men with money to have access to the female quarters.'[15]

The physical condition of the accused women was no barrier to the application of corporal punishment. Homelessness and poverty, universally described as 'vagrancy' in court records usually warranted a whipping. In *The Description of England* published in 1587, William Harrison describes 'several disorders and degrees among our idle vagabonds', and identifies those varieties 'of the woman kind'. He goes on to describe in some detail the punishments laid down in law for women apprehended in pursuit of such criminal activities:

> Demanders for glimmer or fire, Bawdy-baskets, Morts, Autem Morts, Walking Morts, Doxies, Dells, Kinching Morts and Kinching Coes. The punishment that is ordained for this kind of people is very sharp, and yet it cannot restrain them from their gadding: wherefore the ends must need be martial law, to be exercised upon them, as upon thieves, robbers, despisers of all laws, and enemies to the commonwealth and welfare of the land. The rogue being apprehended, committed to prison, and tried at the next assizes (whether they be of gaol delivery or sessions of the peace), if she happen to be convicted for a vagabond, either by inquest of office or the testimony of two honest and creditable witnesses upon their oaths, (she) is then immediately adjudged to be grievously whipped and burned through the gristle of the right ear with an hot iron of the compass of an inch about, as a manifestation of her wicked life,

and due punishment received for the same. And this judgment is to be executed upon her except some honest person worth five pounds in the Queen's books in goods, or twenty shillings in land, or some rich householder to be allowed by the justices, will be bound in recognizance to retain her in service for one whole year. And if she be taken the second time, and proved to have forsaken her said service, she shall then be whipped again, bored likewise through the other ear, and set to service.

Third offences were punishable by death.

Seventeenth-century court records are full of examples of such laws being rigorously applied. August 1640 saw Richard Banister and his wife Elizabeth convicted of 'vageinage and wandering', that is to say they were nothing more than homeless, but nevertheless were sentenced to 'be whipt naked until they be bloodie'. In Northampton, homeless Eleanor Childe appears before the bench for vagrancy and is handed down a savage sentence: 'To be whipt on Saturday next twixt 12 and 2 of the clock in the open market in the town of Northampton, and then be sent with a Pass to the place of her last settlement'.

Occasionally a woman's pregnancy was allowed to get in the way of a whipping sentence: 'Sarah Liscombe a woman two months gone with child (by own declaration & the observation of our Apothecary Mr Haslam) having been ordered to be whipped, the whipping is to be omitted in that account.'[16]

The courts had obviously become more lenient in the seventeenth century – back in 1533, a heavily pregnant woman had been whipped at Cheapside in London and then afterwards nailed by the ear to the pillory for suggesting that Catherine of Aragon and not Anne Boleyn was the true Queen of England!

Even a woman suffering from a serious illness was not immune from corporal punishment. In January 1699, the court at Wendover in Buckinghamshire heard a complaint from the inhabitants of Beaconsfield, that they had been forced to maintain one Ann Hone, a vagrant, who was clearly suffering from small-pox. She was being conveyed on a pass signed by the constables of Chesham, who stated therein that she had been apprehended in their town, 'sick and weak and in a low condition and that they had relieved and whipped her'. The good inhabitant's complaint was not that a very sick woman had been flogged, but that her detention in their town posed a serious risk to the health of the parishioners![17]

Conversely, as always, having friends in high places might help. During the reign of Charles II, the Duke of York interposed to save the Lady Sophia Lindsay from being publicly whipped through the streets of Edinburgh, to which she had been sentenced as a punishment for assisting in the escape of her father-in-law, the Earl of Argyle.

Many of the offences for which whippings were ordered would now be considered of a very trivial nature. In 1630, the Edinburgh Town Council sentenced a number of women to a public whipping for the wearing of plaids in the street, while in Dunfermline, Margaret Robertson and Catherine Westwood were flogged in 1653 for swearing and scolding. Insobriety, especially in church, was not tolerated. In 1627 at Beeston, a group of women became drunk and disorderly after attending church and taking the sacrament. They were sent to the local House of Correction where each of them was immediately stripped naked to the waist, tied to the post and given a whipping. On Sunday 30 April 1690 at Durham, one 'Eleanor Wilson, a marryed woman', was found to be drunk in church and as a result was publicly whipped in the market-place the following day between the hours of noon and 1 p.m. On 28 September 1699 at Burnham in Buckinghamshire, one Mrs Smat was punished for begging in the street, her sentence to be: 'Openlie whipt at Boveney in the parish of Burnham in the county of Buckinghamshire according to ye laws.'

The degree of punishment meted out to the victims took no account of age. On this occasion not only she and her husband, but also her three children each took their turn at the whipping-post for the same offence. Also at Burnham, a 60-year-old widow named Isobel Harris and Mary Webb, a 13-year-old girl were both publicly flogged on the same day and with equal severity. At Oxford in June 1654, neither youth nor her apparently diminutive size saved 14-year-old 'Little Elizabeth' Fletcher from being 'publicly and severely' whipped for blasphemy on the orders of the Vice Chancellor. In 1663, 13-year-old Alice Fautlie was 'publicly and severely' whipped at Hastings in Sussex for stealing a handkerchief. In London as late as 1800, Elizabeth Anderson was also just 13 years old when she was tried for stealing one leather bag and three silk sheets, value 10*d*. She was sentenced to be whipped in the pillory and to serve one year in Newgate prison. Even younger girls could be publicly flogged. At the Old Bailey in London on 12 December 1683, the court records record that: 'Elizabeth Howel, a Child of about Ten Years of Age, Indicted for Stealing some Childrens Clothes; and, when first Examined, having confest [*sic*] the same, she was found Guilty of Felony to the value of 10 pence.' She was tried in company with several adults, and all were 'Sentenc'd to be Whipt from Newgate, to the several Places where their respective Facts [crimes] were committed.'

Even as late as 2 April 1800, one Elizabeth Clarke, indicted for 'feloniously stealing', was sentenced to be 'whipped in the jail' at just 12 years of age.

Flogging as administered in the seventeenth and eighteenth centuries was not an insignificant punishment. In England, the instrument of punishment was often a nine-thong lash, knotted seven times along each of the thongs, the dreaded 'cat o'nine tails', although other instruments for inflicting the punishment might be specified.

The sentence of the court usually specified the time and place that the punishment would be executed and often the degree of severity to be used in its application.

This usually called for the whip to be applied until the victim's back was thoroughly flayed, as in the case of Mary Allen and Elizabeth Couch sentenced in 1772 for the theft of a hundred gallons of flour; typical of thousands of such sentences, the court ordered that they were 'to be stript naked from the middle upward and whipt till their bodies are bloody'. Similarly, the Buckinghamshire Session Records of 1696 record that: 'Jane, wife of John Inwood of Stewkley, wheelwright, for stealing 1¾ yards of serge and two pairs of stockings from William Giles junior. To be whipped by the executioner till her body is bloody.'

The following eighteenth century action for damages alleges that two women were not only falsely accused but were so injured by their flogging in the Bridewell that they were rendered seriously ill, almost to the point of death:

> Boys & uxor vers. Jenkinson Kt. & al.; Sending two Women to the House of Correction without cause.; Misleading the Justice on the Benen.; 50 l. of a piece damage to these no Parties to the Suit. The Defendants bearing malice to the Plaintiff, Susan Boyes, and to one Grace Tubby, plotted how to disgrace them, and to effect it Carsey and Pulkham caused them to be convented before the other Defendants, Sir Tho. Jenkinson and Sir John Rowse Knights, two Justices of Peace in Comitat. Suffolk, and there falsly accused them to be Persons of ill life and quality, and that the Plaintiff Susan, looking Mr Guthery a Preacher in the Face in Sermon-time, jeered and made mouths at him, and that the said Grace also had carry'd her self uncivilly and insolently towards the said Mr Guthery, when he was in the Pulpit preaching, and procured some of the Neighbours to come before the Justices, and to in. form them of their said supposed ill carriage, and that they were of ill Life and Conversation: And upon this bare Information without Oath, the said Justice (notwithstanding the said Susan and Grace upon their Examination deny'd it) made their Warrant, and sent them to the House of Correction to be there whipt, by reason of which whipping they fell dangerously sick, and one of them was in danger of death: And complaint being made to the Justices at the Bench, at the next Quarter-Sessions, and Witnesses being there offer'd to testify the danger they were in by reason of their whipping, Sir Tho. Jenkinson, to hinder the Examination, falsly and maliciously informed the Justices, that the said Susan and Grace continued in their bold Courses, and after their whipping drank a Health to him and Sir John Rouse, and caused the Bell to be tolled in derision of Justice; and by this means got the Justice not only to forbear to examine the Witnesses, but to make an Order to commit them again to the House of Correction. And for the first of these

Offences they were committed, and fined 200 Marks apiece, and, to pay 50 l. apiece damage to *Susan* and *Grace*; and Sir Tho. Jenkinson, for misleading the Justice, 20 l. Fine more, and the Decree to be read at the Assizes.[18]

Unlike military punishments of the period, the number of lashes was not usually specified, although occasionally the magistrate felt obliged to be specific in this regard; in 1778 Elizabeth Sargent was arraigned for stealing silver to the value of 2*d* and one pair of silver scissors valued at 2*d* (two old pence – less than a modern penny, or about half a US cent). In this case both the route and the number of lashes being specified – a relatively modest flogging of eighteen strokes of the whip:

> To be stript from the waiste upwards and ty'd to the Cart's Tayl and whipt at the Old Market Place, the Fishe Market and att The Sundial … sixe stripes at each place.

Rather than the number of strokes, a period of time during which the whip would continue to be applied was specified by the court. This period was commonly an hour and often as much as two. Thus at Glastonbury in 1630:

> One Joan shall tomorrow sennight [i.e. one week hence] be whipt up and down the market street between 12 and 1 of the clock, stript from neck to girdle.

If the flogging were to be administered at the 'cart's tail', the victims wrists would be tied to the back of the vehicle and would therefore follow behind it through the town as the lash was applied by the beadle. The court would specify the route to be taken – obviously the longer the route the more severe the punishment. Thus Maria Pritchard was sentenced at Bristol in 1705:

> To be stripped naked to the waist on Friday next and whipped from the Tolzey, down one side of the high street and up the other side between twelve and one o'clock.

The distance and therefore the duration of a flogging ordered by the justice could be substantial. On 23 January 1725, Sarah Kettleby from Stepney in London was convicted of 'keeping an ill-govern'd and disorderly room, and receiving and entertaining lewd and disorderly persons, whoring and misbehaving themselves'. Sarah was unable to pay the fine assessed by the court so was sentenced instead to be whipped at the cart's tail. Her punishment commenced at the Angel & Crown tavern in Crispin Street, Spittlefields. From there, the painful procession moved onto

Lamb Street, Red Lion Street and Paternoster Row before making its way back to the Angel & Crown tavern from whence it had begun. By the most direct route this represented a journey of at least 2,000 meters, or almost 1¼ miles. Even this agony was deemed to be insufficient punishment, as Sarah was further sentenced to two weeks incarceration with hard labour in the house of correction.[19]

The back of the victim after such a fustigation has been described as resembling chopped raw liver, bloody from the lacerated flesh and in severe cases, with hardly an inch of skin remaining. The contemporary description of the punishment of Mary Hamilton in 1746 (see Chapter 'Male Impersonators') horrified observers with its severity and elicited unusual sympathy. It is hardly surprising, therefore, to find that given the chance, a woman might elect an alternative punishment, even to spend many years in penal servitude, rather than undergo such an experience. This Breconshire woman took such an opportunity in 1759:

> Elizabeth Thomas single woman being indicted and convicted this present Sessions for felony. It is ordered that she be transported to some of his Majesty's Plantations in America for the Term of Seven Years. It being at her own request to avoid Corporal Punishment.

Although a single flogging was a punishment severe enough to persuade a woman to elect an alternative if she had the chance, the magistrates might be of the opinion that one application was not enough. Even for minor offences, it was often deemed necessary and desirable to flog a female culprit more than once. Typical of a double punishment was that to which Joanna Bonner was sentenced in October 1757, the sentence requiring that she be:

> Publicly whipped on Friday next and the Friday following at the parish of St Martin Stamford Baron, each day from the foot of the Stamford Bridge to Mr Neal's house.

Bearing in mind that the first flogging would have left her back raw and bleeding, it is clear that her second fustigation only a week later would have fallen on her unhealed back and must therefore have been doubly agonising. Joanna was sentenced for the theft of three pieces of brass valued at 10*d* [4½p] and the unbelievably the sentence might well have been more lenient than it might at first appear. The value may have been set at this sum to save the lady from being hanged – theft of goods valued at more than a shilling [5p] was punishable by death during this period.

Ordering that a woman be publicly whipped on two occasions until the blood ran down her back was not enough for some judges, particularly if the woman was well known to the courts. In 1764, a woman described as 'an old offender' was conveyed in a cart from the Clerkenwell Bridewell to Enfield, where she was whipped at the cart's tail by the common hangman for cutting wood on Enfield Chase. She was obliged to undergo this same punishment on no less than three separate occasions.

Even the most callous of magistrates might feel that three such floggings to be sufficient punishment for any minor theft. Nevertheless, in July 1744, a Saffron Waldon woman was convicted of stealing four different articles (a shirt, a pot and two pairs of stockings) from four separate people. If the direction of the court is understood correctly, she was sentenced to be publicly whipped on four consecutive market days for each offence, a flogging every seven days for sixteen weeks!

Sometimes the unmitigated brutality of the punishment awarded to what was – more often than not – an impoverished woman, defies belief. Martha Philipson, a widow, was indicted for stealing some ironwork of the value of 10*d*. [4½p] and was ordered on 7 October 1791:

> to the custody of the House of Correction, there to be confined and kept to hard labour in the day time and to solitary confinement in a cell at night time. On Saturday the 15th between twelve and one o'clock to be stripped naked from the waist upward and publicly whipped *at* the cart's tail till her body be bloody, from the said House of Correction round the High Cross and back again. And again to be whipped in like manner on that day four months next ensuing, and a third time on that day four months hence and finally at the expiration of the year's confinement to be again whipped in like manner.[20]

Hard labour, solitary confinement and four severe floggings over the course of a year, handed down to a middle-aged widow for what would now be regarded as a petty misdemeanour.

As has already been noted, when the magistrates decreed that a woman must be flogged at the cart's tail, the sentence usually specified the route through the town that the procession must take. In some places 'by cause of the narrowness of the streets', it was necessary to use only the broader thoroughfares in order to accommodate not only the horse and cart dragging their screaming victim, but the large crowds of jeering spectators as well. In Truro, for example, the route for flogging women generally began outside the prison, went round Middle Row and the Market Place, past 'The King's Head' inn and thence back to the prison. More usually, the magistrates had a choice of route. For example, in Northampton the magistrates could decree the 'short round' – from the Town Hall, along the Parade, the Drapery and Mercers Row. Where a more severe punishment was called for – the 'long round' could be specified – from the Old City Gaol, along the Parade, Sheep Street, Bearward Street, the Horse Market, Gold Street and George Row.

One might be forgiven for thinking that the severity of such punishments might engender some sympathy from the onlookers. Sympathy was not always with the culprit however, and then as might well be the case now, there were some folk who felt that the punishment was richly deserved. John Collier, a Hastings man writing to his wife in 1742 described the flogging of a widow by the name of Elizabeth Arthur, whom he had witnessed being whipped round the town for a period of an hour. The cart had apparently stopped at every street corner on the specified route for the lash to be applied. The culprit had obviously upset the local populace in some way by her behaviour as Mr Collier wrote to his wife that the widow had not been sufficiently punished, as she had 'hadde some strokes at every lanes ende, but I fynde that it is thoughte she hadde nott half enough'.

In the newly founded colonies of New England, society was governed with a patriarchal system of justice; magistrates and religious leaders, (often one and the same people) made the laws, and set the penalties for disobeying them, which were severe: 'The earliest criminal codes mirrored the nasty, precarious life of pioneer settlements.'[21] In addition to the usual laws governing the theft or misappropriation of property and those designed to ensure a peaceful and ordered society, much attention was given to the regulation of individual religious and sexual behaviour. Attendance at church was mandatory, especially on the Sabbath, when failure to attend twice could earn a severe public whipping. In all colonial settlements, the law set very high standards of sexual conduct; in the Plymouth Colony for example, sodomy, rape, buggery, and (for a time) adultery, were all crimes punishable by death. The Massachusetts Bay General Court declared adultery a capital crime in 1631. In 1641 John Winthrop, the first Governor of Massachusetts Colony, described one such case in his diary:

> At this court of assistants one James Britton, a man ill affected both to our church discipline and civil government, and one Mary Latham, a proper young woman about 18 years of age, whose father was a godly man and had brought her up well, were condemned to die for adultery.

The most commonly prosecuted crimes in New England during the Puritan area were sex crimes, according to Gettysburg College. Any sexual activity, besides that engaged in within a marriage, was considered criminal behaviour. Later for adultery, the punishment was more usually a whipping and a fine. In 1658 the law was finally rewritten to formalise how it had been administered previously; it defined the punishment for adultery as two severe whippings, once immediately after conviction and a second time to be determined by the magistrates; and the individual would have to wear the letters 'AD' for adulterer 'cut out in cloth and sowed on their uppermost garment on their arm or back.' If at any time they were found without the mark within the jurisdiction of the Colony, they would again be publicly whipped.

That was the case for Anne Linceford, who confessed to committing adultery and was punished by 'an immediate severe whipping at the public post in Plymouth [and] a second whipping at the public post in Yarmouth [where the act was committed]'.

Adultery was considered a more serious offence for women, who were often viewed as having tempted the man into sin. In the 1639 case of Mary Mendame, her lover was 'only' whipped at the whipping-post, a much less severe punishment than the whipping Mary received at the cart's tail, because the judges said she had enticed him:

> Mary, the wife of Robert Mendame, of Duxborrow ... using dalliance diverse times with Tinsin, an Indian, and after committing the act of uncleanness with him ... the Bench doth therefore censure the said Mary to be whipped at a cart's tail through the town's streets, and to wear a badge upon her left sleeve during her abroad within this government; and if she shall be found without it abroad, then to be burned in the face with a hot iron; and the said Tinsin, the Indian, to be well whipped with a halter about his neck at the post, because it arose through the allurement [and] enticement of the said Mary, that he was drawn thereunto.

Mary was joined on the day of her flogging by Jane Winter, also sentenced to a severe whipping for having had sexual intercourse with her husband Christopher, before they were married.

As was often the case in the mother country, the woman in such cases was more severely punished than the man. In the colonies of New England it was generally the case that married men who had sex with a single woman were charged with 'fornication', while married women who had sex with a single man were charged with the much more serious crime of 'adultery'.

Women continued to be flogged in the colony throughout the eighteenth century. General George Washington was a strong advocate of corporal punishment, as was Thomas Jefferson. In Jefferson's 1778 Bill for Proportioning Crimes and Punishments, he provided for up to fifteen lashes for individuals pretending to witchcraft or prophecy, and in the case of polygamy, a minimum half-inch hole bored in the nose cartilage with a red-hot iron of any women convicted of that crime.

The public flogging of women in the colonies of America continued until well after they had ceased to be part of the British Empire. A description of the whipping of Abigale White has come down to the present day, as she is thought to be the last woman to be publicly flogged in Vermont and probably in the New England colonies. Abigale and her husband were members of a gang of counterfeiters, forging $10 bills, and who were tried and imprisoned for their crimes. Reported as 'Strayed or Stolen' from the Newfane gaol the night of 30 September 1808, Abigail is described as 'about six feet high, very straight, and very pleasing in her conversations and manners, light complexion, she was very genteely dressed, the last time she was seen in the custody of the gaoler, when she travels she commonly wears laced boots.'

Abigale had served only fifty-one days of her sentence when she escaped. Recaptured, she was sentenced by Judge Royall Tyler to thirty-nine strokes with the cat o' nine tails, payment of a fine and court costs. On 10 August 1808 at five o'clock in the afternoon a great crowd assembled to witness the statuesque Abigail being led to the whipping-post. There she was stripped to the waist and her arms bound to the post with its crossbar near the top. The High Sheriff of Windham County, Mark Richards, and his seven deputies took it in turns to apply the cat 'o nine tails to the woman's bare back. Many decades later, eyewitness Charles K. Field, who was in the crowd as a 4-year-old child, told interviewers that 'near the close of the whipping her back became raw, and she suffered excessive pain and she shrieked and screamed terribly in her agony.'

Her husband Converse White was tried in his absence and merely fined.

Chapter 6

Burned Alive

Probably the worst example of the law punishing women more severely than men for the same crime arises from the Treason Act of 1351. That act decreed that the killing of a superior by a subordinate individual was not simply murder, but was a crime against the natural order of things and therefore an attack on the state. It would apply should a servant kill their master or mistress or a senior ecclesiastical figure be murdered by a junior one. Given the subordinate status of women at that time, it also included the murder of a husband by his wife, so instead of being punishable by hanging, the crime was classified as 'Petty Treason' and was punished by the guilty woman being drawn to the place of execution on a hurdle before being burned at the stake. It therefore joined high treason, counterfeiting and coining as punishable by a most gruesome and agonising death.

Typical of the women who were put to death in this way is Catherine Hayes, who was burned to death at Tyburn on Monday 9 May 1726. Catherine had arranged for her two lovers, Thomas Wood and Thomas Billings, to murder her husband, who was alleged to be sexually inadequate. They obliged by getting him drunk and then cutting off his head with an axe before throwing it in the Thames and disposing of the rest of the dismembered body (Wood was a butcher) in a pond at Marylebone. At their trial, and in the face of overwhelming evidence, the two men admitted to the crime, but Catherine continued to plead her innocence and claimed that Thomas Billings was in fact her son whose real name was Hayes. Nevertheless, she was found guilty of Petty Treason and sentenced to be burned at the stake. The two men were sentenced to be hanged and afterwards to have their bodies exhibited on the gibbet.

Catherine's execution was horrifically botched by the executioner, Richard Arnet. Dragged to Tyburn tied onto a hurdle, she was first forced to watch as the two men were hanged before she was secured to the stake by an iron chain around her waist. A cord was passed round her neck and through a hole in the stake, in order that the executioner could strangle her before the flames reached her, a small mercy that had become the normal practice in such cases. Two cartloads of dry brushwood were piled up around the hapless woman and set alight. She was heard begging Arnet to strangle her, but as he took hold of the cords the wind blew the flames over his hands and he was forced to let go. Catherine was heard shrieking as the flames reached her and she was observed trying to push the faggots away with her hands to no avail. As she writhed in agony, contemporary reports claim that Arnet threw a log at her head which 'broke her skull, when her brains came plentifully out.' Whether or not this is true, it was more than an hour before her body was completely reduced to ashes.

Such occasions were a huge public event, attracting thousands of people eager to watch the ghoulish spectacle. In a similar manner as Catherine Hayes, Elizabeth Herring was indicted at the Old Bailey on 8 September 1773:

> feloniously, traitorously, and of malice aforethought, making an assault upon Robert Herring, her husband, with a certain case knife giving him a mortal wound on the right side of the throat, of the length of one inch, and the depth of two inches, of which wound he instantly died, on August 5th of that year.

Elizabeth was found guilty and sentenced by the judge to be 'burnt with fire until you are dead'. She too died at Tyburn, on Monday 13 September 1773, in front of a crowd of about 20,000 spectators.

Also condemned to be burned for murdering her husband by stabbing him with a knife was one Prudence Lee, and a pamphlet of April 1652 described her execution. It recounted how she was brought on foot, between two sheriff's officers and dressed in a red waistcoat, to the place of execution in Smithfield. There she confessed to having 'been a very lewd liver, and much given to cursing and swearing, for which the Lord being offended with her, had suffered her to be brought to that untimely end'. The executioner placed her in a barrel of pitch, piled the straw and faggots around her and set them alight,

> whereupon she lifting her eyes towards Heaven, desired all that were present to pray for her; and the Executioner putting fire to the straw, she cried out, Lord Jesus have mercy on my soul; and after the fire was kindled she was heard to shrike [*sic*] out terribly some five or six several times.

The second offence for which women could be burned to death was that of 'coining' – the artificial colouring of base metal coins to resemble silver. This was the offence for which the last woman to be burned in England was found guilty. Catherine Murphy (also known as Christian Murphy or Bowman) was indicted together with her husband Hugh Murphy for 'falsely and deceitfully, feloniously and traitorously did colour with materials [base coins] producing the colour of silver.' She and her husband were executed on 18 March 1789 outside Newgate prison in a mass execution together with seven other men who had been convicted of other offences.

The eight men, including Hugh Murphy, were hanged, but as a woman, the law required that Catherine was guilty of Petty Treason should be burned at the stake. She was led from the prison past the hanging bodies of her husband and the other men, and made to stand on a 12-in high [30cm] 10-inch square [25cm] platform in front of the stake. She was secured to the stake by an iron ring around her waist and allowed a moment for prayers. When she had finished praying, the executioner, William Brunskill, piled faggots of straw around the stake and lit them. According to later testimony to Parliament given by Sir Benjamin Hammett, the Sheriff of London, he gave instructions that she should be strangled before being burned. She had been tied to the stake with a rope around her neck, after which the platform was removed from under her feet and thirty minutes were allowed to elapse before the fire was lit, and therefore she was not actually burned alive. Nevertheless, Catherine Murphy remains the last person to have been sentenced and, officially at least, executed by the method of burning.

As with other capital offences, women who were pregnant might obtain a delay in their execution, or even have the sentence commuted to a lesser one such as transportation, by 'pleading their belly', (i.e. that they were pregnant).

> In the late seventeenth and early eighteenth centuries around half of all women sentenced to death pleaded their bellies, and almost two thirds were found 'quick with child' and their punishment was respited. The remarkably large number of women who avoided punishment in this manner suggests that some women were making false claims, and that, as one observer complained, they found sympathetic female friends who made themselves available to serve on the jury of matrons, and colluded with them.[1]
>
> Unlike a trial jury, the jury of Matrons received their evidence in private, normally conducting an intimate physical inspection of the convicted woman after being led by the court bailiff to a closed room. Several tests were employed though most were not conclusive. For example, the convict's belly might be felt and her breasts squeezed for signs of lactation. Exactly how reliable these tests were, like the matrons degree of expertise, were debatable.[2]

Inevitably, not all claims were successful and the hapless women concerned would find themselves condemned to a terrible fate:

> Record of the arraignment and trial, at Session 9 July, 4 Charles I., of Alice Davies, for killing her husband Henry Davies, with record

of verdict of 'Guilty' (followed by her plea of pregnancy, which was disallowed, because a jury of matrons found her 'Not Pregnant'), and of her sentence to 'be burnt'.[3]

Despite the early success rate of such a ploy, by the last quarter of the eighteenth century only two per cent of those sentenced to be executed made such a plea and only a quarter of these were found to be pregnant. This seems to imply that the courts had either become very much better in detecting false claims, or that the recruiting of sympathetic matrons to the jury had been stopped.

Perhaps even more shocking than women being burned at the stake (if that were possible) is the fact that at least three of the victims during the period were teenagers. Mary Grote (or Troke or Groke) guilty of Petty Treason by virtue of the murder by poison of her mistress, Justin Turner, was aged just 16 when she was burnt in Winchester on Saturday 18 March 1738. Mary was tied a hurdle and dragged along in a procession behind a cart containing two men, John Boyd and James Warwick, to Gallows Hill on the outskirts of Winchester. Here she was held as usual until the two men had been hanged before being executed.

Mary Fawson, aged 19, was found guilty of Petty Treason for the murder of her husband by poisoning with white mercury in a mess of Bread and Beer, three days after their wedding in the parish of Weston. She was tied onto a sledge and drawn to the stake on Northampton Heath and there burned.

Susannah Bruford, also aged 19 and found guilty of Petty Treason of the murder, by poison, of her husband John was sentenced to be drawn to the place of execution on a hurdle at Wells, Somerset, and burned.

An unidentified 14-year-old girl imprisoned at Newgate was more fortunate. Found guilty in 1777 of being an accomplice to high treason for concealing (at her master's request) whitewashed farthings under her stays (corsets), she had been sentenced to be burned to death. She was saved by the intervention of Thomas Thynne, 1st Marquess of Bath and Secretary of State, who happened to be passing.

Although the last execution for Petty Treason by burning was of Catherine Murphy in 1789, women convicted of the crime were still liable to be burned at the stake until 1793. They were still to be drawn to the place of execution on a hurdle, but then hanged in the usual way until 1825, when the crime of Petty Treason was abolished, the offence being reclassified as ordinary murder.

Chapter 7

An Exiled World

To most Englishmen this place seemed not just a mutant society but
another planet – an exiled world.

(*The Fatal Shore* Robert Hughes, 1987).

It has already been shown that in the seventeenth and eighteenth centuries, criminal justice could be severe and cruel. This was due to both the particularly large number of offences punishable by death, usually by hanging (but in the case of some women, by burning) and to the limited choice of other sentences available to judges for convicted criminals. Many offenders were pardoned as it was considered unreasonable to execute them for relatively minor offences, but under the rule of law, it was equally unreasonable for them to escape punishment entirely. With the development of the colonies, transportation was introduced as an alternative punishment, thus convicted criminals who it was thought represented a menace to society were sent away to distant lands. Transportation had originally taken place to America, but following independence from Britain in 1776, an alternative had to be found. The shipping of felons to Australia began in May 1787 and was to continue for eighty-one years. In all, around 164,000 people[1] were transported, of which 24,960 were women, twenty per cent of whom were first offenders.

The brutal treatment of these women often began on the ships that would carry them halfway round the world, on a voyage that lasted up to eight months. In 1796 the *Britannia* sailed for Australia from Cork with 188 Irish convicts on board, including forty-four women. The *Britannia* was captained by a sadist named Thomas Dennot, who had several convicts flogged to death during the voyage, handing down a staggering total of 7,900 lashes. In the midst of this horror a woman named Jenny Blake tried to commit suicide. To punish her attempt, Dennot had her seized up and gagged, cut off her hair, and used the bosun's cane to publicly beat her over the back and shoulders before slashing at her face and neck. He then ordered that she be confined below and double-ironed. This latter punishment is not as innocuous as it might at first be thought. A weight of up to 22lb [10kg] of iron around the ankles meant that the woman not only would be unable to walk, but medical journals of the time recorded that that they caused severe groin pain, bruising of the skin, lesions and skin ruptures.

The voyage to Australia took up to eight months, during which time the female convicts were sharing the relatively small sailing ships with dozens of men – the male convicts may have been physically constrained but the sailors were not. Lord Auckland, chairman of the 1812 Parliamentary Select Committee on Transportation, asked the captain of a brig that lay in the Thames estuary loaded with convicted women 'as to the means of preventing improper intercourse between the sailors and the women'. To his horror, the captain informed him that, far from being segregated, every sailor on board was allowed one woman to cohabit with him for the duration of the voyage.

When the ship docked in Sydney Cove, it landed in a country where the population was overwhelmingly male, most of whom were desperate for female company:

> the upper deck became a slave-market, as randy colonists came swarming over the bulwarks, grinning and ogling and chumming up to the captain with a bottle of rum, while the female convicts, washed for the occasion and dressed in the remnants of their English finery – they were mustered before them, trying as hard as they could to set themselves off to the best advantage. Military officers got the first pick, then non-commissioned officers, then privates, and lastly such ex-convict settlers as seemed respectable enough to obtain the governor's permission to keep a female servant.
>
> (*The Fatal Shore,* Robert Hughes, 1987)

Given that the majority of the women were not prostitutes but merely petty thieves, many contemporary witnesses found the 'slave-market' process 'morally barbarous', and one which brought disgrace upon both the colony and the British Government.

Once in Australia, convicted women were subject to the local laws set by the governor, infringement of which brought down the usual corporal punishments of the time. The summary chastisement of the 24,960 female convicts who had already been punished by deportation to Australia while it served as a remote prison was every bit as savage and brutal as that inflicted upon their sex in the mother country. In a letter from a male convict from Wexford to his sister back in Ireland, he described how women in Sydney Cove convicted of whoring were disciplined:

> They are so accustomed to their lude [*sic*] way of life that the most severe punishments will not restrain them. I have been witness to some flogged at the Tryangle, more led through the Town [with]

a rope round their waist held by the common Executioner, and a label on their necks denoting the crime. The mode of punishment mostly adopted now is mostly shaving their heads and Ducking, and afterwards [they are] sent up to Hard Labour with the men.[2]

The worst brutality seems to have occurred on Norfolk Island while Joseph Foveaux (1767–1846) was governor. In common with many Justices in Britain, Foveaux obtained sexual gratification from watching women being flogged: 'To be remembered by all there was his love for watching women in their agony while receiving a punishment on the triangle.' (*The Fatal Shore*, Robert Hughes, 1987)

Foveaux increased the erotic appeal of such occasions by offering the woman the chance to obtain a lesser number of lashes by agreeing to strip naked to receive her punishment – the usual requirement was to be stripped only to the waist. Most women readily agreed to save themselves some of the agony and having been stripped would then be paraded before the assembled male convicts before being trussed up to the triangle and flogged with the cat o' nine tails.

The usual number of lashes awarded was twenty-five, ironically referred to as the 'Botany Bay dozen', but Foveaux's sentences could go as high as 250! What this implied for the victim can be clearly imagined from this description of the flogging of a man named James Kenworthy, awarded fifty lashes of the 'cat' for pilfering:

> The first lash elicited loud cries from the prisoner; at the eighteenth lash the blood appeared; at the 25th lash the blood was trickling; at the end of the 32nd, flowing down his back … the sufferings of this prisoner were evinced by his unnerved state of body when cast loose; he could hardly stand.[3]

Sexual gratification obtained in witnessing or administering corporal punishment in the colony was not confined to men, or its application to adult women. The Reverend Robert Crooke (1818–88) in his work 'The Convict – A Fragment of History' described the punishment of female pupils in the Queen's Orphan School in Hobart, Tasmania:

> The slightest offence … was punished by unmerciful flogging and some of the officers, more especially females, seem to have taken a delight in inflicting corporal punishment … the female superintendent was in the habit of taking girls, some of them almost young women, to her own bedroom and for trifling offences … stripping them naked, and with a riding whip or a heavy leather strap, flagellating them until their bodies were a mass of bruises.

Flogging was not the only physical punishment inflicted on female convicts in the Australian colony. Once the lash had been outlawed as a punishment for women, other equally brutal punishments were instigated, isolated cells without light or sound and the wearing of spiked collars among them. In 1823 a treadmill was installed in the Parramatta Female Factory and in 1837 another was installed in Hobart:

> Within the Factories women were subjected to punishment as well as incarceration. Most despised by the women was the shaving of their heads as punishment for refractoriness. Women were supposedly not allowed to be flogged, but the Rev. Samuel Marsden, a member of the Managing committee of the Parramatta Factory had one women, Susanah Denford, flogged and then dragged through the streets of Parramatta behind a dray.
>
> In 1836, one hundred small dark cells were built at the Factory 'in order to try the effect of solitary confinement on recalcitrant females.' A frequent form of punishment in Van Diemen's Land prior to governor Arthur's administration was to force around the women's necks an iron collar which had a long prong on each side of it. This, says Robson, 'gave them the appearance of horned cattle'. Evidently this was considered an eminently suitable mode of apparel for what was, in the 1812 Select committee's opinion, a herd of prime breeders.
>
> In 1837 a treadmill was erected at the Cascades Factory; such punishment had been meted out to women in Sydney since 1823. This horrendous form of torture had especially deleterious effects on those women sentenced to periods on it. An English surgeon, Dr John Goode, who reported on its effects found that its main consequence was 'a very horrible pain in the loins' which precipitated a greatly intensified menstruation.[4]

Troublesome female prisoners were sent to various 'Female Factories', where they made rope and span and carded wool. The 'female factory' at Parramatta was in fact a loft above a gaol, 60ft long and 20ft wide. The floor was so warped that any attempt to wash it resulted in the prisoners in the cells below being soaked in the filthy water which ran through between the boards. The roof leaked and the privies were in a disgusting state. Cooking for all the women had to be done on a single fireplace. Here too, punishment of any misdemeanour could be harsh: the treadmill, solitary confinement with a bread and water diet or, as in the following case, a combination of solitary confinement together with 'gagging' – a wooden bit placed between the teeth and secured with straps passed around the head.

THE VIOLENT ABUSE OF WOMEN

On 19 July 1843, Jane Eskett, who had been transported on the convict ship *Garland Grove*, was charged at Cascades Female Factory on the complaint of the Superintendent John Hutchinson with insubordination in openly resisting his lawfully constituted authority on the night of Monday 17 July. Jane pleaded guilty to the charge. The case of insubordination was dismissed but she was found guilty of misconduct and received fourteen days in solitary confinement. Jane's case is interesting in that John Hutchinson quelled her behaviour by using a gag. At her hearing, the Superintendent gave the following statement:

> I am the Superintendent of the Female House of Correction, and on Monday last at 12 o'clock in the day there was a considerable noise and uproar proceeding from the cells. I first went Mrs Stewart to beg they would desist and to inform them if they did not I should come to them, Mrs Stewart is one of the Officers of the Establishment. I was obliged to go to them with cuffs & gags the noise proceeded from Eskith .... she was in one of the cells confined under a special order of the Governor. I opened the cell door in which she was confined, her conduct was so riotous I was compelled to put the gag on. I repeatedly advised her to desist, and at last she did, her behaviour was such as to cause insubordination in the Building so I was compelled to remove her. After she confessed her fault I took off the gag and she then commenced most violent language in consequence of a noise in the adjoining cell. Her language was not bad but violent. I was compelled to remove her to one of cells. Her language was not bad to me personally. She did not continue violent in the next cell. Eskitt's general conduct up to the time of this disturbance has been very good. There [were] about thirty or thirty five women engaged in the disturbance it did not commence with this woman and she was not worse than the rest. She was using violent language at the time I gagged her she did not fight.[5]

Throughout the eighteenth century, death sentences – especially for relatively trivial offences – were often commuted to one of transportation, commonly for a period of seven years. At first glance this may seem comparatively humane, but the case of Mary Talbot (1766–91) vividly demonstrates what a cruel punishment this could be for a wife and mother.

Mary was an émigré from Ireland whose husband was unable to pursue his trade due to injury. With a child to support, and in the days before any form of social security, Mary took to thieving in order to support her family until she was caught stealing 17*s* [85p] worth of cotton from a shop in King Street, London. At her trial at the Old Bailey in February 1788 she claimed to have been drunk and didn't know what she was doing, a defence which the court did not accept and she was sentenced to transportation to New South Wales for seven years.

Numbers of similarly convicted women were being assembled on the convict ship *Lady Juliana*, being readied for the voyage on the Thames at Gravesend. However, friends and relations of the women hatched an escape plan and Mary, her baby son and three other women escaped from the ship in a small boat. She returned home, but was apprehended in Bloomsbury in January 1790, charged with escaping transportation. Re-tried at the Old Bailey, she was again convicted and this time sentenced to death. Mary 'pleaded her belly' and the jury of matrons who examined her found that she was indeed pregnant. The court ordered that her execution be postponed until after she had given birth, which she did later in 1790 while imprisoned in Newgate. Back at the Old Bailey in October 1790, Mary received a pardon from execution, conditional upon her being transported to New South Wales for the rest of her life. She was denied further access to her children or any contact with her husband, and she sailed together with 137 other women and three children (two more were born during the voyage) on 29 February 1791 aboard the convict ship *Mary Ann*. This ship was part of a fleet of nine containing a total of 978 convicts, which arrived in Sydney on 9 June.

During the whole of this period Mary had been in touch with an unidentified man in England who had endeavoured unsuccessfully to get the whole family transported together to America. Now in Australia, Mary wrote to him begging that he renew his efforts to obtain a pardon for her in order that she might be reunited with her family. She requested that he tell her husband that she had written and was in better health than she had been for a long time, and to send a response via any captain sailing for Botany Bay:

> Pray, Sir, be good enough to let my husband know you have had a letter from me, and beg him to take care of my dear children. I think it hard I did not see him before I sailed for we laid a week at Gravesend, and I should have left my country less sorrowfully had I given him my last charges and bade him farewell.[6]

Her letter was written and posted on 29 March 1791 at St Jago in the Cape Verde Islands, the *Mary Ann*'s only landfall en route to Australia. It was redirected to Dublin where it was published as 'foreign news' in the *Dublin Chronicle* on 1 November, thus making Mary the first letter-writing female transportee to be so identified.

Sadly, Mary's story does not have a happy ending. In spite of telling her benefactor that she was in good health, Mary died only seven weeks after her arrival in the colony, never having seen her children or her husband again. She was buried on 28 August 1791.

THE VIOLENT ABUSE OF WOMEN

The brutal treatment of women en route to Australia which had begun in the convict ship *Britannia* in 1796 continued well into the nineteenth century. As late as July 1849, the *Perth Gazette* was scandalised by an account of four young women being flogged on board the ship *Ramilies*. The following report appeared in *The Perth Gazette and Independent Journal of Politics and News* 27 July 1849:

> We have seen and heard complaints of the treatment of the sailors and passengers on board the above vessel, which however we did not notice, as it was understood, steps were to be taken by the parties concerned. Disagreements so frequently arise on a voyage that they attract little attention until legal redress is sought. But the present case assuming a very important character, and no charge having been as yet preferred, we have felt it our duty to make close enquiries.
>
> As to the general treatment of the passengers we receive various accounts: but this is not the object of our present notice. All are agreed in the fact that four female emigrants were flogged during the passage. Their names are Catherine Morgan, Phoebe Spooner, Jane Downey, and Margaret Mack. Of their conduct we hear conflicting accounts, but this is of no material consequence. The fact is certain that fully grown girls – seventeen or eighteen years old – were flogged by the surgeon with his own hand, a rope's end being the instrument of torture used. Besides the surgeon and captain we cannot learn that any persons were present but two men who acted as constables or surgeons assistants.
>
> The particulars of what passed in the 'Chamber of the Question' we cannot give, but we have spoken with several, both male and female, – one a married, and apparently respectable woman who examined the girl's backs and found them scored with wails of red and blue as large as the finger, and one was bleeding. The mind can hardly dwell on the revolting idea of men holding a half naked girl and flogging her till the blood starts from her skin. We read of such horrors in Russian dungeons, but scarcely give them credit. Of all the charges made against the slave system, the flogging of women was perhaps the most popular. Exertions are yearly making in Parliament, and are seconded by almost every paper, to abolish flogging in the army and navy. Yet in 1849, in a ship sailing under Government guarantee, is the system commenced in its very worst form.[7]

Australia was not the only colony where the scandalous punishment of women by flogging occurred well into the nineteenth century. Nearly forty years after the corporal punishment of women was made illegal in Britain, and despite a highly critical Parliamentary Report in 1838, the females in the colony of Jamaica were still liable to be punished by flogging with a cat o' nine tails. This report followed numbers of similar reports of women in the colony being flogged:

> Jamaica ss., St Catherine – Mary Ann Smith, apprentice to Turnbull's Pen, in the parish of St Catherine, being duly sworn, maketh oath and saith, that about the middle of last year she was sentenced by Mr Special Justice Moresby to punishment on the tread-mill in the house of correction of this parish, and that while undergoing the aforesaid punishment she was flogged with a cat on the legs by the driver thereof. Deponent further declares, that another woman was at the same time similarly punished by flogging.

> Sworn before me, this seventeenth June 1836   Mary Ann Smith
> (signed) Geo. Ousley Higgins   her X mark

Mary Ann Smith went on to state that her legs were so 'mangled' by the whipping, she was unable to work for the remaining term of her sentence. Neither age nor physical condition protected women from corporal punishment. On 20 June 1835, Sarah Jarrett was one of three women to be stripped and flogged – she was eight months pregnant.

Not only were adult females punished in this manner. On 3 March 1836 in Prospect Hill, Jamaica, five juvenile girls were punished for an unspecified offence: Catherine Shaw, Susannah White, Isabella Williams, Becky Walker and Little Farry were, one after another, 'mounted on the back of William Bryant and flogged by Mr Chevannes. N.B. Catherine Shaw aged 12 years, the rest, likewise, children.'[8]

By the mid-nineteenth century, Australia was becoming a country in its own right and no longer willing to accept 'moral sewage' from Britain. The Australian Intercolonial Conference held in Melbourne in 1863 told the British Government that if the colony was to have a future, transportation of convicts to Western Australia must stop. However, it would be another twenty-five years before the last convict ship landed its cargo in Fremantle, docking on 10 January 1868, exactly eighty years to the month after the first convict fleet anchored in Sydney Cove.

Chapter 8

At the Mercy of the Mob

Apart from the lash, magistrates of the day had a number of other physical punishments available to them, among them the pillory, an ancient penalty first mentioned in *Judicium Pillorie*, a statute of Henry III dated 1267. Originally used to punish dishonest traders, by the seventeenth century it was commonly employed to discipline prostitutes, female brothel keepers, common scolds and any convicted of sedition or contempt of court.

The most common form of Pillory[1] was a device comprised of a wooden or metal framework erected on a post, with holes for securing the head and hands, which forced the victim to stand in a slightly bent position with head and face exposed. It was usually to be found mounted on a raised platform and frequently on a revolving turntable, thus enabling the victim to be rotated to face the crowd of spectators that inevitably accompanied its occupation.

Originally intended to subject the individual to public humiliation, it commonly engendered further physical abuse from the public. A significant drawback of being sentenced to the pillory was that the severity of the punishment depended very much on the attitude of the crowd, how they felt about the crime committed, whether or not they liked or approved of the victim, or simply what mood they happened to be in that day. In *A Tale of Two Cities* Charles Dickens observed that the pillory 'inflicted a punishment of which no one could foresee the extent'.

In the same way as a public flogging, the infliction of the pillory as punishment carried a high degree of free entertainment and many no doubt found the sight of a woman trapped in the device and subjected to physical abuse, more than a little titillating:

> The crowd played an important role. As a form of legally sanctioned street theatre, each pillory event relied upon the audience for its success. In a carnival-like atmosphere, people crowded the streets and surrounding buildings in an attempt to get the best vantage point to view the offender's punishment.[2]

On 18 August 1732, Eleanor Beare was tried in Derby for performing illegal abortions, and inciting a man to murder his wife (for which Eleanor supplied him with poison). A number of contemporary reports have survived to provide a vivid picture of what a horrific experience an appearance in the pillory would have been for a woman.

According to *The Gentleman's Magazine*:

> his Lordship summed up the Evidence in a very moving Speech to the Jury, wherein he said, he never met with a Case so barbarous and unnatural. The Jury, after a short Consultation, brought the Prisoner in Guilty of both Indictments, and she received Sentence to stand in the Pillory, the Two next Market-Days, and to suffer dole Imprisonment for Three Years.
>
> This Day Eleanor Beare, pursuant to her Sentence, stood for the first Time in the Pillory in the Marketplace; to which Place she was attended by several of the Sheriff's Officers; notwithstanding which, the Populace, to show their Resentment of the horrible Crimes wherein she has been charged, and the little Remorse she had shown since her Commitment, gave her no Quarter, but threw such quantities of Eggs, Turnips, Etc. that it was thought she would hardly have escap'd with her Life: She disengaged herself from the Pillory before her the Time of her standing was expired, and jump'd among the Crowd, whence she was with Difficulty carried back to Prison.
>
> I saw her, August 18, 1732, with an easy air ascend the hated machine, which overlooked an enraged multitude. All the apples, eggs, and turnips, that could be bought, begged, or stolen, were directed at her devoted head. The stagnate kennels were robbed of their contents, and became the cleanest part of the street. The pillory, being out of repair, was unable to hold a woman in her prime, whose powers were augmented by necessity; she released herself; and, jumping among the crowd, with the resolution and agility of an Amazon, ran down the Morlege, being pelted all the way; new kennels produced new ammunition; and she appeared a moving heap of filth. With difficulty they remounted her [and] by the time they had fixed her, the hour expired, and she was carried to prison, an object which none cared to touch. The next week she was again brought out of prison, and again pilloried. As soon as she mounted the platform, she kneeled down and begged mercy of the still outraged mob. The executioner finding, from her struggling, some difficulty in getting her head through the hole of the pillory, pulled off her head-dress, and therein found a large pewter plate, beat out so as to fit her head, which he threw among the spectators. As soon as she was fixed, a shower of eggs, potatoes,

turnips, &c. assailed her from every direction and it was thought she would not be taken down alive. Having expended all the ammunition of the above description, stones were thrown, which wounded her to such a degree, that her blood streamed down the pillory. This somewhat appeased the resentment shewn [*sic*] against her, and she was returned to gaol a shocking spectacle to behold. The next Friday she appeared again not as a young woman, but an old one, ill, swelled, and decrepid [*sic*]; she seemed to have advanced thirty years in one week. The keeper suspecting some finesse from the bulk of her head, took off ten or twelve coverings, among which was a pewter plate, fitted to the head, as a guard against the future storm. He tossed it among the crowd, and left no covering but the hair. The pillory being made stronger, and herself being weaker, she was fixed for the hour; where she received the severe peltings of the mob; and they, her groans and her prayers. She afterwards sustained the three years imprisonment, recovered her health, her spirits, and her beauty; and at her enlargement [release from prison] was preceded by a band of music.

One case illustrates perfectly how women sometimes suffered physical abuse and humiliation, far from committing a crime, simply dared advocate new feminine ways of doing things, especially if it trespassed on what had been exclusively a male preserve, such as the practice of medicine. Elizabeth Cellier is best known as the seventeenth-century pioneer of female midwives. The authoress of a controversial pamphlet that argued for the value of midwives' practical experience over the theoretical knowledge of male physicians, she also advocated the formation of what was to become the Royal College of Midwives. This did not endear her to the male establishment, particularly as she was also a Catholic. In 1680, Mrs Cellier was implicated in an alleged Catholic conspiracy to assassinate the king and other high profile Protestants. Brought to trial she was acquitted of that charge, but then rashly published a pamphlet entitled *Malice Defeated, or, a Brief Relation of the Accusation and Deliverance of Elizabeth Cellier*, an account of her trial in which she claimed that Catholics were being tortured in Newgate prison, where she had heard 'the cries of tortured prisoners [which] so resembled those of a woman in labour that she had offered her services'. She was brought to court again, and this time found guilty of libel. Her sentence was that she pay a fine of £1,000 (equivalent to around £100,000 today), to be kept in prison until that was paid; to stand three several times in the pillory, on each occasion for one hour. First, by the Maypole in the Strand, secondly, in Convent-garden (Covent Garden), and thirdly, at Charing Cross. At each occasion, a parcel of her pamphlets was to be burned under the pillory by the common hangman and after her punishment to find sureties for her good behaviour during the remainder of her life.

During her first appearance on the pillory she was 'much pelted but not hurt'. This was hardly surprising as she had managed to keep her head from being thrust through the aperture and had obtained permission to hold a wooden paddle in front of her face – which seems to indicate that her wrists were not pinioned either! When she was pilloried for the second time she was not so lucky:

> she had been hauled out of bed, though she could not rise, set on the pillory, twice struck down with stones by the rabble but lifted up again by the sheriff's officers, and had been kept there till 2 o'clock, though her sentence was to remain only between 12 and 1. She had been grievously bruised and, several officers had been wounded in her defence.

After she had been pilloried three times, she was once more returned to prison until she could pay the £1,000 fine, not being finally released until 1687.

Some women were even more unfortunate than Elizabeth Cellier. Elizabeth Needham (also known as Mother Needham), an English procuress and brothel-keeper, has been identified as the bawd greeting Moll Hackabout in the first plate of William Hogarth's series of satirical etchings, *A Harlot's Progress*. Although she was notorious in London at the time, little is known for certain of her life, and no genuinely accredited portraits of her have survived (if indeed they were ever painted). Her brothel was the most exclusive house in London and her clientele were drawn from the most wealthy and fashionable men in society. However, moral reform was the order of the day. In 1730, Justice of the Peace Sir John Gonson, a fervent supporter of the Society for the Reformation of Manners, began conducting raids on brothels all over London. He eventually arrived at St James's, where residents of Park Place had reported 'a Notorious Disorderly House in that Neighbourhood'.[3] Elizabeth Needham was arrested and committed to prison.

On 29 April 1731, she was convicted of keeping a disorderly house, fined one shilling [5p] and sentenced to stand twice in the pillory, and 'to find sureties for her good behaviour for 3 years'. On 30 April she was taken to the pillory near Park Place to stand for the first time. Perhaps because of her high level social connections, she was allowed to lie face down in front of the pillory and a number of men were paid as guards to shield her from the mob. Despite these precautions she received such a pelting that it was thought likely she would die before her punishment was completed. The crowds that had gathered to see her pilloried were so large that one boy fell on an iron fencing rail while trying to get a better view and was killed. Needham was taken down from the pillory still alive, but badly injured. She died on 3 May 1731, the day before she was due to stand in the pillory for the second time. With her last words she apparently expressed great fear at having to stand in the pillory again after the severe punishment she had received the first time.

However, the crowd could also be remarkably lenient to certain individuals with whom they felt sympathy, as this contemporary newspaper report clearly shows:

> Yesterday at Noon Sarah Thomas stood in the Pillory in the Old Bailey, opposite to Fleet-Lane, for keeping a disorderly House, pursuant to her Sentence at the last Quarter Session in Guildhall. The Mob behaved to her with great Humanity, she standing on the Pillory all the Time drinking Wine, Hot-pot, &c. It was Diversion to her rather than a Punishment.[4]

As is often the case, ladies of high social status or connection could avoid punishment altogether. The seventeenth century witnessed an epidemic of gambling among the higher social classes, very often for huge sums of money. Such a scandal had the matter become that the Gaming Act of 1738 made two of the most notorious card games 'Hazard' and 'Faro' (often rendered as 'Pharaoh') illegal. This of course did not stop clubs from running gambling sessions, which continued to give rise to regular financial scandals. Sitting at a trial to recover the relatively paltry sum of £15 won by gambling, Chief Justice Kenyon threatened that he would set in the pillory any who were brought before him for gambling 'though they be the first ladies of the land'. As fate would have it, four such ladies were to appear before Justice Kenyon, charged with running gambling houses in and about Covent Garden, where illegal card games were played: Albinia, Countess of Buckinghamshire; Sophia, Viscountess Mount Edgecombe; Mary, Baronesse Mordington and Susan, Countess of Cassilis. In the end none of the ladies were either flogged or pilloried as the law required, but suffered a rebuke from the Justice and a modest fine. The satirical cartoonist James Gillray famously illustrated Albinia stripped to the waist and whipped at the cart's tail by Chief Justice Kenyon, a cynical comment on how those of aristocratic rank avoided the rigours of the law suffered by the rank and file.

Following two deaths in the pillory on the same day in April 1780 at the hands of the mob, Edmund Burke in Parliament described the adverse consequences of the pillory and argued unsuccessfully for its abolition. It would not be until the Pillory Abolition Act of 1816 that the use of the pillory was restricted in England to punishment only for perjury and subornation (procurement by underhand means). In the early nineteenth century there grew a more general rejection of violence in society, with the pillory seen by some contemporaries as an endorsed form of mob violence, anarchy and barbarity, which made criminal justice something of a lottery. Nevertheless, it was 1837 before the pillory as a form of punishment was abolished completely.

Chapter 9

Locked in the Cage

Although it took until the nineteenth century for the pillory to become obsolete as a form of punishment, another form of confinement was to be generally abandoned during the eighteenth century. Although Genghis Khan executed his enemies by locking them naked in a cage hung from the city walls and leaving them there to die, the cage was used in Britain more as a form of minor humiliation – a sort of public prison, almost exclusively for the incarceration of women.

The practice of locking women convicted of 'harlotry' or other minor crimes such as slander or vagabondage in a cage first appears in Scotland in the twelfth century, when the Countess of Buchan defied both her husband and Edward 1 in 1306 by crowning Robert Bruce King of Scotland. This was not to go unpunished and Edward had instructions sent to the Chamberlain of Scotland that he should 'make a cage in one of the turrets of the [Berwick] castle'. One chronicler described her cage as a 'little house of timber … the sides latticed so that all there could gaze on her as a spectacle'. The cage was to be 'cross-barred with wood and well strengthened with iron' so that she could not escape; she was viewed like a captive animal by visitors to the castle and was forbidden to speak to any except the English women who tended her. The countess was not released from her confinement until 1313.

Women were punished by being exposed in the cage for the usual range of minor offences – vagrancy, begging or unruly behaviour. In 1501, the Lord Mayor of London, Sir John Shaa (Shaw) ordered that a cage was 'to be sett up in everie ward for the punishment of vacabunds', a provision echoed by Lord Mayor William Cappell in 1509 who instructed that 'smal howses [sic] to be put up in every ward and stocks fixed inside theym'. This mode of punishment continued to be employed throughout the sixteenth century; in 1558 Queen Mary instigated a campaign to 'cleanse the towns of mislyvynge women' and ordered a cage to be set up on London Bridge for the purpose.

Although intended as a temporary incarceration, the punishment was clearly too much to bear for one woman in 1586; Mary Keys alias Beck had been locked in the St John's Street cage in London. In the morning she was found to have killed herself by 'binding her girdle round her neck and hanging it from a pole.'[1] This was not a unique event – in 1609 Elizabeth Smith, described as a poor woman, died while confined in the cage at Newbury.

Little is recorded with respect to the use of the cage, as it was not seen as a punishment in itself, merely a way of imprisoning women apprehended by the constable for 'harlotry' or as vagrants, pending their appearance in court, after which they would usually be sent to the house of correction to be whipped. This meant that cages were often erected where they would be most needed, for example in July 1612, King James ordered that a cage be erected 'at some convenient place' near St John's Street in Clerkenwell, a district notorious for civil disturbances, being adjacent to the notorious Bartholomew's Fair.

The provision of these facilities was funded from local taxation, an imposition that caused much resentment. In 1610, George Thorogoode and William Harvey were fined £10, after they had 'threatened to pull downe ye Cage [in St Giles-without-Cripplegate, London] and within a whyle afterwards ye Cage was throwne downe'.

Being in the open air, cages were much less secure than a prison cell. In January 1614, a constable named Thomas Bignell sought authority from Middlesex magistrates to indict Edward Sommer for breaking open the cage in Kensington and thereby 'helping a woman to escape, that was kept there by the constable.'

By the beginning of the eighteenth century, almost all surviving cages had fallen into disrepair and disuse, although some – such as the example at Saffron Waldon in England – continued to be employed until around 1840.[2]

Another method of restraint reserved exclusively for the punishment of women was a device called the 'thew' or 'thewe', a word, which may originate from the old German 'thau' meaning discipline. It appears as early as 1084 where an entry in the Doomsday Book for Ipswich where it is prescribed as a punishment for women that are 'comoun chiderers and stryvers'. It appears to have taken the form of a neck ring by which the victim was locked and thereby attached by a chain to a stake. In London in 1375 a woman's neighbours were: 'Greatly molested and annoyed and it was awarded that she should have punishment of the pillory, called the 'thewe' for women ordained.'

It occurs commonly throughout the fourteenth century as a punishment for a variety of offences, other than that of chiding or scolding. On 23 November 1364, Alice de Caustone sold a quart of ale in a pot that had 1½in of pitch concealed by sprigs of rosemary and was duly 'punnyshed by the pyllorie of the thew for women'.

Short measure was not the only crime committed by female vendors that would result in a stint manacled by the neck. Selling unmarketable produce would likewise incur a similar penalty. In 1372 on the Saturday after the feast of St Giles, Margery Hore was caught, 'With certayne fisshe call'd soles, stynking and rotten and unwholesome for humans, exposed for sale at ye Stokkes which shee dyd nott denye. Punishment of the thewe with the fysshe burnt abowte her'.

LOCKED IN THE CAGE

In the fourteenth century as now, begging was often more successful if one was accompanied by a small child to excite the sympathies of the passers-by. London, 1373:

> On Monday, the feast of St Benedict the Abbot (21st March) Alice de Salisbury, a beggar, was adjudged to the pillory called the 'thewe' for women ordained, by award of the Mayor and Aldermen there to stand for one hour in the day, for that on the Sunday before, she had taken one Margaret, daughter of John Oxwyke, grocer, and had carried her away and stripped her of her clothes that she might go begging with the said child. Punishment one hour on the thewe.

This might seem a modest punishment for what in modern times would be regarded as the abduction of a minor. However, other relatively serious crimes were also punished with a similarly modest period of humiliation. On 27 July 1385, Elizabeth Moreing was accused of being a procuress and having elected to be tried by jury, was found guilty. She was sentenced to be taken to Cornhill in the City of London and put upon the thewe for one hour a day and thereafter to be ejected from the city, not to return upon pain of three years in prison and a further appearance in the thewe for each and every time she broke the sentence.

A similar punishment still seems to have been in use in British army garrisons as late as the eighteenth century. The Gibraltar Garrison Order Book records that in January 1728 a gentlewoman of the Foot Guards (presumably the wife of an officer) was pinioned for three hours in the market place, with her neck and hands fastened by chains.

Chapter 10

Hot Iron & Cold Steel

As with flogging, branding and maiming was often used as a punishment for a variety of offences including theft, vagrancy and prostitution. As usual, the bible has its store of Mosaic law, usually biased unfavourably towards women:

> If two men are fighting and the wife of one of them comes to rescue her husband from his assailant, and she reaches out and seizes him by his private parts, you shall cut off her hand. Show her no pity.
>
> (*Deuteronomy* 25:11–12)

In medieval times, the England of King Canute (994–1035) adjudged adulteresses to have their noses slit and their ears cut off, a punishment that continued through into Tudor times. Women in the Channel Islands had their ears amputated for sorcery throughout the reigns of Elizabeth I, James I and Charles I. Other parts of the anatomy might also be mutilated; at Henley in 1646 it was reported that:

> A woman taking notice of the unwonted taxations imposed upon her and others by this Parliament, expressed (yet in civil terms) some dislike thereof, which made known to a committee there, she was by them ordered to have her tongue fastened with a nail to the body of a tree, by the highwayside [*sic*] on a market day, which was accordingly done, and a paper in great letters (setting forth the heinousness of her fact) fixed to her back to make her the more notorious.

At Portsmouth in the fourteenth century, the law decreed that a female thief's 'tetys shall be kyt'. while the *New Law Dictionary* of 1752 informs us that prostitutes were even sometimes hamstrung (the sinews of their legs or thighs being cut, thus rendering them permanently crippled).

A statute of Edward VI made it mandatory for vagrants who refused to work to be branded on the breast. Whores were branded on the face, which meant of course that they would thereafter find it impossible to obtain honest work and were condemned to a life of prostitution. The *Branding Act* of 1623 was extended so

JUDGE THUMB.
or — Patent Sticks for Family Correction: Warranted Lawful !

Judge Thumb. Cartoon by James Gillray 1782. Judge Sir Francis Buller (1746-1800) was reported to have said that a husband could thrash his wife with impunity provided that the stick was no bigger than his thumb, thus his nickname.

Judge – 'Who wants a cure for a rusty wife? Here's your nice Family Entertainment for Winter Evenings. Who buys here?'

Wife – 'Help! Murder for God's sake, Murder!'

Husband – 'Murder hay? Its Law you Bitch, it's not bigger than my thumb!'(British Museum)

How came this Flogging Whim into thy Skull._
Thou'rt sold to endless Shame and Laughter. Hull,_
Each Lash that did the Wife's Posteriors wound._
Shall spread the shameless Husbands Tale around.
Ladies prepare your Scourges, lay them on_

Let Horsing Joseph smart with whipping John
Nor scape the Strumpet Wench her Share of Fame
Oftner turn'd up than was her injur'd Dame._
Nor let unnotic'd Hend'k slink away_
Somewhat methinks he should for Peeping pay.

Whipping John of Islington. An etching dated 1748 the origin of which appears to be unknown. It shows an interior view of a room in which a man holds a bare-bottomed woman with a pained expression on her face on his back as another woman holds up the woman's skirts and points to her naked buttocks; a second man, named as Whipping John, prepares to apply a birch to her exposed posterior. In the background, peeping in at the door, stands a third man apparently deriving gratification from the scene.(United States Library of Congress, British Cartoon Prints Collection)

Bridewell Prison, London in 1666 before the Great Fire. Wood engraving from 'Old and New London' 1880. (Collection of the author)

Bridewell Prison, London in 1765. Copper engraving from William Maitland's 'The History and Survey of London from its Foundation to the Present Time'. The original Bridewell was left in ruins after the Great Fire of 1666 and rebuilt with two quadrangles – one a prison, the other a hospital for paupers, 'hospital' in this 18th century context meaning a hostel, shelter or lodging.(Collection of the author)

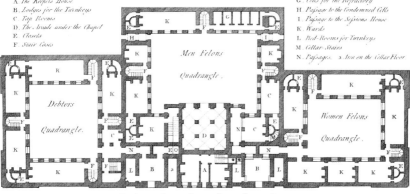

Plan of Newgate Prison, London, designed by Charles Dance 1782. (Collection of the author)

Under the Birch. Illustration of a woman undergoing punishment in prison from 'Lenchen im Zuchthause' published in Germany 1848. First published in Britain in 1900 as 'Nell in Bridewell' it purports to describe the corporal punishment of women incarcerated in Bridewell prisons, both in the UK and Germany. (Collection of the author)

Whipping posts and stocks from the 18th century. Many survived in Britain well into the 20th century. This photograph was taken as the subject of a postcard in Rock, Worcestershire, England in 1906.(Collection of the author)

A whipping post and stocks surviving into the 21st century in Aldbury, near Tring in Hertfordshire, England.

An earlier photograph of the Aldbury whipping post and stocks taken around the beginning of the 20th century shows the stocks and whipping post to be in a rather better condition. (Collection of the author)

his hand, the other end faſtned to an Engine called the Branks, which is like a Crown, it being of Iron, which was muſled * over the head and face, with a great gap or tongue of Iron forced into her mouth, which forced the blood out. And that is the puniſhment which the Magiſtrates do inflict upon chiding, and ſcoulding women, and that he hath often ſeen the like done to others.

(B) He this Deponent further affirms, that he hath ſeen men drove up and down the ſtreets, with a great Tub or Barrel opened in the ſides with a hole in one end, to put through their heads, and ſo cover their ſhoulders and bodies down to the ſmall of their legs, and then cloſe the ſame called the new faſhioned Cloak, and ſo make them march to the view of all beholders; and this is their puniſhment for Drunkards, or the like.

(C) This Deponent further teſtifies, that the Merchants and Shoe-makers of the ſaid Corporation, will not take any Apprentice under ten years ſervitude, and knoweth many bound for the ſame terme, and cannot obtain freedome without. 5. *Eliz.* 4.

Theſe are ſuch practices as are not granted by their Charter Law, and are repugnant to the known Laws of *England.*

(D) Drunkards are to pay a Fine of five ſhillings to the poor, to be paid within one week, or be ſet in the Stocks ſix hours, for the ſecond offence, to be bound to the Good B.haviour, 1 K. *James* 9.21.7.

(E) Scoulds are to be Duckt over head and ears into the water in a Ducking-ſtool.

(F) And Apprentices are to ſerve but ſeven years 5. *Eliz.* 4.

I was certainly informed by perſons of worth, that the puniſhments above, are but gentle admonitions to what they knew was acted by two Magiſtrates of *Newcaſtle*, one for killing a poor Work-man of his own, and being queſtioned for it, and condemned, compounded with King *James* for it, paying to a Scotch Lord his weight in gold and ſilver, every ſeven years or thereabouts, &c. The other Magiſtrate found a poor man cutting a few horſe-ſticks in his Wood, for which offence, he bound him to a tree, and whipt

---

A page from 'England's Grievance Discovered in Relation to the Coal Trade' by Ralph Gardiner (born 1625) in which he describes the Branks or Scold's Bridle as an instrument for punishing women. (British Library)

A illustration from 'England's Grievance Discovered in Relation to the Coal Trade' by Ralph Gardiner (born 1625) showing a woman wearing a Scold's Bridle being led through the streets.(British Library)

Mary Reynald a Pauper in the House having embezzled Bread Cheese Beef and Candles belonging to this Corporation Ordered that she be publicly whipped in the Hall immediately before Dinner on Wednesday next.

An entry from the minute book of the Powys, Wales workhouse; 'Mary Reynald a Pauper in the House having embezzled Bread Cheese Beef and Candles belonging to this Corporation Ordered that she be publicly whipped in the Hall immediately before Dinner on Wednesday next.'(Copyright Powys County Council Archive)

The whipping at the cart's tail of three Quaker women in Dover, colony of New Hampshire, 1662. Illustration from 'The Whip and the Rod' Professor R.G. Van Yelyer 1942. (Collection of the author)

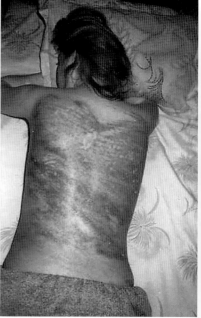

50 Lashes. The back of a woman allegedly given fifty lashes by a court in Saudi Arabia 2016. Although undoubtedly painful, the punishment was moderate as the skin is not broken. In 17th and 18th century Britain, the sentence of whipping was usually specified by the court to be carried out until 'her body be bloody'. (Multiple websites)

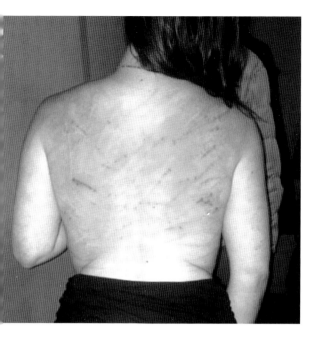

Another modern flogging, this time in Iran. (Multiple websites)

A Narrative of the Proceedings at
the Seffion for London *and* Middlefex,
holden at the Old Bailey, *on the Third
and Fourth days of* July, 1678.

THe firft brought to a Tryal was a young man charged with Stealing a Silver Tankard of the value of 5 *l.* 10 *s.* out of a Gentlemans Houfe in the Parifh of St. *Brides*; The Prifoner appeared to be of an idle loofe Converfation, but no proof being made directly of his taking the Plate, nor its being found with, or difpofed of by him, (for indeed it never was heard of) he was thereupon brought in not Guilty.

An elderly comely Woman was Convicted of Stealing a Green Silk Petticoat on the firft of *July*, from a Shop keeper near *Pauls*, whither fhe came on pretence of buying, but it being miffed before fhe was out of fight, fhe was brought back, and at the end of the Shop, droped the Petticoat, but the Jury were fo favorable, as to value it but at 10 *d.* fo that her Back is like to pay the wages due to the activity of her Fingers.

The next was a young fellow for a filthy bruitifh offence being Arraigned on the Statute of 18 *Eliz.* *cap.* 7. for having the Carnal knowledge

Black humour – an extract from Old Bailey Proceedings July 1678; '...the jury were so favourable, as to value it but at 10d. so that her Back is like to pay the wages due to the activities of her fingers'. Had the jury valued the stolen goods any higher, she would have been hanged rather than publicly flogged. (www.oldbaileyonline.org)

'Indecency' Cartoon print by Isaac Cruikshank 1799 showing a woman urinating in the street, saying, 'Blast you, what are you stareing [sic] at?' The print reflects contemporary public concern over the behaviour of prostitutes, reflected in public support for 18th century moral reforming societies. (United States Library of Congress, British Cartoon Prints Collection)

A woman wearing a Brank or Scold's Bridle. Lithograph illustration from 'A Brief History of the United States' by Joel Dorman Steele and Esther Baker Steele, 1885. (United States Library of Congress)

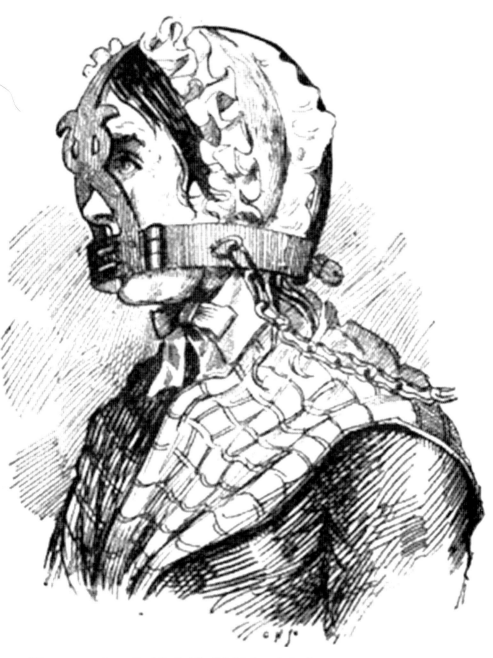

Woman wearing a Scold's Bridle (Multiple websites)

Woman being flogged in the Bridewell. Illustration from 'The Annals of Bristol in the Eighteenth Century' John Latimer (born 1824). Latimer was editor of the Bristol Mercury for 25 years, but his life work was the production of his famous Annals, recording the day-to-day history of Bristol from the 17th century onwards. (Multiple websites)

Tothill Fields Bridewell (also known as the Westminster Bridewell) was a prison located in the Westminster area of central London between 1618 and 1884. The catholic Westminster Cathedral, started in 1895, now stands on the site of the prison and the prison's foundations were re-used for the cathedral. All that remains of the prison is a stone gateway dating from the 17th century. (Authors collection)

Chapbook Illustrations of Witch Ducking. Chapbooks were small booklets, cheap to make and to buy. They provided simple reading matter and were commonplace across the country from the 17th to the 19th century, covering a very wide range of subject matter. (British Library)

Society for the Reformation of Manners Eleventh Black List containing the names of 830 people, approximately 90% being women, against whom the Society had obtained conviction in the courts for moral offenses. This list brought the total number of persons thus prosecuted and convicted to 7,995. The list notes that they have been punished either by carting, whipping, fining, imprisonment or the suppression of their licences. (Houghton Library, Harvard University, EB65.A100.B675b v.5 no.43.)

Mary Hamilton whipped –a print of 1813 showing Mary Hamilton undergoing one of four severe public whippings to which she had been sentenced in 1746, in addition to six months imprisonment. Between 1740 and 1742 Jacob Bicker Raye in Holland counted the number of strokes administered during public floggings; between 36 and 41 for a regular whipping and between 60 and 83 for a severe whipping. It is likely that Mary received more than 300 lashes altogether. The picture rather fancifully shows her still wearing men's breeches during her flogging, no doubt giving a frisson to some but unlikely. (Multiple websites)

Ducking Stool preserved in Leominster Priory, Herefordshire, last used in 1809. The 'ducking' or 'cucking' stool first appears in 'Piers Plowman' 1378 where it is described as 'wyuen pine' - women's punishment. (Multiple websites)

Wives & Daughters of imprisoned debtors being sexually assaulted by the gaolers. Illustration from 'Cry of the Oppressed' Moses Pitt 1689 (Multiple websites)

A woman being simultaneously birched and her breasts torn with pincers. Illustration from 'A General Martyrolojie' Samuel Clarke 1651.

that any woman convicted of stealing goods worth more than 12*d* [5p] would be branded with the letter 'T' on the left thumb, in addition to the whipping or other punishment the court might impose.

It is alleged that sometimes criminals convicted of petty theft, or who were able to bribe the executioner, had the branding iron applied when it was cold, so branding was usually inflicted in the court immediately following sentence, so that the magistrates could see 'the smoke from the offender's singed skin'. Such an occasion took place at Taunton in 1706, when the sheriffs' officers were fined 40*s* (£2) for not causing two women to be 'well burnt.'[1]

For a short time, between 1699 and January 1707, convicted thieves were branded on the cheek in order to increase the deterrent effect of the punishment, but this rendered those convicted as unemployable and in 1707 the practice reverted to branding on the thumb.

As with whipping, branding proved to be an ineffectual deterrent, even when applied over and over again to the same culprit. Ann Harris was 20 years old when she was hanged on 13 July 1705. She was sentenced to be branded before execution, but was: 'A notorious shoplifter so often burnt in the hand that there was no more room for the hangman to stigmatize her.'

Women transported to the American colonies were often branded before they were shipped aboard the transports. In 1720, Jane Clarke was convicted of theft and sentenced to be transported for a term of seven years, after 'the proper officer kiss'd the hand with a red hot iron'. Sometimes, even this double punishment was not thought sufficiently harsh. Isabella Chapman was convicted of sheep stealing in 1721 and was sentenced not only to be 'burnt in the hand', but also to be whipped before beginning her seven years transportation.

Branding as a punishment for those receiving 'benefit of clergy' (see Appendix I) ended in 1779 and the last convict sentenced to be branded at the Old Bailey received the sentence in 1789.

Chapter 11

Hanged by the 'Bloody Code'

The English legal system between 1688 and 1815 has been called the 'Bloody Code' for good reason; in 1688 around fifty offences carried the death penalty, but by 1815 this had risen to a staggering 225. The substantial increase in commercial activity following The Glorious Revolution of 1688 led to an ongoing plethora of laws mainly designed to protect wealth and property. Why this was considered necessary is a matter of debate; Lord Chancellor Hardwicke (1690–1764) remarked that they were made necessary 'by the egregious wickedness of the age'. Whether or not this is true, the perceived 'egregious wickedness' led to people being hanged for pick-pocketing more than a shilling [5p] or stealing five shillings [25p] in a shop, for cutting down trees in a garden or orchard, or allowing fish to escape from a pond. Sir Erskine May famously described eighteenth justice thus:'The lives of men [and women] were sacrificed with a reckless barbarity worthier of an eastern despot, than of a Christian state'.[1] '… those unlucky enough to be caught up in the web of exemplary punishment the criminal code was unjust, irrational and exceptionally severe.'[2]

Between 1735 and 1799, a total of 1,596 women were condemned to death, although more than seventy per cent of those would be reprieved, most being transported to the colonies – first in America and then to Australia; 353 women were executed in England for a wide variety of crimes, including murder but also for 'receiving', embezzlement and fraud, returning illegally from transportation and, in one case, 'sacrilege'.

When a woman stood convicted of a capital crime, the judge would ask if there was any reason why sentence of death should not be passed on her. Many women took this opportunity to 'plead her belly,' i.e. that they were pregnant. She was often not sentenced to death at this point, but kept in prison and examined by a jury of matrons to see if she actually was pregnant. If she was found to be 'quick with child', her execution was delayed until after she had given birth or her sentence was commuted to one of transportation. There is evidence that female prisoners would sometimes try to get pregnant while in prison to save themselves from execution. To this end, they would offer themselves to the jailer or to male visitors, as the law did not permit the execution of a pregnant woman. Many of the claims of pregnancy proved to be false, in which case she would be returned to court to be formally sentenced to death and then included in the next batch of executions.

The Murder Act of July 1752 required that murderers must be hanged within two working days of receiving the death sentence. (Sunday alone was a non-working day). This meant that the condemned murderers were often the only execution on any given day, in order to comply with the requirements of the Act, which incidentally also stipulated that they be given only bread and water between sentence and execution.

Women convicted of other crimes at the Old Bailey in London were usually executed several weeks after sentence when the Recorder had submitted his report indicating which prisoners sentenced to death should be reprieved or had their sentences commuted and which were to be 'left for execution'. These women would be executed together with all others under similar sentence, including convicted men, on the next execution day. This led to the mass executions later seen at Tyburn and Newgate in London. Those condemned in the provinces were usually executed on the next local market day, thus ensuring a big crowd to witness the spectacle, thought to be a deterrent against individuals emulating the crimes being thus punished. When the day's executions included the burning of a woman (see chapter 6 'Burned Alive') the hangings would take place first, thus ensuring that the woman would be obliged to watch as her fellow condemned, who often included her male co-defendants, were put to death.

Before 1789, executions would usually take place in an open space outside the town to which the condemned would be taken in a procession consisting of the Sheriff, a religious minister, the hangman and a troop of guards. Later, there was a trend to execute the condemned in front of the county gaol. Before 1783, women were executed by being thrown off a ladder or the back of a cart with the noose around their neck, thus rendering their death to be both protracted and painful. In that year, the new 'drop' gallows was introduced which allowed for a fall of up to 18in (35cms), although whether this made death any easier or quicker is somewhat doubtful.

Before 1752, women who had been hanged were able to have their bodies reclaimed by family and friends who would arrange for their interment with whatever religious rites accorded with their beliefs. After this date, women executed for murder were further punished after death by having their bodies made available for dissection by surgeons and not returned to their families for a decent burial.

Not only were women disadvantaged in law by being burned at the stake for certain crimes, while their male accomplices were merely hanged, but often they were left to face the judicial penalty for their crime alone while their male partner escaped justice altogether. Their general lack of independent means, social conventions surrounding women travelling alone, encumbering clothing and weaker physical strength often resulted in their being less likely to make good their escape when the law caught up with them. Sometimes they stood in the dock alone in order to protect their loved one from the legal consequences of their actions. Whatever the reason, the court did not take any excuse as mitigation, and the woman was as savagely dealt with as the letter of the law demanded.

Such a case was that of a young woman named Sophia Pringle. Sophia was probably born in 1767, the daughter of a journeyman tailor of Cannon Row, London. When she was 19, she went to work as a servant to an American lady in Duke Street, where she apparently fell in love with and intended to marry a lottery-office keeper, whose name has been lost to history. For whatever reason her employment was short-lived and she went to lodge with one William Lewis, a hairdresser in Oxford Street, where she cohabited with her unidentified lover. Unfortunately, he apparently became sick and unable to work, throwing responsibility for both their financial upkeep on Sophie.

In December 1786, the pair embarked on a bold plan to obtain money by producing a forged power of attorney, Sophia posing as the daughter of her father's lodger, one William Winterbourne. The document was made out, she tricked someone into notarising it for her, and then went to the Bank of England, which paid her the requested £100 without question. However, when she tried the same trick again a week later, this time for £150, the broker became suspicious that she was not who she claimed to be and by the time she presented herself at the Bank of England, the bank was on notice that all was not as it seemed. The real Mr Winterbourne was contacted and he identified Sophia Pringle as being the daughter of his landlord.

Sophia's trial caused huge public interest, attracting huge crowds wishing to view a young woman facing such serious charges of fraud and forgery. The crowds of people trying to get into the court were so large that the key witness, William Winterbourne, was unable to push past them in order to get into the courtroom when called to give evidence. Throughout her trial, Sophia fainted continuously and her head had to be forced up for witnesses to identify her, so a surgeon was called who gave her wine and water in an effort to revive her. Found guilty and sentenced to be hanged, she tried to save herself by claiming she was pregnant, but a jury of matrons found that this was not the case. A periodical of the time snappily entitled 'The New Ladies Magazine, Or, Polite, Entertaining, and Fashionable Companion for the Fair Sex', saw fit to report Sophia's execution in vivid and disturbing detail:

> Yesterday morning were executed in the Old Bailey, pursuant to sentence, Sophia Pringle [plus eight others listed]. Sophia Pringle, the unhappy woman convicted of forgery at a former sessions, for two hours, prior to her execution, was in strong convulsive fits, and at every interval raved incessantly. The Sheriffs, judging that her being placed upon the scaffold with others doomed to the same fate, might

have interrupted their devotion, and taken off their attention from the great concern which must necessarily occupy them at that dreadful moment, kept her within the prison until a few minutes before eight. When orders were sent for her to be conducted from her cell, she again fainted, and was obliged to be brought forth by the Sergeants at Mace. Recovering her senses, in some measure, she frequently cried out 'Mother, mother, what have I done!' with other wild expressions. She was supported on either side by two men, until the scaffold dropped, and put a period instantaneously to her existence. She was dressed in plain mourning, and had a kind of veil over her face, which being removed, her head appeared very neatly dressed in a morning cap. Her deplorable situation affected the spectators with the most poignant grief, every one present lamenting her miserable end.

We hope the fate of this deluded and unhappy girl, will operate forcibly on the rest of her sex; for there scare remains a doubt, but that she was the victim of an artful and designing villain who imposed upon her too easy credulity.

The other eight, who were executed at the same time, behaved themselves with piety and resignation.

The number of spectators assembled, were more numerous than on any occasion for some years.

No evidence has come to light that Sophia was in fact ever offered a pardon in return for denouncing her accomplice and lover, but it was clearly thought to be the case at the time, and that whoever he was, he had got away scot free, as expressed by the Reverend William Cole (1714–82) in his poem *To the Feeling Heart, Exalted Affection or Sophia Pringle*:

> Mark well the tale, thence dread example take
> Reflect, and weep for poor Sophia's sake.
> Yet act those tears a mean, a mimic part
> Which grace the cheek, but not amend the heart.
> 'Tis persevering innocence alone,
> 'Tis wedded love, that makes sweet peace your own.
> Law, mildly stern, and yet severely wise,
> Spare a mean culprit, but a forger dies.

Perhaps the worst example of a woman suffering for the crimes committed by a man, who escaped scot-free, was that of Deborah Churchill. Deborah was born in or around the year 1677, in a village near Norwich. Her maiden name is unknown, but she married a Mr Churchill, with whom she apparently had several children, whose fate is unrecorded. Unfortunately her husband took to drink and died as a result, whereupon Deborah took herself off to London to seek employment.

Having no way of supporting herself, she quickly ran into debt and cast around for a way of obtaining money. Upon entering a public house in Holborn, she met a soldier, who obviously must have appeared to be a good catch, as Deborah asked him to marry her. He agreed and the couple took coach to the Fleet, where they entered into a 'fleet marriage', the best-known example of an irregular or a clandestine marriage taking place in England before the Marriage Act of 1753 made them illegal. The 'marriage' did not last long however, as Deborah is alleged to have enticed her husband to drink until he passed out, whereupon she made her escape, clutching the marriage certificate which guaranteed that she could no longer be pursued for her debts, now the legally enforceable responsibility of her hapless husband.

Following this episode, Deborah began cohabiting with a young man by the name of Hunt, with whom she was apparently genuinely in love as they happily stayed together for some six years, a relationship which the Ordinary of Newgate would later describe at her trial as a 'lascivious and adulterous'. One fateful night, the couple were returning from a visit to the theatre accompanied by a male friend, when a violent argument broke out between the two men, both of whom drew their swords. Deborah, anxious for her husband's safety, interposed herself between the two men, whereupon Hunt took the opportunity to stab his opponent, killing him instantly.

Hunt fled the scene and escaped abroad to Holland, but Deborah was apprehended at the scene, taken before the magistrate and committed to Newgate prison. In June 1708, at the Old Bailey, Mrs Churchill was indicted as an accomplice under an Act established during the reign of James I called the 'Statute of Stabbing', which stated that 'If any one stabs another, who hath not at that time a weapon drawn, or hath not first struck the party who stabs, is deemed guilty of murder, if the person stabbed dies within six months afterwards.'

The Newgate Calendar recorded that at her trial it was revealed that Deborah had been arrested and committed to the Clerkenwell Bridewell on no less than twenty previous occasions for pick-pocketing or whoring, and had been stripped half naked and whipped at the post on each and every occasion. Moreover, she had been 'kept to beating hemp from morning till night for the small allowance of so much bread and water, which just kept life and soul together, she commonly came out like a skeleton, and walked as if her limbs had been tied together with packthread.'

Unsurprisingly, Deborah was convicted, but pleaded her belly to avoid being hanged. The jury of matrons were unable to say whether she was pregnant or not, so the judge remanded her for six months to await developments. Sadly at the end of that time, there was no sign of the claimed pregnancy and Deborah was duly sentenced to death. *The Newgate Calendar* reported that 'This woman's behaviour was extremely penitent; but she denied her guilt to the last moment of her life, having no conception that she had committed murder, because she did not herself stab the deceased. She suffered at Tyburn, seventeenth of December 1708.'

The Ordinary [chaplain] of Newgate recounted her last moments, which seem to have been mainly occupied in prayer and concern for the welfare of her children: 'She desired the Standers-by to pray for her, That God would be pleas'd to be merciful to her Soul. And turning to one she call'd Nurse, she earnestly begged of her to take care of her poor Children, for whom she seemed to be very much concern'd.' Perhaps the saddest part of the story is the postscript to *The Newgate Calendar*'s report, tardily acknowledging the unjust nature of Mrs Deborah Churchill's fate: 'Though this woman's sins were great, yet we must admit some hardship in her suffering the utmost rigour of the law for the crime of which she was found guilty.'

The Ordinary recorded his opinion that 'let what punishment would light on this common strumpet, she was no changeling, for as soon as she was out of jail she ran into still greater evils, by deluding, if possible, all mankind.' Be that as it may, but there is no escaping from the fact that Deborah was hanged for a crime committed by her husband, for which he was never punished, and for which she was 'deemed' to have been his accomplice although no evidence was ever offered to support this conjecture.

On 16 December 1966, the International Covenant on Civil and Political Rights (ICCPR) was adopted by the United Nations General Assembly, and was ratified on 23 March 1976. Article 6[5] of the treaty states: 'Sentence of death shall not be imposed for crimes committed by persons below eighteen years of age.' (sadly at least ten countries have since breached this treaty). The niceties of an international treaty did not trouble the judges administering the 'bloody code' in the eighteenth century, and underage felons suffered the same penalties as their adult counterparts, including numbers of teenage girls.

Elizabeth Morton, aged 15, was hanged at Gallows Hill, Nottingham on 8 April 1763 for the murder of the 2-year-old child of her employer, John Oliver. Elizabeth, a servant girl employed by the farmer John Oliver and his family in the parish of Walkeringham, was caught after attempting to kill one of the Olivers' other children.

> In August 1762, Mrs Oliver found one of her children under some straw in a barn, 'struggling in the agonies of death, the blood gushing from its mouth, nose and eyes.' The child recovered and accused Elizabeth. The servant was immediately suspected of having strangled the family's two-year-old daughter Mary, who had been found dead in her cradle months earlier. Elizabeth confessed to the crime, but said she had been incited to commit it by a gentleman

in black who came to bed with her and told her she must murder two of her master's children. She could not feel easy, she said, until she had done as he directed. Despite the fact that the report in the Annual Register suggested she was an 'idiot' (which would have been grounds for a pardon), she was executed.[3]

After she was hanged her body was sent for dissection and afterwards buried in a village near her home.

Susannah Underwood was hanged at Gloucester on Friday 19 April 1776 for setting fire to a barn and a hay stack at Longhope on 31 January. *The Hereford Journal* criticised the bad manners of the 15-year-old girl for refusing to shake hands with her master at her execution, but did not criticise the authorities for hanging her.

Catharine Connor, aged 17, went to the gallows at Tyburn on Monday 31 December 1750 for publishing a false, forged and counterfeit Will, purporting to be the Will of Michael Canty, a sailor in the navy, on 29 October of that year. She told the court that she could neither read nor write and that the forgery was made by a Mr Dunn, although she was present at the time. The court did not trouble itself with testing that defence and Catherine was hanged together with fourteen other people that day.

Susannah Minton, aged 17, was hanged at Hereford for arson on Saturday 16 September 1786. She was described as being simple, and worked as a servant at the house of Paul Gwatkin. Susannah had watched her mistress Anne Gwatkin 'exhibit some articles of finery', (handkerchiefs, caps etc.) and she coveted them for herself and planned a theft. She decided to create a diversion by setting fire to a barn close to the house in the hope that everyone would rush to the fire leaving her way clear. The plan worked and she managed to steal the box containing the finery, but the fire destroyed a great quantity of barley, oats, feed clover and hay that the farmer had stored in the barn.

Elizabeth Marsh, aged 15, was convicted of the murder of her grandfather, aged 70, by giving him two blows to the head while he slept. She was hanged on Monday, 17 March 1794 at Dorchester. At her trial, Elizabeth claimed that she was bred in such extreme ignorance that she had been wholly unacquainted with the difference between good and evil, heaven and hell. She was executed according to her sentence, forty-eight hours after her conviction.

Mary Stracey, aged 18, was hanged at Tyburn for highway robbery on 15 March 1745 for assaulting a man named Will Humphreys and robbing him of one guinea [£1.05p] a few months earlier. Mary was about 18 or 20 years old, was a prostitute and pickpocket who was, according to the Newgate Ordinary, 'a perverse, vicious Girl, void of all good Dispositions, and wholly untractable and unadviseable, giving herself up to the vilest Company on Earth, both of Men and Women'. The Ordinary goes on to give a brief biography and character assassination of the hapless girl. Having no interest in honest work and,

> renounc[ing] everything resembling Goodness or Virtue, [she] went idling her Time away on the Streets with her hellish wicked Companions, who induc'd her to commence Whore[ing], upon which she turn'd a meer [*sic*] reprobate-Creature' and 'became known to all the Constables, and inferior Officers of Justice in that End of the Town.

Stracey, says the Ordinary, 'own'd she was naturally inclined, and not over-persuaded by others, as some of them may or do allege in Extenuation of their Guilt'.

Mary Jones, aged 18, was charged under the Shoplifting Act and hanged at Tyburn 16 October 1771 for stealing four pieces of muslin valued at £5 10s. Mary was thought to be about 18 or 19 years old but was already married with two children when her husband, William, was press ganged into the navy to go to the Falkland Islands, leaving her virtually destitute. She lived with her friend Ann Styles in Angel Alley in the Strand and was at times reduced to begging to feed herself and the infants. It is said that she had her baby with her in the cart as she was taken to Tyburn to be hanged.

Sarah Shenston, aged 18, was hanged at Moor Heath on the outskirts of Shrewsbury in Shropshire on Thursday, 22 March 1792. She suffered for the murder of her illegitimate male child whose throat she had cut immediately after birth, on 30 September 1791

In 1778, the Papist Act was passed, relaxing certain restrictions on inheritance and schooling for Catholics. Lord George Gordon raised a petition against this and marched on Parliament in June 1780, drawing huge crowds. Matters got out of hand and the rioting lasted for a week. The mob raged against the Catholics, attacking chapels, houses, public buildings, and even Catholic people in the streets; 12,000 troops were deployed and 700 people were killed.

The nineteenth century saw numbers of attempts in parliament to de-capitalise many minor crimes. Sir Samuel Romilly (1757–1818) introduced a Bill in 1813 'to repeal so much of the Act of King William as punishes with death the offence of stealing privately in a shop, warehouse or stable, goods of the value of 5 shillings', but it was thrown out by the House of Lords. In 1819 Sir James Mackintosh, who had supported Romilly's proposals, carried a motion against the government for a committee to consider capital punishment. In 1820, he introduced six bills embodying the recommendations of the committee, only three of which became law. In 1823, Mackintosh put forward a further nine proposals to parliament for abolishing the punishment of death for less serious offences, succeeding in having shoplifting removed from the list of capital crimes.

THE VIOLENT ABUSE OF WOMEN

Between 1832 and 1837, Sir Robert Peel's government introduced various Bills to reduce the number of capital crimes. Sheep, cattle and horse stealing were removed from the list in 1832, followed in 1834/5 by 'sacrilege', letter stealing and returning from transportation, forgery and coining in 1836, arson, burglary and theft from a dwelling house in 1837. Nonetheless, in the period 1800 to 1833 a further thirty-three women were hanged for crimes other than murder, the last of these being Charlotte Long who was hanged for arson in August 1833 at Gloucester.

Chapter 12

Male Impersonators & Female Actors

Although women regularly dressing in male attire became common practice in the twentieth century (at least in the Western world), women have dressed as men since time immemorial and for a wide variety of reasons. We have no way of knowing for certain, but Boudicca probably did not go to war with the Romans wearing a frock! Other than going to war, the wearing of masculine cloths invariably arose from a need to ensure anonymity or avoid recognition, perhaps to evade creditors or to illicitly seek employment as a man in order to claim a man's income. It might also have been to masquerade as a man in order to pursue a lesbian relationship, as was the case with Mary (aka Charles) Hamilton, born in 1721, who in order to have a sexual relationship with other women allegedly 'used vile and deceitful practices, not to be mentioned'.

One of the most common reasons for adopting such a subterfuge in the seventeenth and eighteenth centuries seems to have been to follow a husband or lover into the armed services, being unable to face the months or even years of separation (and lack of income) that having a partner in such an occupation entailed. Sometimes the woman was in pursuit of an absconding partner, as in the case of Hannah Snell, whose husband deserted her while she was pregnant with their first child. Determined to trace her errant husband, she served under the name of James Grey for several years in the 6th Regiment of Foot and subsequently the Marines, seeing action in both services. Amazingly, she remained undiscovered, despite having been stripped and flogged with 500 lashes in the army on a trumped-up charge of dereliction of duty, and later being wounded with a musket ball in the groin while on service in India. Hannah remained undiscovered while being flogged, apparently because she had small breasts and was tied pressed against a wrought iron gate while the cat o'nine tails was applied to her back. She had actually been sentenced to 600 lashes, but such was her stoicism under the agony of the lash that the officer overseeing her punishment rescinded the last 100.

Other women had their true identities discovered when being similarly stripped in readiness for corporal punishment, although of course their punishment had been awarded as men. In 1771 naval seaman Charles Waddall was revealed as a woman when, unlike Hannah Snell, she was being stripped to the waist in order to receive a flogging. Likewise in 1781 another naval seaman named George Thompson was shown in fact to be Margaret Thompson while being similarly prepared for punishment.

Phoebe Hessel was born in London in 1713 and after marriage, in order to follow her soldier husband overseas, joined the 5th Regiment of Foot as a man and fought with them at the Battle of Fontenoy in 1745 under the Duke of Cumberland, where she received a bayonet wound to the arm. She also served in Gibralter and later in America, where she fought at the Battle of Bunker Hill. However, she was eventually detected when she was sentenced to be flogged for some offence she had committed, as described by a sergeant of the 13th Light Dragoons: 'A misdemeanour at length put an end to her martial career. She was brought to the halberts to be whipped, and having her neck and shoulders bared, her sex was discovered.'

When the drummer who was to wield the cat o'nine tails hesitated, she called out 'Strike and be damned'. Pheobe survived and continued to live on a state pension into a ripe old age, allegedly dying at 108 years of age in Brighton, Sussex, where she is buried in St Nicholas's churchyard.

Unlike in the case of Hannah Snell and Phoebe Hessel, the motivation for impersonating a man and joining up for military service was not always made clear:

> Last Saturday [4 February] Betty Blandford, of Pimperne in Dorsetshire, a young woman about twenty, dressed herself in man's cloaths, and inlisted in Gen. Elliot's regiment of light horse (a party being in this city) and was immediately sworn in; but soon after being discovered, she was discharged, and committed to Bridewell [where she would undoubtedly have been whipped upon admission as was the custom].[1]

Sometimes, a woman's motivation to dress as a man was not even admitted. One woman, travelling to Uxbridge in a sailor's outfit was stopped by three gentlemen who were suspicious of her 'odd shape'. Discovered to be a woman, and unable or unwilling to give any explanation of her male attire, she was suspected of planning some 'evil design' and taken before a magistrate. He sentenced her to a term of hard labour in the Tothill Fields Bridewell.[2]

Although flogging may seem a harsh punishment for cross-dressing, earlier centuries had imposed similarly brutal penalties – during the fifteenth century, military articles required that an offender's money be confiscated (assuming that she had any) and that she then be driven from the camp by being beaten with a staff, and with one arm broken. Henry VIII merely mandated that the woman be branded on the cheek.[3]

By no means were all of these cross-dressing women, including the many who served as men in the armed forces, punished for this deception per se – indeed many of them, like Hannah Snell, were later rewarded with a pension. Women wearing male attire did not in itself constitute a criminal offence, but the society of the day found any suggestion of lesbianism offensive, and when presented with an example the law invariably sought some sinister motivation deserving of punishment. Women found to be wearing male attire in circumstances that suggested the motivation for male impersonation was sexual in nature brought down the law in its severest and most savage form. Prosecutions involving women disguising themselves as men, with a view to seducing or marrying other women, were regularly reported in the seventeenth and eighteenth centuries; for example, in 1694 the Oxford antiquarian and diarist Anthony Wood recounted in a letter that there had:

> appeared at the King's Bench in Westminster hall a young woman in man's apparel, or that personated a man, who was found guilty of marrying a young maid, whose portion he had obtained and was very nigh of being contracted to a second wife. Divers of her love letters were read in court, which occasion'd much laughter. Upon the whole she was ordered to Bridewell to be well whipt and kept to hard labour till further order of the court.[4]

In 1746 Mary Hamilton, alias Charles, George, and William Hamilton, was put on trial at the Quarter Sessions at Taunton in Somerset, for posing as a man in order to marry a woman. It was claimed by the prosecution at the trial that she had at various times married a total of fourteen women. Some initial confusion arose as no one was quite able to define exactly what crime Mary Hamilton had committed, as no statute covered such an outrageous act. Most of the laws banning illicit sexual activity in Britain only date from the late nineteenth century, and that legislation which made homosexuality illegal only ever applied specifically to men. In the upshot, upon the advice of a learned counsel, she was prosecuted under a clause of the vagrancy act, 'for having by false and deceitful practices endeavoured to impose on some of his Majesty's subjects'. Mary Hamilton was duly convicted of fraud and received a savage sentence; the justices delivering their verdict that:

> the he or she prisoner at the bar is an uncommon, notorious cheat, and we, the Court, do sentence her, or him, whichever he or she may be, to be imprisoned six months, and during that time to be whipped in the towns of Taunton, Glastonbury, Wells and Shepton Mallet.

A contemporary report describes how severely inflicted was her punishment:

> These whippings she has accordingly undergone, and very severely have they been inflicted, insomuch, that those persons

95

who have more regard to beauty than to justice, could not refrain from exerting some pity toward her, when they saw so lovely a skin scarified with rods, in such a manner that her back was almost flead [flayed]: yet so little effect had the smart or shame of this punishment on the person who underwent it, that the very evening she had suffered the first whipping, she offered the gaoler money, to procure her a young girl to satisfy her most monstrous and unnatural desires.

With its sexual connotations, the cross-dressing and the prospect of an attractive woman undergoing a public stripping and whipping, not once, but four times, the case fascinated the prurient interest of the public and was reported at length in the local newspaper, the *Bath Journal*. It related that after news of the arrest was made public many people visited the prison to get a look at Hamilton, who was described as very 'bold and impudent'. It added that 'it is publickly talk'd that she has deceived several of the Fair Sex by marrying them' and the author promised to 'make a further Enquiry' into these allegations for a later report. The final report was repeated in the *Daily Advertiser* on 12 November, where it was probably seen by the author Henry Fielding, who subsequently wrote a pamphlet on the subject entitled 'The Female Husband: or, The Surprising History of Mrs Mary, alias Mr George Hamilton' (London, 1746).

Incidentally, savage as Hamilton's sentence was, it was as nothing compared to those handed down for similar offences in other countries. German court records of 1721 gives an account of the case of two women named Catherina Lincken and Catherina Mühlhahn who were living together as husband and wife, being charged with a number of offences including sodomy! Upon their conviction, the lawyer representing the pair asked for nothing worse than life imprisonment for Lincken, and that Mühlhahn be released. However, the sentence of the court was for Lincken to be executed by hanging and then her body to be burned, and that Mühlhahn was to be tortured in order to ascertain the truth of her testimony.[5]

Sometimes however, the penalty imposed was intended to be publicly shaming rather than physically agonising, although the public often made sure that a severe physical punishment was added to that imposed by the magistrate:

On Saturday last a Woman was convicted at the Guildhall, Westminster, for going in Men's Cloaths, and being married to three different Women by a fictitious Name, and for defrauding them of the Money and Cloaths: She was sentenced to stand in the Pillory at Charing-Cross, and to be imprisoned six Months.

Daily Advertiser 8 July 1777

MALE IMPERSONATORS & FEMALE ACTORS

> Yesterday a Woman stood in the Pillory at Charing-Cross, for going in Mens Cloaths, marrying three Women, and obtaining a Sum of Money from each.[6]
>
> *Daily Advertiser* 23 July 1777

One of these unnamed women was undoubtedly Ann Marrow. Ann Marrow was convicted of fraud in July 1777. She was found guilty of 'going in man's cloaths [*sic*] and personating a man in marriage with three different women and defrauding them of their money and effects.' It is unclear if these accusations of theft were true as there is no record of Marrow's side of the story. She was sentenced to three months in prison and to stand in the pillory at Charing Cross on 22 July 1777. It is said that she was pelted so severely by the female spectators that she was blinded in both eyes and later died of her injuries in the Bridewell.[7]

Occasionally, the desire by a woman to dress in masculine clothes was engendered neither by sexual desire nor by a need to disguise her identity. One such was Mary Frith who was born in Aldersgate Street in London on or about 1584. Her parents were relatively well to do and tried to provide an education for their daughter, providing the young Mary with private tutors. A tomboy from an early age, she rebelled against her parent's authority and took up with London's pickpockets, becoming notoriously successful and earning herself the nickname Moll Cutpurse. She found dramatic fame as the subject of two plays: *The Roaring Girl* (1607) by Thomas Dekker and Thomas Middleton and later in *Amends for Ladies* (1612) by Nathan Field. Several times apprehended for theft, she was 'burnt in the hand' (branded) on no less than four occasions. Subsequently sentenced to death, she escaped the noose by paying a bribe of £2,000 to the roundhead General Fairfax who obligingly dropped the charges.[8]

Ironically, women have also been abused for appearing in female attire! Actresses first appeared on the English stage in 1629, when a troupe of French players, comprising both male and female actors, dared to give a performance at Blackfriars in London. According to a letter addressed to Laud, then Bishop of London, by one Thomas Brande, the public were indignant. The French actresses were 'hissed, hooted, and pippin-pelted from the stage,' so that the writer 'did not think they would soon be ready to try the same again.' Until then, female parts in stage drama had been enacted invariably by boys or young men, specifically trained to take female roles. The employment of women upon the stage was seen as an obscenity and it is not surprising therefore that the playgoers of the day were suitably shocked. In 1632 the puritan author William Prynne published his thousand-page work *Histriomastix*, in which he stigmatised all 'woman-actors' as 'monsters' and 'notorious whores' and applied to their performances such adjectives as 'impudent', 'shameful', and 'unwomanish'. This attitude to women in the theatre was slow to change; as late as the 1860s, the actress Anna Cora Mowatt stated that 'being an actress, people considered her and all the actresses as immoral, flighty, silly buffoons who are not to be taken seriously for a moment.'[9]

Chapter 13

Seen But Not Heard

Xanthippe, the wife of Socrates, the Greek philosopher (fifth century BC) became eponymous for subsequent centuries as the archetypical scolding and nagging wife, whose bad temper once led her to tip a bucket of dirty water over her husband's head. Two thousand years later, Shakespeare's Petruchio in *The Taming of the Shrew* was assuring audiences that he would wed a wealthy woman, even 'be she as foul as was Florentious' love, as old as Sibyl, and as curst and shrewd as Socrates' Xanthippe'. In the seventeenth century, the name Xanthippe had become an eponymous term for any scolding or shrewish wife.

More than twenty centuries after poor nagged Socrates, an unknown eighteenth-century balladeer was expressing an opinion about how (probably he) felt the ideal woman should conduct herself:

> A woman should like echo true
> Speak but when she's spoken to;
> But not like echo still be heard
> Contending for the final word.
> Like a town clock a wife should be
> Keeping time and regularity;
> But not like clocks harangue so clear
> That all the town her voice might hear.

The great (but somewhat misogynistic) Doctor Samuel Johnson would most certainly have agreed with such sentiments: 'I am very fond of ladies, I like their beauty, I like their delicacy, I like their vivacity and I like their silence.'[1]

In an age when women had no official voice, and subservience to men in all matters both public and private was considered a cornerstone of society, women who were liberal with their tongues, expressed shrill opinions, nagged their husbands or argued garrulously with their neighbours, were perceived to be possessed of unwomanly aggressiveness, requiring public penance, restraint, punishment or possibly all three.

Although almost certainly in use in Scotland from a much earlier date, the instrument considered ideal for this purpose was first recorded there in 1560, where it had become known as the 'branks', the origin of which is uncertain. It is possible that it derives from the Norman French word 'branques', the branches of a horses bridle or alternatively that it derives from the Old French 'bernac', meaning barnacle, a device put on a horse's nose to keep it quiet. The town council of Edinburgh in that year decreed that 'all persons found guilty of blasphemy shall be punished by the Iron Brank' although it was probably already being prescribed for shrewish women; in 1600 the Kirk Session in Stirling recorded that they would prescribe 'the brankes for the punishment of the shrew'.

In England it was also commonly referred to as the 'Scold's Bridle', the earliest reference to which appears in the 1380s when Geoffrey Chaucer (1343–1400) has one of his characters say:

> But for my daughter Julian
> I would she were bolted with a Bridle
> That leaves her work to play the clack
> And lets her Wheel stand idle.

Although never formally legalised as a judicial penalty, it was often awarded by village or parish councils as well as occasionally by local magistrates. Described in England around 1500 as being 'efficacious and safe … and not dangerous', throughout the seventeenth and eighteenth centuries it was developed from an instrument of simple humiliation into one of torture and severe punishment. For the best part of 300 years it was used to discipline 'shrewish' or 'scolding' women; those whose speech was deemed to be 'riotous' or 'troublesome' as well as for silencing those suspected of practicing witchcraft. Furthermore, in the workhouses of the nineteenth century, it was employed as an instrument of corporal punishment on female inmates. As late as 1856 it was allegedly still in quasi-judicial use at Bolton-le-Moors in Lancashire, and even later in 1876, a Newcastle-upon-Tyne magistrate threatened to use it on some loudly contending women in his courtroom.

The earliest design of the bridle consists of a harness of leather straps secured under the jaw to prevent the mouth from opening. Later, a flat iron bit was added to be inserted in the wearer's mouth and depress the tongue, making it impossible for the wearer to speak. By the mid-seventeenth century, this iron bit had been modified to include a sharp point or even a revolving wheel of spikes. Other branks included an adjustable gag with a sharp edge, causing any movement of the mouth to result in laceration of the tongue. When wearing the device, it was impossible for the woman to either eat, drink or speak, and the agony was often further increased by the wearer being tied to the whipping-post for hours at a time, or worse, being led through the town like an animal, on a lead attached to the bridle. Its employment in this manner was described by a visitor to Newcastle-upon-Tyne in 1648:

> John Willis of Ipswich, upon his oath, that he this deponent was in Newcastle six months ago, and there he saw one Anne Bidlestone drove through the streets by an Officer of the same Corporation, holding a rope in his hand, the other end fastened to an Engine called the Branks. Which is like a Crown, It being of Iron, which was musled [muzzled] over her head and face, with a great gap or tongue of iron forced into her mouth, which forced the blood out. And that is the punishment which Magistrates do inflict upon chiding, and scolding women, and that he hath often seen the like done to others.[2]

The *Reliquary* magazine for October 1860, provided a detailed illustration of a bridle then preserved in Chesterfield, together with an explicit account of the way in which it was secured on the head of the victim:

> The Chesterfield brank is a good example, and has the additional interest of bearing a date. It is nine inches in height, and six and three-quarters across the hoop. It consists of a hoop of iron, hinged on either side, and fastening from behind, and a band, also of iron, passing over the head from back to front and opening dividing in front to admit the nose of the woman whose misfortune it was to wear it. The mode of putting it on would be thus: The brank would be opened by throwing back the sides of the hoop, and the hinder part of the top band by means of the hinges. The constable would then stand in front of his victim and force the knife or plate into her mouth, the divided band passing on either side of her nose, which would protrude through the opening. The hoop would then be closed behind, the band brought down from the top to the back of the head, and fastened down upon it, and thus the cage would at once be firmly and immovably fixed so long as her tormentors might think fit. On the left side is a chain, one end of which is attached to the hoop, and the other end is a ring by which the victim was led, or by which she was at pleasure attached to a post or wall. On the front of the brank is the date 1688.

First-hand accounts by women forced to wear the bridle are unsurprisingly extremely rare. However, one such account has been left by Dorothy Waugh, a disciple of the Quaker preacher James Parnell (1636–56). Dorothy was arrested for preaching in Carlisle in 1655 and although she had committed no offence in law, on the orders of the local mayor, was twice punished with the device before being flogged as a vagrant:

Upon the 7th day about the time called Michaelmas in the year of the world's account 1655, I was moved of the Lord to go into the market of Carlisle, to speak against all deceit and ungodly practices, and the mayor's offer came and violently haled [hauled] me off the cross and put me in prison, not having anything to put to my charge: and presently the mayor came up where I was and asked me from whence I came, and I said out of Egypt where thou lodgest. But after these words he was so violent and full of passion, he scarce asked me any more questions, but called to one of his followers to bring the bridle, as he called it, to put it upon me and was to be on three hours. And that which they called so was like a steel cap, and my hat being violently plucked off, which was pinned to my head, whereby they tore my clothes to put on their bridle, as they called it, which was a stone weight of iron by the relation of their own generation, and three bars of iron to come over my face, and a piece of it was put in my mouth, which was so unreasonable big a thing for that place, as cannot be well related, which was locked to my head, and so I stood their time with my hands bound behind me with the stone weight of iron upon my head and the bit in my mouth to keep me from speaking. And the mayor said he would make me an example to all that should ever come in that name. And the people to see me so violently abused were broken into tears, but he cried out onto them and said 'for foolish pity, one may spoil a whole city'. And the man that kept the prison door demanded two-pence of everyone that came to me while the bridle remained upon me. Afterwards it was taken off and they kept me in prison for a little season, and after a while the mayor came up again and caused it to be put on again and sent me out into the city with it on, and gave me very vile and unsavoury words, which were not fit to proceed out of any man's mouth, and charged the officer to whip me out of the town: from constable to constable, till I came to my own home, when as they not anything to lay to my charge.[3]

In addition to being used to punish 'scolds', the bridle was also employed in the treatment of those women accused of practising witchcraft or sorcery. In1661, Forfar in Scotland possessed a brank specifically for this purpose, describing it as 'the bridle with which the wretched victims of superstition were led to execution'. The most notorious employment of the device as an instrument of torture inflicted upon a woman suspected of witchcraft was during what became known as the North Berwick witch trials.

In 1590, James VI of Scotland returning from Oslo after marrying Anne, daughter of the King of Denmark and Norway, was nearly drowned by violent storms. In that year a great witch hunt was instituted in Copenhagen. One of the first victims was Anna Koldings, who under torture divulged the names of five other women, one of whom was Mail, the wife of the burgomaster of Copenhagen. They all confessed that they had been guilty of sorcery in raising storms that threatened the king and queen's voyage, and that they had sent devils to climb up the keel of their ship. In September two women were burned as witches at Kronborg and when this story was recounted to James, he immediately decided to set up his own witch hunt. One of the first to be apprehended was a woman named Geillis [Gillis] Duncan who had began to exhibit miraculous healing abilities and furthermore had been observed sneaking out of her house during the dead of night on unexplained errands. Betrayed by her employer, Gillis was tortured into a confession of witchcraft and named several others.

Among those accused was Agnes Sampson, a respected and elderly woman from Humbie. Brought before King James and a tribunal of nobles in Holyrood Palace, Agnes strenuously denied the allegation and as a result was ordered to be tortured into making a confession. The executioner's assistants opened the proceedings by first stripping her naked and shaving off all her head and body hair. Next they brought an iron 'witches bridle' to be locked onto her head, this device further refined to cause additional pain by being equipped with four sharp prongs – two that pressed against the tongue and two against the inside of the cheeks. Thus fitted, she was fastened to the wall of her cell by the bridle, every slight movement of her head causing excruciating pain, yet even in this agony she refused to confess. Additional torture was employed but still she remained obdurate 'vntill the Diuels [devil's] marke was found vpon her priuities [privates], then she immediatlye confessed whatsoeuer was demaunded of her, and iustifying those persons aforesaid to be notorious witches'.[4]

Agnes Sampson confessed to the fifty-three indictments against her, including having attended a Sabbat with 200 other witches. She was finally garrotted (strangled) before being burned at the stake.

The bridle as a device for punishing women never seems to have crossed the ocean to the American colonies. However, they invented their own device for the same purpose in the form of a 'cleft stick', a split piece of wood that clamped on the tongue like a simple clothes peg to prevent the victim from speaking. On 4 June 1651, the little town of Southampton, Long Island, saw a well-known resident, for her 'exorbitant words of imprication' [sic] sentenced to stand for an hour in public with her tongue in a cleft stick. It was obviously catching on as a penalty – soon after another woman in the neighbouring town of Easthampton received a similar sentence from the magistrate (2 February, 1652):

> It is ordered that Goody Edwards shall pay 3 Lb or have her tongue in
> a cleft stick for contempt of court warrant in saienge [sic] she would
> not come, but if they had been governor or magistrate then she would
> come, and desireing the warrant to burn it.[5]

In Salem, a town governed under a rigid and narrow puritan ethic, the system of petty surveillance followed by demeaning and painful public punishment meant that women must be careful about what words passed their lips: 'one Oliver, his wife', was sentenced to be publicly whipped for reproaching the magistrates and for prophesying. However, she was obviously a woman of strong willpower, for having been carried to the whipping-post and stripped to the waist in readiness for her flogging:

> She stood without tying, and bare [*sic*] her punishment with a masculine spirit, glorying in her suffering. But after (when she came to consider the reproach which would stick by her, etc.), she was much dejected about it. She had a cleft stick put on her tongue half an hour for reproaching the elders.[6]

By the nineteenth century in Britain, other than for one or two unsubstantiated occurrences, the bridle had fallen into disuse as a form of quasi-judicial punishment for women. However, there remained one place where it still found favour as an instrument for the disciplining of unruly women – the workhouse. Women who found their way into the workhouse included those who had been left destitute by a disappearing husband, girls who found themselves to be unmarried mothers, and those forced to earn a living as what were euphemistically termed 'fallen women'.

In 1792, Montgomery and Pool, together with thirteen other parishes, were incorporated under a local Act of Parliament (32 Geo.3. c.96) 'For the better Relief and Employment of the Poor, belonging to the Parishes of Montgomery and Pool, and certain other Parishes and Places therein mentioned in the Counties of Montgomery and Salop'. Conditions were harsh, with men being separated from their wives and children, and all inmates who were physically able subjected to a twelve-hour working day in addition to cleaning the workhouse from top to bottom. Corporal punishment was used regularly – even for the smallest of offence, the minute books faithfully recording each application of whip or bridle:

> 1801. Maria Clayton having been detected in embezzling potatoes, ordered that she be punished by whipping.
> 12th May 1802. Anne Davies to be placed in stocks with scolding bridle for 2 hours at dinner time to-morrow, and Mary Nicholas in stocks, same time for disorderly behaviour.
> 5th Oct 1808. That a bridle for the punishment of scolds be purchased that lately in the house belonging to Montgomery Corporation being sent for back and returned.[7]

After 1834 Poor Law Unions were created and each union was required to build a workhouse. These unions were groups of parishes that joined together in an effort to reduce the escalating cost of caring for the poor. In the Powis workhouse the minute books record that inmates were often noisy and violent and fighting was common, especially in the women's yard: 'Punishments – Ordered that Mary Davies wife of Robert Davies for riotous and other ill behaviour be confined with a Bridle for two hours.'

The last recorded use of the device seems to have been as late as 1856 at Bolton-le-Moors, Lancashire. In chapter eight of the novel *Three Men in a Boat* (Jerome K. Jerome, 1889) one of the characters makes light of the scold's bridle they come across in Walton church: 'They used these things in ancient days for curbing women's tongues. They have given up the attempt now. I suppose iron was getting scarce, and nothing else would be strong enough.'

It's doubtful that any of the women subjected to this form of punishment would have seen the joke.

A different way to punish scolds which was in use from time immemorial involved public humiliation rather than physical torture. Town and village communities would stage a 'charivari' (defined as a noisy mock serenade performed by a group of people to celebrate a marriage or mock an unpopular person) also often referred to as a 'skimmington'. This involved members of the public assembling in the streets, and clanging pots and pans as the offending woman was led among them, facing backwards mounted on a horse, a mule, or simply carried, tied into a chair or behind a cart.

Shakespeare devoted one of his plays to portray a scold; in *The Taming of the Shrew*, Katharina is said to be 'renowned in Padua for her scolding tongue', and Petruchio is the man who is 'born to tame [her] ... from a wild Kate to a Kate conformable as other household Kates.' Shakespeare was obviously familiar with the practice of mounting 'skimmingtons'; one character suggests instead of courting Kate, Petruchio should 'cart her'!

Amazingly, the legal crime of being a 'scold' or 'shrew' was not removed from English and Welsh law until 1967; the Criminal Law Act 1967, Section 13 states that:

> The following offences are hereby abolished, that is to say (a) any distinct offence under the common law in England and Wales of maintenance (including champerty [a sharing in the proceeds of litigation by one who agrees with either the plaintiff or defendant to help promote it or carry it on] but not embracery [an attempt to influence a judge or jury by corrupt means, as by bribery, threats, or promises] challenging to fight, eavesdropping or being a common barrator, a common scold or a common night walker.

Chapter 14

Gracing the Stool

First mentioned as 'wyuen pine' (women's punishment) in William Langland's *Piers Plowman* (1367) the Ducking Stool falls into that category of quasi-judicial corporal punishments that, like the 'scold's bridle', were punishments suffered almost exclusively by women. The device comprised of a wooden or iron chair into which the victim was strapped, usually fully clothed. The chair was mounted at the end of a long beam, counter weighted at one end and located beside a pond or river of sufficient depth that, when the chair was lowered into the water, the victim became completely submerged.

The ducking stool seems to have been a development of the 'cucking-stool', a commode-like device with a hole in the seat into which the woman identified as a 'scold' was partially stripped before being strapped into the chair and publicly exposed at her door or paraded through the streets amid the jeers of the crowd. A ballad, dating from about 1615, called 'The Cucking of a Scold', describes how the punishment was inflicted:

> Then was the Scold herself,
> In a wheelbarrow brought,
> Stripped naked to the smock,
> As in that case she ought:
> Neats [calves] tongues about her neck
> Were hung in open show;
> And thus unto the cucking stool
> This famous scold did go.[1]

The punishment seems to have been in use since Saxon times, 'cucking' being derived from 'cukken' meaning to defecate. As the victim was originally secured into this device often for days at a time, further elucidation is left to the reader's imagination! It remained in use in parallel with the watery version well into the eighteenth century, being mentioned in *Poor Robin's Almanack* (1746) and appears in law books of the same period:

> Lastly, a common scold, communis rixatrix, (for our law-latin confines
> it to the feminine gender) is a public nuisance to her neighbourhood.

For which offence she may be indicted; and, if convicted, shall be sentenced to be placed in a certain engine of correction called the trebucket, castigatory, or cucking stool, which in the Saxon language signifies the scolding stool; though now it is frequently corrupted into ducking stool, because the residue of the judgment is, that, when she is so placed therein, she shall be plunged in the water for her punishment.[2]

As is made clear by Blackstone, both the 'cucking stool' and 'ducking stool' seem always to have been punishments reserved for women, a fact which puzzled Mr J. Neild, the self-described 'benevolent visitor of prisons', writing in 1766:

In the [Liverpool] Bridewell I saw a ducking-stool complete, the first I had ever seen; we had two at Knutsford: one in a pond near the Higher Town, and another in a pond near the Lower Town, where the schoolboys were accustomed to bathe: in these, scolding and bawling women were ducked, but the standard [pivot] in each was all that remained in my memory. I never remembered them used, but this at Liverpool enables me to describe it. A standard was fixed for a long pole, at the extremity was fixed, a chair, on which the woman was placed and soused three times under water until almost suffocated. At Liverpool, the standard was fixed in the court [yard], and a bath made on purpose for ducking; but why in a prison this wanton and dangerous severity was exercised on women and not on men, I could no where learn. This, however, was not the only cruel punishment used at this Bridewell, for the women were flogged weekly at the whipping-post.[3]

The eighteenth-century poet John Gay (1685–1732) in his work *Pastorals* was also certain that the ducking stool was for women only:

I'll speed me to the pond, where the high stool
On the long plank hangs o'er the muddy pool;
That Stool, the dread of ev'ry scolding Queane …

The French traveller Francis Misson on a visit to England describes this way of punishing scolding women in terms that make it sound almost therapeutic:

The way of punishing scolding women is pleasant enough. They fasten an armchair to the end of two beams twelve or fifteen feet long, and parallel to each other, so that these two pieces of wood with their two ends embrace the chair, which hangs between them by a sort of axle, by which means it plays freely, and always remains in a natural horizontal position in which a chair should be, that a person may sit conveniently in it, whether you raise it or let it down. They set up a post on the bank of a pond or river, and over this post they lay, almost in equilibrio [*sic*], the two pieces of wood, at one end of which the chair hangs just over the water. They place the woman in this chair and so plunge her into the water as often as the sentence directs, in order to cool her immoderate heat.[4]

The reality of course was very different; women were usually ducked several times and left submerged for half a minute or more each time. Apart from the shock of the cold water, that could be icy at certain times of the year, the victim was left in sodden clothes, half-drowned and gasping for breath. In 1731 the mayor of Nottingham, Thomas Trigg, was prosecuted for not providing an official or a constable to supervise a woman's punishment, thus allowing the woman to 'be duck't too much and severely' by the mob with the result that she drowned.

Such a fate was more common than might be supposed. In December 1729 a woman was arrested in Westminster, London, accused of fraudulently obtaining money by begging, pretending to be suckling a baby when in fact she was carrying a small kitten. The magistrate ruled that in asking for alms the woman had not committed a fraud and discharged her. However, the public had been made aware of the case and upon her release she was seized by a large mob, who ducked her repeatedly in a horse-pond, causing her to expire the following day.[5]

Death by drowning was obviously an ever present risk if the authorities or the mob became excessively incensed by the woman's offence, something that apparently occurred regularly – the description of the Liverpool Bridewell informed us of 'a chair, on which the woman was placed and soused three times under water until almost suffocated'. A public enquiry in 1803 found that women incarcerated in the House of Correction were ducked with 'wanton severity' as well as being whipped too frequently.

The ducking stool device spawned many variations on the theme. The antiquary John Cole writing in 1780 described how as a boy he watched a woman being ducked into the river from a footbridge adjacent to Magdalene College in Cambridge:

The chair hung by a pulley, fastened to a beam about the middle of the bridge; and the woman having been fastened in the chair, she was let under water three times successively, and then taken out.[6]

THE VIOLENT ABUSE OF WOMEN

The practice of punishing women found guilty of 'scolding' soon found its way to the British colonies in the new world, where Virginia passed a specific law for the purpose;

> In December 1662, the General Assembly passed a law stating that any woman found guilty of slander could be punished by being ducked, or plunged underwater, to save her husband from paying a fine. WHEREAS oftentimes many brabling women often slander and scandalize their neighbours for which their poore husbands are often brought into chargeable and vexatious suites, and cast in greate damages; Bee it therefore enacted by the authority aforesaid that in actions of slander occasioned by the wife as aforesaid after judgment passed for the damages the women shal be punished by ducking; and if the slander be soe enormous as to be adjudged at a greater damage then five hundred pounds of tobacco, then the woman to suffer a ducking for each five hundred pounds of tobacco adjudged against the husband if he refuse to pay the tobacco.[7]

Why Virginia needed to enact a law at this late juncture is not clear as the penalty had obviously been in use in the colony for many years. Thomas Hartley, who was on a visit to Hungars Parish, Virginia from Massachusetts, wrote home to Governor Endicott in 1634 about the ducking stool:

> They endeavor to live amiably, keep the peace in families and communities, and by divers means try to have harmony and good will among themselves and with Strangers who may sojourn among them. For this they use a device ... to keep foul tongues that make noise and mischief silent.... They have a law which reads somewhat in this wise: 'Whereas it be a sinn and a shame for scolding and lying tongues to be left to run loose, as is too often the way among women, be it therefore enacted that any woman who shall, after being warned three severall time by the Church, persist in excessive scolding, or in backbiting her neighbors, shall be brought before the Magistrate for examination, and if the offence be fairly proved upon her, shee shall be taken by an Officer appointed for the purpose, to the nearest pond or deepe stream of water, and there ... be publicly ducked ... in the waters of said pond or streame, until shee shall make solemn promise that shee'l never sinn in like manner again.

Indeed, Hartley recommend that the Governor of Massachusetts institute a similar program, and described in detail the ducking of one such scolding woman:

108

GRACING THE STOOL

The day before yesterday at two of the clock in the afternoon I saw this punishment given to one Besty, wife of John Tucker who, by the violence of her tongue, had made his house and the neighborhood uncomfortable. She was taken to the pond near where I am sojourning by the officer, who was joyned by the Magistrate and the Minister, Mr Colton, who had frequently admonished her, and a large number of people. They had a machine for the purpose, that belongs to the Plaris, and which I was told had been so used three times this Summer. It is a platform with 4 small rollers or wheels, and two upright posts, between which works a Lever by a Rope fastened to its shorter or heavier end. At the end of the longer arm is fixed a stool, upon which Betsy was fastened by cords, her gown tied fast about her feete. The Machine was then moved up to the edge of the pond, the Rope was slackened by an officer and the woman was allowed to go down under the water for the space of half a minute. Betsy had a stout stomach, and would not yield untill shee had allowed herself to be ducked 5 severall times. At length she cried piteously, 'Let me go! Let me go! By God's help I'll sinn no more.' Then they drew back the Machine, untied the Ropes, and let her walk home in her wetted clothes, a hopefully penitent woman. Methinks such a reformer of great scolds might be of use in some parts of Massachusetts bay, for I've been troubled many times by the clatter of scolding tongues of women, that like the clack of the mill, seldom cease from morning 'til night.[8]

The lack of a proper ducking stool did not deter the judicial authorities in the new world from imposing similar brutal punishments on women. On 12 October 1626 we learn that the court in 'James-Citty' Virginia ordered one woman to be punished …

for ye several offences aforenamed, of ye said Margaret Jones, yt shee be toughed or dragged at ye boat's Starne in ye River from ye shoare unto the Margaret & John and thence unto ye shoare again.

Likewise, in 1634, two women were sentenced to be drawn from King's Creek 'from one Cowpen to another at the starne of a boat or kanew'.

The use of ducking as a punishment for women continued in some parts of the new United States until well into the nineteenth century. In 1811, the Supreme Court in Georgia ordered that one Miss Palmer, who 'seems to have been rather glib on the tongue' be punished for scolding by being ducked in the Oconee River. Apparently, 'numerous spectators attended the execution of the sentence'. Eight years later, the court in Burke County also sent Mary Cammell to be ducked in the same river. As late as 1824, a woman was sentenced to be ducked by the Court of Sessions in Philadelphia, but the punishment was not inflicted being deemed to be obsolete and contrary to the spirit of the time.[9]

The common law offence of 'common scold' was still on the statute book of New Jersey until 1972 when Circuit Judge McCann found that it had been subsumed in the provisions of the Disorderly Conduct Act of 1898, and offended the 14th Amendment to the US Constitution for sex discrimination.[10]

In Britain, the last recorded cases are also in the nineteenth century; in 1808 a Mrs Ganble at Plymouth; in 1809 one Jenny Pipes and in 1817 one Sarah Leeke, both of Leominster. In the case of Sarah Leeke, the pond water was found to be too low to cover the miscreant, so she was placed in the ducking stool and wheeled around the town.

Chapter 15

Religious Belief: Persecution & Punishment

The persecution of women for their religious beliefs had a long history before the seventeenth century. Elizabeth Barton, the 'holy maid of Kent' had been hanged (and then beheaded) at Tyburn in 1534 for claiming to have seen a vision in which King Henry VIII had been refused the holy sacrament by an angel.

Margaret Clitheroe was killed in 1586 by being crushed to death by a process known as 'peine fort et dure', a hideous torture reserved for those who refused to plead upon being charged in court, in spite of the fact that she was allegedly pregnant. Margaret had sheltered Catholic priests at a time when adherence to the Catholic religion was illegal.

Margaret Ward assisted a Catholic priest to escape from the London Bridewell. Arrested, she was taken to the Tower of London where she was suspended in irons for eight days and flogged in order to extract a confession. She was hanged at Tyburn on 30 August 1588.

A similar fate befell Anne Line, tried at the Old Bailey and hanged on 27 February 1601 for harbouring Catholic priests and holding a Catholic Mass in her home.

The seventeenth century in particular was an age of tremendous religious enthusiasm and the period of the Commonwealth (1649–60) probably the most oppressively religious period in British history. Most people believed that God and the Devil had a powerful influence on their lives, fates and fortunes. In spite of this, the period is marked by much religious dissent, the most extreme example being the banning of any celebration of the Catholic faith. Even within the protestant church, there was much disagreement and the sixteenth and seventeenth centuries were fertile times for the formation of non conformist religious groups, of which some seventeen were founded in the 200 years between 1580 and 1780. The 'Dissenters' as they were called opposed state interference in religious matters, and founded their own churches, educational establishments and communities; while some emigrated to the 'new world' of America (where sadly some were to find much 'old world' persecution). In the field of religion, nothing demonstrates quite so clearly the undeserved and violent reaction against women who were finding a voice in society where they had had none before.

Amongst the plethora of such dissenting groups, the 'Ranters' were a short-lived sect that existed during the time of the Commonwealth (1649–60) and who denied the authority of the church, of holy scripture, of the ministry and of formal church services, instead calling upon men to listen to the voice of God within them. As such they were regarded as heretical by the established church and seen as a danger to social order, thus making them a serious threat to the stability of society in general and the government of the day in particular.

William Franklin, a London rope-maker became one of the sect, abandoned his wife and took several mistresses, one of whom was a woman named Mary Gadbury. Mary was an eccentric woman with a penchant for religious visions, one of which was that Franklin was the reincarnation of Christ and thus claimed herself to be the spouse of God. In late 1649, she and Franklin set out to bring their gospel to the inhabitants of the Southampton countryside. It was not too long before she and Franklin were arrested and charged with blasphemy and additionally for Mary, adultery. The Adultery Act of 1650 had made adultery a felony for women, another example of gender-specific legislation aimed at controlling the behaviour of the female sex. Many Ranters quickly retracted their beliefs when faced with the full rigour of the law, and William Franklin very quickly did so, although being unable to produce sureties for good behaviour, he still found himself imprisoned.

Mary however, refusing to give her name and condition to the court, she was declared 'a lewd woman and a rogue in law' and committed to the Bridewell, the notorious 'house of correction'. She was apparently 'not sensible of the dangers she exposed herself to' with the result that over a period of several weeks in the Bridewell she was intermittently taken to the whipping-post and flogged until, according to the Ordinary, 'having tasted somewhat the smart of the whip the height of her spirit began to be somewhat abated'. Mary was sent for trial at the next quarter sessions in Winchester, where she was sentenced to yet another flogging – this time at the public whipping-post. Following the infliction of her public chastisement she left on a cart for London and disappears from history.

Few religious bodies have been singled out for persecution more than the Society of Friends, or Quakers, as they are popularly known. Barbara Blaugdone (c.1609–1704) was converted to Quakerism in 1654. She was an unusually well-educated woman and a teacher until her religious conversion caused her pupils to be withdrawn from her school. Published in 1691, she left an autobiographical account of her travels, evangelism, and religious and political views, as well as details of the many persecutions she suffered as a result of her religious beliefs. Barbara's maiden name is unknown and there is very little information as to her early life, marriage, or from whence she acquired the independent financial means that enabled her to fulfil what she saw as her God-given calling as a travelling minister: 'In all my Travels, I Travelled still on my own Purse, and was never chargeable to any, but paid for what I had.'

The activity of travelling Quakers such as Barbara met with much public resentment which often led to violence. They were also held to breach several laws, including the Act of Uniformity 1662 for not attending church, the Vagrancy Acts of 1596 and 1601 for illegal assembly, and the Blasphemy Act of 1650, which punished any who claimed to be godlike or equal to God; the Quaker belief in moral perfection and the possibility of transcending sin through communion in God were often interpreted in that light.

Her early travels took her to the town of Marlborough, where she was imprisoned for six weeks during which time she went on hunger strike. Upon her release, she moved to Devonshire where she was variously incarcerated in prisons at Molton, Barnstable, Bideford and Great Torrington, where the local priest endeavoured to have her publicly whipped as a vagabond. Instead of whipping her, the local mayor sent her to Exeter prison to await trial at the assize court. She seems not to have been arraigned in court, but nevertheless was severely whipped by the Sheriff and the Beadle who took it upon themselves to punish her as a vagrant – Barbara takes up the story in her own words:

> and there I was until the Assizes, and was not called forth to a Tryal: but after the Assizes was over, a petty Fellow sent for me forth, and read a Law, which was quite wrong, and did not belong to me at all, and put me to lodge one Night among a great company of Gypsies, that were then in the Prison; and the next day the Sheriff came with a Beadle, and had me into a Room, and Whipt me till the Blood ran down my Back, and I never startled at a blow; but the Lord made me rejoyce, that I was counted Worthy to Suffer for his Name's sake, and I Sung aloud; and the Beadle said, 'Do ye Sing; I shall make ye cry by and by': and with that he laid more Stripes, and laid them on very hard. I shall never forget the large Experience of the Love and Power of God which I had in my Travels, and therefore I can speak to his Praise, and glorifie his Name: for if he had Whipt me to Death in that state which then I was in, I should not have been terrified or dismayed at it; Ann Speed was an Eye Witness of it, and she stood and lookt in at the Window, and wept bitterly. And then the Sheriff, when he saw that the envy of the man could not move me, he bid him forbear, for he had gone beyond his Orders already. So when he had left me, Ann Speed came in and drest my Wounds; and the next day they turned me out with all the Gypsies, and the Beadle followed us two Miles out of the City.[1]

Not discouraged by her brutal treatment, Barbara's sufferings continued throughout her long life; a stabbing at the hands of an angry member of the public which nearly killed her and imprisonment in various other cities including Dublin where in addition to being imprisoned she was also put to hard labour. Even these events seem not to have been the total of her sufferings, as the closing words of her autobiography reveals:

> And much more could I declare of my Sufferings which I passed through, which I forbear to mention, being not willing to be over-tedious. And I have written these Things that Friends may be encouraged, and go in the Faith, in the Work of the Lord: For many have been the Tryals, Tribulations and Afflictions the which I have passed through, but the Lord hath delivered me out of them all; Glory be given to him, and blessed be his Name for ever, and evermore.

Barbara died in London in 1704.

The sect known as the 'Levellers' were active during the English Civil War (1642–1651) advocating extended suffrage, equality before the law, and religious tolerance. Richard Overton, a Leveller and a Baptist had campaigned against the rule of Oliver Cromwell, but was also well known as a pamphleteer, writing and printing broadsheets, including one entitled 'Women will have their will'.

In January, 1647, his wife Mary Overton was arrested, together with her brother Thomas Johnson, when they were discovered producing seditious pamphlets written by her husband. She was taken before the House of Lords, but she refused to answer any of the questions they put to her. Their Lordships had Mary, who was visibly pregnant and with a six month old baby in her arms, committed to prison on suspicion of being complicit in the production of seditious libels. She later complained that she was dragged there 'headlong upon the stones through all the dirt and mire of the streets' with her baby in her arms. Whilst being dragged along, she was also subjected to a tirade of verbal abuse from the officers who called her a scandalous wicked whore and a strumpet. A pamphlet later recounted that she was 'caste into the most infamous Gaol of Bride-well, that common Centre and receptacle of Bauds [sic] whores and strumpets.'[2]

The treatment she received resulted in her miscarrying her unborn child while in prison. In March she petitioned the House of Commons begging for a speedy sentence. If wrong had been done, then she was prepared to face execution, if not she should be granted her freedom; but arbitrary imprisonment at the orders of the House of Lords was utterly intolerable. Mary was released in July 1647 after nearly six months in prison without ever being tried in a court of law.

'English Dissenters' or 'English Separatists' as they were sometimes known were Protestant Christians who separated from the Church of England in the sixteenth and seventeenth centuries. They opposed state interference in religious matters, founded their own churches, schools and communities and agitated for wide-ranging reformation of the established church. This was clearly not behaviour likely to endear them to the establishment of the day.

In June 1654, Elizabeth Heavens (or Leavens – both names appear in different documents) and Elizabeth Fletcher were preaching in Oxford when they were seized by a mob of university students. According to the Quaker preacher Richard Hubberthorn, the two women were speaking 'the word of the Lord in boldness against the deceits of the Priests and People, in the streets, in the Market-place, in the Synagogues, and in the Colleges'.

There had been earlier complaints from some citizens of the town concerning the disruption of Dissenter services by unruly students and a petition seeking intervention had been presented to Parliament, who in turn had written letters of rebuke to the mayor of the town and the Vice Chancellor of the university, requiring them to take remedial action. As a result, Daniel Greenwood, the Vice Chancellor had issued a number of declarations, strictly enjoining the students to desist from such disturbances. This did not discourage the students (all of whom would have been male) from now violently abusing the two women. They were dragged to St John's College, where they were mocked, buffeted and shamefully used, being forcibly held under a water pump by the youths and 'where they pump'd water upon their necks and into their Mouths, till they were almost dead'. Not satisfied with this cruelty, their behaviour took an even more obscene turn: 'then they took one of them and bound her knees together and set her upon her head, saying '... they would pump at the other end' after which they tied them arm to arm and dragged them up and down the college and through a pool of water'. [known locally as 'Giles pool']. The younger woman of the two, the now half-drowned Elizabeth Fletcher, was then dragged into a nearby churchyard where they threw her 'over a Grave-stone into a Grave, whereby she received a Contusion on her Side, from which she never recovered'.[3]

A few days later, the badly bruised women attended a church service, where they found themselves confronted by two Justices of the Peace, who ordered them incarcerated in the Bocardo prison, part of the city's north tower. The following day, the women were brought before the city magistrates and the Vice Chancellor, who tried to force the mayor into having the women whipped out of the city. To his credit, the mayor Thomas Williams refused 'because he could not in Conscience consent to a Sentence he thought undeserved'. Nevertheless, despite the mayor's reluctance, he was overruled and the women were stripped to the waist and severely flogged at the public whipping-post before being driven out of the city. Elizabeth Fletcher never completely recovered from the severe flogging and the injuries she had received at the hands of the students when being thrown into a grave and she died four years later in 1658, then being about 20 years of age.

THE VIOLENT ABUSE OF WOMEN

In December 1653, two women arrived in Cambridge from the north of England intent on preaching the word according to the Quaker sect to which they belonged – the so-called 'Northern Army'. Elizabeth Williams and Mary Fisher, aged about 50 and 30 years respectively, soon fell into a religious discourse with the scholars of Sidney Sussex college, who mischievously asked them how many gods there were. The women answered that there was but one God, and added that the scholars clearly had many gods and began reproving them for their lack of piety. The discourse became increasingly antagonistic, with the scholars mocking the two women, who unwisely retaliated by telling them that they were the Antichrist, that their college was a cage of unclean birds and the synagogue of Satan. Not surprisingly, their sarcasm resulted in them being dragged before the mayor, William Pickering, who, trying to show them to be vagrants, demanded that they reveal from whence they had come the previous night and to what purpose. The story of their subsequent brutal treatment is described in detail nearly two centuries later in the Quaker periodical *The Friend*:

> They answered that they were strangers and knew not the name of the place, but paid for what they had and came away. He asked their names; they replied that 'their names were written in the Book of Life'. He then demanded their husbands' names. They told him that they had 'no husband but Jesus Christ' and he had sent them. Upon this the mayor grew angry, called them opprobius [*sic*] names [accusing them of being common whores] and issued his warrant to the constable 'to whip them at the market-cross till the blood ran down their bodies' and ordered three of his sergeants to see that [the] sentence, as cruel as it was unlawful, severely executed. The virtuous women, kneeling down in the spirit of the suffering Redeemer, besought the Lord to forgive him, for he knew not what he did. They were led to the market-cross, calling upon God to strengthen their faith. The executioner commanded them to take off their clothes, which they refused. He then stripped them to the waste [*sic*] and put their arms in to the whipping post, and executed the warrant far more cruelly, than is usually done to the worst of malefactors, so that their flesh was miserably cut and torn.[4]

This is clearly not an exaggeration as a more contemporary account informs us that 'their bodies were cut and slashed and torn, as never were the bodies of any rogues, or whores … as those poor Christians were'.[5]

The anger against female Quakers who preached was such that the perpetrators were hard-pressed to think of sufficiently brutal reprisals:

Katharine Evans, for exhorting people to repentance in Salisbury market-place, in the 3rd month, 1657, was, by the mayor's command, tied to the whipping-post in the market-place, and there whipped by a beadle, and then sent away with a pass. On this woman's return to execute the commission with which she imagined herself to be intrusted [sic], the mayor ordered her to Bridewell, there to be put in a close, nasty place, called the 'Blind-house', where two madmen had lately died, with a charge to the keeper that no friend should come at her, and that she should have no food but what she earned in that place, which was too dark to see to work in. The magistrates were taking council to have her whipped again; but one of them, Colonel Wheat, zealously opposed it, and told the mayor 'they might as well have whipped the woman of Samaria, that brought the glad tidings into the town.' This stopped their proceeding, so that, after some time of imprisonment in the aforesaid nasty place, they sent her privately out of the town' One Justice Cole was so virulent, that a sheep-stealer being before him, he spake to him thus; 'I will send you to gaol to the Quakers, and you shall go to the gallows together.'[6]

As is often the case, when such cruelty to allegedly saintly Christians is reported at a later date (for example in the savage treatment of Barbara Blaugdone), the women are stoical when subjected to the agony of the lash, claiming their faith rendered them oblivious to the pain:

The constancy and patience which they manifested under this barbarous usage, was astonishing to the spectators; for they endured the cruel torture without the least change of countenance, or appearance of uneasiness, singing and rejoicing while under the lash, saying 'The Lord be blessed, the Lord be praised, who hath thus honoured us, and strengthened us to suffer for his Name's sake.'[7]

Released from the clutches of the executioner, and with torn clothes and bleeding backs, the two women were run out of town 'no man daring to show them any countenance, or give them any relief; many secretly commiserated their pitiable condition, yet none had [the] courage to oppose the current of popular prejudice, and the misapplied power of those who governed.'

Having been persecuted all over Europe, Quakers turned their sights to the American colonies and in 1656 a vanguard comprised mainly of women set off for the new world, where they expected to be free from oppression and tyranny. They were soon to be sadly and painfully disillusioned, the Massachusetts Bay

Colony was not a friendly or tolerant world for women. Women did not participate in town meetings and were excluded from all decision making processes, in both secular and religious matters. Puritan ministers furthered male supremacy in their writings and sermons. They preached that the soul had two parts: an immortal masculine half, and a mortal feminine half. Women and children were treated particularly harshly in the Puritan commonwealth. Women were commonly viewed as being the instruments of Satan, believing that Eve's role in original sin exemplified woman's inherent moral weakness. They feared that women were much more susceptible to temptations, and that they possessed qualities that could be exploited and become sinful. Children were regarded as the property of their parents and any child disobedient to their parents could be ordered a whipping by the local magistrate.

However, the Puritans of Massachusetts had struggled and sacrificed much to protect their independence and their state religion. The Quakers ill-advisedly launched an attack against both. They loudly 'trespassed' in Boston and other towns, burst into church services, disrupted baptisms, shouted in the streets, sent letters to ministers questioning their religion and predicted that divine wrath in the form of great calamities would befall the colony.

The Puritan magistrates responded harshly to the Quaker troublemakers, imposing severe punishments. The first three women to arrive in Boston – Ann Austin, Mary Fisher and Mary Clark were quickly to fall foul of the law: stripped naked to the waist, whipped at the cart's tail by the public hangman, and thrown into prison until they could be deported from the colony. Likewise, on 3 May 1669, Mrs Wilson, Mrs Buffum, and others, were stripped and whipped at the cart's tail through the town for 'making a disturbance in the meetinghouse'. Even more severe sentences of corporal punishment were handed down to Alice Ambrose, Anne Coleman and Mary Tomkins. The warrant for their punishment read as follows:

> To the constables of Dover, Hampton, Salisbury, Newberry, Rowley, Ipswich, Wennam, Linn, Boston, Roxbury, Dedham, and until these vagabond Quakers are carried out of this jurisdiction: You, and every of you, are required in the King's Majesty's name, to take these vagabond Quakers, Anne Coleman, Mary Tomkins, and Alice Ambrose, and make them fast to the cart's tail, and driving the cart through your several towns, to whip upon their naked backs, not exceeding ten stripes a piece on each of them, in each town; and so to convey them from constable to constable till they are out of this jurisdiction, as you will answer it at your peril; and this shall be your warrant.
>
> Per me, Richard Weldon.
> At Dover, dated December 22 1662

So it was that on a bitterly cold winter's day with snow on the ground, constables John and Thomas Roberts of Dover seized and stripped the three women and executed the first part of their sentence, giving each ten lashes with ten more such floggings to follow: 'Deputy Waldron caused these women to be stripped naked from the middle upwards, and tied to a cart, and after awhile cruelly whipped them, while the priest stood and looked and laughed at it.'

Samuel Sewall's *History of the Quakers* continues:

> The women thus being whipped at Dover, were carried to Hampton and there delivered to the constable. The constable the next morning would have whipped them before day, but they refused, saying they were not ashamed of their sufferings. Then he would have whipped them with their clothes on, when he had tied them to the cart. But they said, 'set us free, or do according to thine order' He then spoke to a woman to take off their clothes. But she said she would not for all the world. Why, said he, then I'll do it myself. So he stripped them, and then stood trembling whip in hand, and so he did the execution. Then he carried them to Salisbury through the dirt and the snow half the leg deep; and here they were whipped again. Indeed their bodies were so torn, that if Providence had not watched over them, they might have been in danger of their lives.[8]

In Salisbury, Dr Walter Barefoot convinced the constable to swear him in as a deputy. He duly received the women and the warrant, and put a stop to the persecution. Dr Barefoot dressed their wounds and returned them to the Maine side of the Piscataqua River.

The savagery with which the floggings were sometimes administered upon these and other Quaker women is clear from historical evidence that additional cruel refinements were often added to the judicial sentence: 'Sarah Gibbons and Dorothy Waugh were whipped in Boston's House of Correction; Lydia Wardel, tied to a post in such a position that her bare breasts were forced against the rough splintered wood, was given thirty strokes.'

Even where the judicial sentence was adhered to, it was not unusual for it to be administered with the severest cruelty; Anne Coleman (presumably the same woman who had been sentenced to be flogged through the eleven towns) was so severely lashed that the knotted thongs wrapped around her torso and split open one of the nipples on her breasts 'which so tortured her that it very nearly proved fatal.'

Sometimes, starvation was added to the punishment:

> Two women named Sarah Gibbons and Dorothy Waugh, being come to Boston, and having in the public meeting place, after the

lecture was ended, spoken a few words, were brought to the house of correction, and [for] three days before their being whipped, and [for] three days after, were kept without victuals, though they offered to pay for them.[9]

Elizabeth Hooton (1600–72) was born Elizabeth Carrier in Nottinghamshire and later married Oliver Hooton, to whom she bore several children. She was converted to Quakerism in 1646 by the preaching of George Fox and subsequently became one of the first Quaker women missionaries. She began her ministry by organising the local Baptist group in her house, later to be known as the 'children of light', but her preaching soon got her into trouble, being imprisoned in Derby in 1651 for 'reproving a priest' and a year later being imprisoned in York for preaching in a church in Rotherham. Undeterred, she was again gaoled in Lincoln in 1654, and while incarcerated wrote letters to the authorities protesting against the poor conditions in the prison and calling for segregation of the sexes and useful employment for the prisoners.

In 1661, at the age of 60, Hooton made her first trip to New England with her friend Joan Brocksop. Prosecution of non-conformist religious groups was well established in the colony; even severe floggings had not discouraged the Quaker women and ultimately the death penalty was invoked. Mary Dyer (born 1611), an English Puritan turned Quaker, was hanged in Boston, Massachusetts Bay Colony on 1 June 1660 for repeatedly defying a Puritan law banning Quakers from the colony, becoming one of the four executed Quakers known to history as the Boston martyrs.

Though the death penalty had since been revoked by King Charles II, other punishments had been devised for Quaker 'blasphemers', of which the harshest was the 'Cart and Tail Law' – those condemned were stripped naked to the waist, and dragged behind a cart from town to town, in each of which they were whipped.

Ships bringing Quakers to Massachusetts were threatened with steep fines, so Elizabeth and Joan travelled via Virginia. Having reached Boston by small boat and overland, they attempted to visit fellow Quakers imprisoned there, but were waylaid and taken before Governor Endicott:

> The sixty years old Elizabeth Hooton, upon arrival at Cambridge, New England, was thrust into a stinking dungeon, in which there was neither a bed nor a chair. Here she was confined for two days and two nights without food. Following her appearance in court, she was sentenced to be publicly whipped in three towns. So, starting at Cambridge, she was tied to the whipping-post and given ten strokes. Then at Water Town she received another ten lashes, this time with a willow rod; and finally, at Dedham, in the most severe weather,

she was tied to the cart's tail and given the third lot of ten lashes. Beaten and torn, she returned to Cambridge, to her daughter and an aged friend named Sarah Coleman. She wished to gather together her clothes and personal belongings, which the executioner had forbidden her to take with her.[10]

Her back scarred and raw from the lashes she had already received, the unfortunate woman was destined to pay a number of further visits to the whipping-post and the cart's tail. After they had been imprisoned for days without food, put in the stocks and publicly flogged in several towns, the two women were taken out into the wilderness and left to die. They survived by following wolf tracks through the snow till they found a settlement and thence made their way to Rhode Island and subsequently to Barbados, from where the two women returned to England.

Once there, Hooton petitioned the king to stop the persecution of Quakers in Massachusetts Bay Colony and gained his approval, authorising her to buy land in Massachusetts and use it to make a safe haven for Quakers in the colony, also writing to Governor Endicott to desist from the prosecution of Quakers. However, upon returning to the colony, Elizabeth and two companions were arrested, sent to the House of Correction, and there whipped. Finally, Elizabeth was yet again flogged at the cart's tail through Boston and other towns.

In 1672, George Fox planned a trip to Jamaica, his first and only voyage to the New World. Elizabeth was determined to accompany him, although she was now 71. Fox fell ill on the voyage and Hooton nursed him, probably ensuring his survival. However, within one week of their arrival, she herself fell suddenly ill and died the next day.

As if flogging a 60-year-old woman for her religion wasn't bad enough, even a breastfeeding mother could be flogged, simply for being a Quaker:

> Hored Gardner, an inhabitant of Newport, Rhode Island, came with her sucking babe, and a girl to carry it, to Weymouth: from whence, for being a Quaker, she was hurried to Boston, where both she and the girl were whipped with a three-fold knotted whip.[11]

Chapter 16

Suffer a Witch

'Thou shalt not suffer a witch to live' says Exodus 22:18, although some authorities believe the word 'witch' to be a mistranslation for 'poisoner'. Whether or not this is true, from 1484 until around 1750 some 200,000 witches were tortured, burned alive or hanged in Western Europe. Within Britain the belief in witchcraft was most virulent in Scotland, where between 1660 and 1700 more than 1,000 people, mainly women, were thus charged. Also in Scotland, women found to be witches were not hanged but covered with pitch and burned (albeit after allegedly being mercifully strangled) at the stake, the last one to be so executed not until 1727.

Many offences that became felonies and punishable by law during the seventeenth century were aimed at regulating the behaviour of women; adultery (a crime for women but not for men), sexual promiscuity, gossiping, scolding, failing to attend church etc. The regulation of female behaviour through the application of secular law falls into two categories: those relating to non-conformity with accepted religious norms (after Charles I, generally Christian Protestantism) and those relating to women's susceptibility to the pursuit of witchcraft and the black arts. In juxtaposition to extreme religious convictions, this period is also a time of extraordinary belief in other supernatural and occult forces. For example, so many people suffering from scrofula (a form of tuberculosis) also known as the 'King's Evil' believed that being touched by the king on the cheek would heal them that in 1684 several of those waiting to be thus cured were killed in the crush!

The full rigour of the secular common law was invoked to control women who were thought to have succumbed to the Devil's wiles, their susceptibility being due to their perceived inherent weakness. The conduit thus provided to the powers of evil posed a threat to the established church and its earthly authority, ample justification for violent retribution to be brought down upon the head of any woman found to have been dabbling in dangerous demonic powers. Such opinions of women's vulnerability had persisted since time immemorial; 'Woman is the Gate of the Devil' said St Jerome 'the road to iniquity, the sting of the serpent ... a perilous object'. Specific laws were obviously needed to counteract this threat and thus Henry VIII had passed the Witchcraft Act in 1542, which made it an offence punishable by death to:

use devise practise or exercise, or cause to be devysed practised or
exercised, any Invovacons or cojuracons of Sprites witchecraftes
enchauntementes or sorceries to thentent to fynde money or treasure
or to waste consume or destroy any persone in his bodie membres,
or to pvoke [provoke] any persone to unlawfull love, or for any other
unlawfull intente or purpose.

Although repealed by Edward VII five years later, another similar act was passed
during Elizabeth's reign in 1563. This act was slightly less draconian in that it only
demanded the death penalty if actual harm could be proven – lesser offences were
punishable by imprisonment. However, it was the Act of 1604, the year following
the accession of King James I, well known as an active pursuer of witches – 'An
Act Against Conjurations, Enchantments and Witchcrafts' which broadened the
Elizabethan Act and brought in the penalty of death without 'benefit of clergy' to
anyone who invoked evil spirits or communed with 'familiars'.

In English law, the 'benefit of clergy' was originally a provision by which could
claim that they were outside the jurisdiction of the secular courts and be tried instead
in an ecclesiastical court under canon law. Various reforms limited the scope of this
legal arrangement to prevent its abuse. Eventually the benefit of clergy evolved into
a legal fiction in which first-time offenders could receive lesser sentences for some
'clergyable' crimes. The legal mechanism was abolished in 1827 with the passage
of the Judgement of Death Act which gave judges the discretion to pass lesser
sentences on first-time offenders.

In 1590 the first major witchcraft persecutions in Scotland were held when a
number of people from East Lothian were accused of witchcraft in the St Andrew's
Auld Kirk in North Berwick. What was to become known as the North Berwick
witch trials continued for two years and implicated more than a hundred people,
alleged to have been members of a local coven. The suspected witches were
arrested, and many confessed under torture to having met with the Devil in the
church at night, and devoted themselves to doing evil, including poisoning the king
together with other members of the royal household, and attempting to sink the
king's ship. King James VI had sailed to Copenhagen to marry Princess Anne,
the sister of Christian IV, King of Denmark. During their return to Scotland they
experienced terrible storms and had to shelter in Norway for several weeks before
continuing their journey.

Alleged to be leading the coven were Agnes Sampson, a respectable elderly
woman from Humbie, and Dr John Fian, a schoolmaster and scholar in Prestonpans.
Agnes was brought before King James VI himself, sitting together with a council
of nobles, but she denied all the charges, so was taken to the Old Tolbooth in
Edinburgh to be tortured into making a confession. First, she was stripped of her
clothes and her head and body hair was shaved off. Next, she was fastened to the

wall of her cell by a 'witch's bridle' (see chapter 13 'Seen but not Heard') an iron instrument designed to lacerate the mouth with four sharp prongs forced inside, two prongs pressed against the tongue, and the two others against the inside of her cheeks. The bridle prevented her from sitting or lying down, which kept her without sleep for several days and nights. Next, she was 'thrawen' with a rope tightened around her head, stripping the flesh from her skull.

Eventually the agony of these ordeals broke her will and Agnes Sampson confessed to the fifty-three indictments against her. On 16 January 1591 she was taken to the scaffold on Castlehill, where she was garrotted (strangled) then her body burned at the stake. Dr Fian was also severely tortured. His fingernails were forcibly extracted before having iron pins thrust into the wounds, his thumbs crushed by the 'pilliwinks' (thumbscrews), and his feet by the 'boot'. He was finally taken to the Castlehill in Edinburgh and burned at the stake on 16 December 1590.

The original account of Agnes's torture and execution was told in a pamphlet published in the same year as her death:

> This aforeaside Agnis Sampson which was the elder Witch, was taken and brought to *Haliruid house* before the Kings Maiestie and sundry other of the nobility of Scotland, where she was straitly examined, but all the perswasions which the Kings maiestie vsed to her with ye rest of his counsell, might not prouoke or induce her to confesse any thing, but stood stiffely in the deniall of all that was laide to her charge: whervpon they caused her to be conueied awaye to prison, there to receiue such torture as hath been lately prouided for witches in that country: and forasmuch as by due examination of witchcraft and witches in Scotland, it hath latelye beene found that the Deuill dooth generallye marke them with a priuie marke, by reason the Witches haue confessed themselues, that the Diuell dooth lick them with his tung in some priuy part of their bodie, before hee dooth receiue them to be his seruants, which marke commonly is giuen them vnder the haire in some part of their bodye, wherby it may not easily be found out or seene, although they be searched: and generally so long as the marke is not seene to those which search them, so long the parties that hath the marke will neuer confesse any thing. Therfore by special commaundement this Agnis Sampson had all her haire shauen of, in each parte of her bodie, and her head thrawen with a rope according to the custome of that Countrye, beeing a paine most greeuous, which she continued almost an hower, during which time she would not confesse any thing vntill the Diuels marke was found vpon her priuities, then she immediatlye confessed whatsoeuer was demaunded of her, and iustifying those persons aforesaid to be notorious witches.[1]

The Scottish historian and author Thomas Smout has estimated that between 3,000 and 4,000 accused witches may have been killed in Scotland in the years 1560–1707.

The first major witch trial in England following the act of 1604 occurred in Lancashire in 1612, described in great detail in a chapbook entitled *The Wonderful Discovery of Witches in the County of Lancashire*, a document of 188 pages in the original. The record was made by the clerk of the court, Thomas Potts and approved by the judge, Sir Edward Bromley, and thus became a text book for the conduct of all future witch trials.

In March 1612 a blind 80-year-old woman named Mrs Elizabeth Sowthern, known as 'Old Demdike' was brought before Roger Nowell, the local justice, on suspicion of witchcraft by common report. This interrogation resulted in the implication of her granddaughter Alison Device and another woman known as 'Old Chattox'. All three women were committed to Lancaster castle to be tried at the next assizes. A series of unrelated events were attributed to the women; Alison Device was accused of laming an itinerant peddler, whose symptoms appear to modern eyes to be those of a stroke. Old Chattox was indicted together with Old Demdike and their daughters Anne and Elizabeth respectively, with the bewitching to death of one Robert Nutter. Eventually, the number of accused expanded to twelve, all of whom lived in an area surrounding Pendle Hill. They were jointly charged with the murder of ten people using witchcraft. Old Demdike died in gaol, one was found not guilty and all the remaining ten (including two men) were executed by hanging.

Later in the century, the same statute of 1604 was rigorously and brutally enforced by the self-styled 'witch-finder general' Matthew Hopkins (circa 1619–47). Hopkins is thought to have been born of well to do family in Manningtree in Essex, although little factual evidence of his early life survives. In his early twenties he reportedly read several books concerning witchcraft, among them *Demonology* by King James I (1597), *The Wonderful Discovery of Witches in the County of Lancaster* by Thomas Potts (1613) and Richard Bernard's two-volume work *A Guide to Grand Jurymen* (1627 & 1629). Armed with this new found expertise, he set himself up in business in March 1645 as a 'Witchfinder-General'.

His first victim, a poor one-legged woman named Elizabeth Clarke, lived in Hopkins's home town of Manningtree. Sadly, Elizabeth's mother had herself been hanged as a witch and on this evidence alone, the daughter was arrested and thrown into prison. In his own pamphlet *The Discovery of Witchcraft* (1647) Hopkins tells us how this came about:

In March 1644, he had some seven or eight of that horrible sect of Witches living in the Towne where he lived, a Towne in Essex called Manningtree, with diverse other adjacent Witches of other towns, who every six weeks in the night (being always on the Friday night) had their meeting close to his house, and had their solemn sacrifices there offered to the Devil, one of whom this Discoverer heard speaking to her imps and bid them go to another Witch, who was thereupon apprehended.

Hopkins clearly wanted his readers to believe that he had daringly eavesdropped on one of the witches' coven meetings, and he subsequently claimed that they had threatened to kill him because of what he had witnessed.

The next stage was to obtain a confession from the victim. Hopkins recruited an unsavoury and sadistic individual named Jack Stearne to assist him in this task. The use of torture was illegal in England, so Elizabeth was stripped naked, prodded and obscenely searched for 'witches marks', incontrovertible evidence that she was in league with the Devil. Having allegedly 'found to have three teats about her, which honest women have not', Elizabeth was kept without food or sleep for three consecutive nights. On the fourth night of her illegal torture she collapsed and confessed to being a witch, at the same time accusing five other women of witchcraft: Anne West and her daughter Rebecca, Anne Leech, Helen Clarke and Elizabeth Gooding. Elizabeth also confessed that she kept five 'familiars', supernatural beings that assumed the form of domestic animals and assisted the witch with her magic. Hers were said to be a white kitten named Holt, a spaniel dog named Jarmara, a black rabbit named Sack & Sugar, a polecat named Newes and most extraordinary of all, a long-legged greyhound with a head like an ox, named Vinegar Tom. Hopkins claimed to have found eight people who swore that they had seen one or more of these creatures.

In order to cope with the increasing demand for his services Hopkins recruited more assistants. One Mary 'Goody' Phillips whose special responsibility was finding witch marks on the naked bodies of those accused was joined by Edward Parsley and Frances Mills. Together they interviewed and interrogated over one hundred people, thirty-two of whom confessed under interrogation to being witches. They all confessed to having familiars, whose names became more and more outrageous: Elemanzer, Pyewacket, Peck in the Crown and Grizzel Greedigut, to which Hopkins commented that they were: 'names that no mortal could invent'. The local justice remanded all of them to be tried in the county sessions at Chelmsford.

Elizabeth Clarke was charged with 'entertaining' evil spirits, and on 25 March 1645, Hopkins gave the following deposition to the court:

> The said Elizabeth forthwith told this informant and one Master Stearne, there present, if they would stay and do the said Elizabeth no hurt, she would call one of her white imps and play with it on her lap. But this informant told her they would not allow it. And they staying there a while longer, the said Elizabeth confessed she had carnal copulation with the devil six or seven years; and he would

appear to her three or four times a week at her bedside, and go to
bed with her and lie with her half a night together, in the shape of a
proper gentleman, with a laced band, having the whole proportion of
a man. And he would say to her, 'Bessie, I must lie with thee'. And
she never did deny him.

The trials of the other thirty-two accused were held at Chelmsford on 29 July 1645,
in a court set up to deal with a growing hysteria about witchcraft, presided over by
a vehement Presbyterian Robert Rich, the Earl of Warwick. These trials resulted
in twenty-nine people being condemned and Hopkins later commented, '… in our
Hundred in Essex, 29 were condemned at once and 4 brought 25 miles to be hanged
at where their Discoverer lives, this for sending the Devil like a Bear to kill him'. Ten
of the accused were hanged at Chelmsford and the others were executed in various
hamlets and villages throughout the locality, fuelling the growing witch hysteria.

The total number of accused, mainly women, hanged as a result of Hopkin's
accusations is not known for certain – Thomas Ady, writing in 1656, says about a
hundred were hanged in Bury St Edmunds alone. It is certain that the total amounts
to several hundred in the eastern counties of Britain. What is certain is that Hopkins
made a great deal of money, charging extortionate fees for his services. Claiming
that he held a unique commission from Parliament, he levied a special tax on the
residents of Stowmarket in Suffolk to pay his costs. Records show that he extorted
£28 3*d* (£28.02) from them, at a time when the prevailing wage of the day was
sixpence (2.5p), but defended his high fees by arguing that finding witches required
great skill and courage.

How did Hopkins make so many women confess to something which we now
know to be complete nonsense? Firstly, he claimed to have a coded list, somehow
obtained from the Devil, of all the witches in England. Exploiting local grievances
and gossip to identify likely candidates, he then arrested and imprisoned his victims.
Here he and his sadistic assistants stripped the women naked before searching them
for 'devil's marks', not difficult to find, as most people have moles or other blemishes
upon their person. Having found a likely mark, it would then be 'pricked', that is,
pierced with a sharp bodkin to see if it bled or proved insensitive to pain. Lack of
blood or no shriek of agony indicated evidence of witchcraft. The procedure would
then progress to obtaining a confession, the victim being bound cross-legged on a
stool and left in this posture for up to twenty-four hours. Released from their bonds
and in agony from cramp, they would be forced to walk stark naked up and down the
stone floor of their cell until their feet blistered and bled.

Where there was a local water feature, such as a river or pond deep enough to
swim in, Hopkins would employ a technique recommended by King James I in
Demonology and which had been in use in England since around 1612. Witches
rejected baptism by water and therefore water would reject them, making it

impossible for them to sink. Hopkins's technique was to bend the victim double with their arms crossed between their legs and with their thumbs tied to their big toes. With a rope tied around their waist, they were lowered into the water and allowed to sink and rise three times. Many of the accused were allegedly drowned during this process.

The first reported use of this technique is in the notorious case of Mother Sutton and her daughter Mary, reported at length in a pamphlet entitled *Witches Apprehended, Examined and Executed, for notable villanies* [sic] *by them committed both by Land and Water* (Edward Marchant 1613). The pamphlet advertised itself as containing 'a strange and most true triall [*sic*] how to know whether a woman be a witch or not.'

Mother Sutton lived in Milton in Bedfordshire and she and her daughter had no previous record of neighbourly disputes until a falling out with one Master Enger, who reported that his animals had somehow been driven mad and some had drowned themselves in their frenzy.

The connection between these occurrences and the two Sutton women was made when Henry Sutton, one of Mary's three illegitimate children, was caught by Enger's servants throwing mud and stones at other local children. Refusing to desist, he was given a boxing round the ears, which he tearfully reported to his mother.

The next day, Enger's cart was taking corn to market when it was said to have been intercepted on the road by a fat black sow, which apparently bewitched the horses and ran off with the cart. Although the cart was recovered, the whole episode was repeated on the way back. The same black sow was reportedly seen by another of Enger's servants, entering Mother Sutton's cottage (hardly surprising as the women kept hogs). This 'coincidence' was compounded when the original servant was stung by a beetle and fell into a trance. Recovering somewhat, the man claimed that during his suffering, Mary had entered through his bedroom window, sat at the foot of his bed and offered to cure him by making lewd and improper suggestions (literally in his dreams!). Enger and his men dragged Mary by force to his house, where she had blood drawn next to the servant's bedside. This immediately improved his condition, but after she was observed touching the man's neck, he fell back into his trance-like state (and presumably more lewd dreams).

The suggestion of witchcraft seems to have emanated from Enger's 7-year-old son, who subsequently threw stones at Mary and her mother, calling them witches. Within days, the young boy fell ill and mysteriously died. Stricken with grief at the loss of his son and recalling the incidents of the crazed animals and the black sow, Enger again apprehended Mary, demanding that she confess to having bewitched his livestock and caused the death of his son. When she refused to confess, she was beaten by Enger and his servants until she lost consciousness. Bringing her back to consciousness, they dragged her to the mill dam, a rope was tied around her waist, and she was thrown into the water, where she was observed to sink somewhat before floating to the surface 'like a plank'. This clearly indicated that she was a witch, so the services of a group of local wives were enrolled to strip her and search for any devil's marks. The women reported having found something resembling a teat on her left thigh, so Mary was taken back to the mill dam, where her thumbs and big toes were tied together before she was thrown back into the water. She again floated and was seen to spin round and round as if caught in a whirlpool (although how she achieved this with a rope around her waist held at either end on opposite banks by Enger's servants is not explained).

What happened next is inexplicable as the women's fate is sealed by Mary's own son Henry. The boy claims to have overheard his mother and grandmother discussing how they might be revenged upon Enger, tormenting him and killing his son, through the use of their two 'familiars' named Dicke and Jude. Presented with this 'evidence', Mary apparently breaks down and confesses. Mother Sutton and her daughter Mary were imprisoned in Bedford Gaol, before being tried and found guilty of witchcraft on Monday 30 March 1612. Both were hanged a few days later on 7 April.

Matthew Hopkins died in the village of Mistley, Essex, from 'a long sicknesse of a consumption' (probably pleural tuberculosis) and according to church records, was buried on 12 August 1647. Although witch-hunting fell out of favour in England, Hopkins's legacy found its way to the new world and during the year following the publication of Hopkins's book, trials and executions for witchcraft began in the New England colonies where around eighty were accused of witchcraft and fifteen women and two men were executed. Some of Hopkins's methods were once again employed during the Salem Witch trials in Massachusetts (1692–93) where nineteen were executed and a further 150 imprisoned.

It would be a mistake to think that such beliefs were only held by the uneducated masses. John Aubrey (1626–97) was a member of the Royal Society, a 'natural philosopher' and pioneer archaeologist (the 'Aubrey holes' at Stonehenge are named after him). In 1696, the year before his death, Aubrey published *Miscellanies*, a book supporting the phenomena of omens, supernatural manifestations, the power of prophecy and conversations with spirits and angels with documented reports. This comes almost a decade after fellow Royal Society member Isaac Newton had published his treatise on mathematical principles (*Philosophiae Naturalis Principia Mathematica*) that we now know as Newton's Laws.

Not everyone had been convinced by the advocates who demanded the hounding down and execution of women alleged to be witches. *The Moderate Intelligencer* in 1645 had declared with not a little cynicism that 'it was a great wonder that devils should be conversant with silly old women that know not their right hand from their left'. Be that as it may, women continued to be persecuted throughout the seventeenth century until Alice Molland becomes the last woman thus hanged in England in 1685. Significantly, the Witchcraft Act is not repealed from the English Statute Book until 1736.

Chapter 17

Military Wives & Camp Followers

For centuries it was common practice for women of all social classes to accompany the British Army on campaign, both at home and overseas, whether they were the wives or the mistresses of serving officers or common soldiers. Apart from being a civilising influence on their husbands or lovers, their presence also served a more practical purpose. In March 1690, The King's Own Regiment (4th Foot) marched from their camp at Bideford to embark for Belfast. The officers' wives were permitted to ride, while those of the common soldier were obliged to walk in the rear with the baggage train. They were required to remain at the rear of the column and often behaving in an unruly manner, were under the command of the regimental marshal. However, despite being 'attached' in one form or another to the soldiers of the regiment, the women were still required to earn their keep:

> The women were of great assistance to the regiment, for they bought and prepared the food for the company, brought in fuel for the fire, washed the linen, and generally tended the men. Especially were they useful in camp, for then they were permitted to go miles from the regiment in search of victuals and of other necessaries.[1]

Neither did the legal wives of soldiers escape military discipline and might suffer in the same manner, being summarily convicted and sentenced by court martial under the Articles of War and the Mutiny Acts of 1689. This was not an idle threat: 'As the wives were on the regimental strength they were also subject to military discipline, which meant that they could be flogged, and flogged they were!'[2]

> The behaviour of the women, whether wives or camp followers often left much to be desired, as Samuel Pepys discovered when he came across some of them in his role with the colony at Tangiers: 'In the whole place, nothing but vice of all sorts, swearing, drinking, cursing and whoring, the women as bad as the men.[3]

Back in 1639, the Royalist general against the Scots, the Earl of Arundel, had published a document entitled *Lawes and Ordinances Of Warre, For the better*

130

Government of His Majesties Army Royall, a direct ancestor of all subsequent military law, enforceable by courts martial. One section dealt with 'Morall' [*sic*] duties, and included the offences of blasphemy, non church attendance, gambling, drunkenness and 'whoredom'. The treatment of female camp followers was briefly and succinctly dealt with in the latter category: 'suspitious and common women' found with the army for a second time were to be 'soundly whipped like common strumpets'.

The punishments meted out to these women by subsequent courts martial, even for relatively minor offences, became far more imaginative and inventive than mere whipping, and could be equally savage in the extreme:

> One very common punishment for trifling offences committed by petit sutlers, jews, brawling women and such-like persons was the whirligig. This was a kind of circular cage which turned on a pivot: and when set in motion, whirled round with such an amazing velocity, that the delinquent became extremely sick, and commonly emptied his or her body through every aperture – much to the amusement of the spectators.[4]

The effect upon bodily functions proved to be great public entertainment and the punishment was executed 'to the delight of the jaded troops'. Women were frequently sentenced to this cruel device on the grounds of their perceived moral lapses, such as one lady who was thus sentenced for her loose behaviour – an entry in the Gibralter Garrison Order Book gives more precise details of how this device was employed in her punishment:

> 13th March 1727. After being confined to the black hole or dungeon for the space of a night, the next day a poor lady by the name of Chidley was conducted to a whirligig. It contains room enough for one person. It is fixed between two swivels, so is turned round till it makes the person a little giddy and landsick. This office was performed by two gentlemen of the garrison for the space of an hour in the market place, being well attended. All this was to oblige her for the too frequent bestowing of her favours.

A full hour might seem to be a very long period of time to subject a woman to this unpleasant and degrading treatment, yet only five days later the Garrison Order Book records a second woman being similarly punished with even greater severity: 'seventeenth March 1727. Mrs Malone committed to the whirligig for 2 hours. It gave great pleasure to the spectators.'

The Order Book doesn't enlighten us as to why the hapless Mrs Malone was thought worthy of such brutal treatment. The errant wives of common soldiers were generally punished with the whirligig or a flogging with the cat o'nine tails. However, when the wife of an officer was found to be in need of correction, a rather less savage mode of punishment was generally employed: 'January 1728. A gentlewoman of the Foot Guards was pinioned in the market place, with her neck and hands fastened by chains. The time of suffering is 3 hours.'

Sentences for the most serious crimes handed down by military courts marshal also reflected the general brutality of the time. This was equally true when the army was serving overseas in the colonies as it was when at home in Britain. On 10 April 1763, a court marshal under the presidency of Lieutenant Colonel Roger Morris tried three people for the murder of Louis Dodier and found all three variously guilty. Joseph Corriveau was sentenced to be hanged. Marie Josephte Corriveau, his daughter and the widow of the murdered man, was found guilty of being a party to the murder and received a physically brutal sentence; she was sentenced to sixty lashes of the cat o'nine tails on her bare back, at three different locations: 'twenty lashes at each place, firstly under the gallows, secondly upon the market place in Quebec and finally in the parish of St Vallier ... where she is also to be branded in the left hand with the letter 'M'.'

A second woman, Isabelle Sylvain, Joseph Corriveau's niece, was found guilty of perjury and was sentenced to an identical flogging as Marie Corriveau 'in the same manner and at the same time and place.'

Condemned to hang, Joseph Corriveau then told his confessor that he was no more than an accomplice to his daughter, after she had killed her husband. At a second trial, on 15 April 1763, Marie-Josephte confessed to having killed her husband with two blows of a hatchet during his sleep, because of his ill-treatment of her. The tribunal was not sympathetic however and found her guilty, sentencing her to death:

> The general court-marshal having tried Marie Josephte Corriveau, for the murder of her husband, Dodier, the court finding her guilty, the Governor (Murray) doth ratify and confirm the following sentence:-
> That Marie Josephte Corriveau do suffer death for the same, and her body to be hung in chains wherever the governor shall think fit. (Signed) Thomas Mills, Town Major.

Footnote: The place of execution was Quebec, on the Buttes-à-Nepveu, probably on 18 April. Her body was then taken, as directed by the sentence, to be put in chains at Pointe-Lévy, at the crossroads of Lauzon and Bienville, today the Rue St-Joseph and the Boulevard de l'Entente.[5] The body, contained its iron gibbet, was exposed to the public view until some date around 25 May. Following the requests of those living nearby, the Governor James Murray, ordered the captain of the militia of Pointe-Lévy, to take the rotting corpse down and bury it. In 1849, the iron cage in which the body had been hung and subsequently interred was dug up from the cemetery of the church of St-Joseph-de-la-Pointe-Lévy when a pit was being dug. Soon after, the cage was stolen from the church cellar and later acquired by the American impresario P.T. Barnum who put it on display as a 'macabre object'. It was later put on display at The Boston Museum, the museum slip indicating its provenance with the words: 'From Quebec'.[6]

On occasion, the formality of a trial by court marshal was dispensed with and summary punishment – invariably corporal – was inflicted upon the hapless woman concerned. During the English Civil War, prostitution flourished as women sold their services to the soldiers of both sides. In 1642 one particular lady who had followed the Parliamentary army to Coventry committed some offence which even the brutalised soldiery would not condone and who took it upon themselves to administer punishment. The unfortunate woman was taken by the soldiers and led about the city, set for a time in the pillory, then in the cage, ducked in the river, and finally banished from the city.

Often the summary justice meted out by soldiers was even more brutal. After winning the battle of Naseby in 1645, the Parliamentarians turned upon the baggage train that contained the Royalist female camp followers. About a hundred Irish women were slaughtered out of hand and any Englishwomen found were slashed across the face in order to disfigure them.

The Parliamentary army often punished its own soldiers and their paramours for immorality. In 1651 at Leith in Scotland, a woman was sentenced to be ducked twice at high tide, then stripped and whipped at the cart's tail, followed by thirty-nine lashes from the main guard at Leith before being turned out of the town.

Other than immorality, the offence of common theft could bring summary retribution down upon the miscreant's head. Captain Charles Le Poer Trench was Adjutant of the Galway Militia from 1797 to 1799 while the regiment was stationed in Cork. Following his military career he was ordained in the ministry and later became the Honourable and Venerable Charles Le Poer Trench, Archdeacon of Ardagh, otherwise notoriously known as 'the flogging parson'. During his time as adjutant, the wife of a private soldier from Galway serving in the regiment had been accused by another soldier of having stolen two candlesticks belonging to him and had pawned them. Upon receiving the complaint, Trench had the woman arrested and put in the guardroom, where she remained for the whole night. The next morning he ordered her to be brought out, guarded by a file of soldiers, and in the presence of the regiment, which was formed up into a hollow square, she was tied hand and foot to the flogging triangle to undergo punishment. Trench ordered that she should receive fifty lashes of the cat o'nine tails on her bare back. When the drummers assigned to administer the flogging had tried to strip her, she had resisted the removal of her clothes and struggled violently:

> but the adjutant went up to the drum-major, cursed and damned him
> for not tearing off her clothes, and in a great passion, giving him a
> blow with a stick, ordered the drum-major to tear and cut them off.

The drum-major thereupon cut open the woman's gown with a knife, pulling it down before tearing her underclothing from her shoulders, leaving her naked to the waist. Having securely tied her wrists and ankles, the two drummers then went to work with their whips, striking the writhing and screaming woman alternately from the left and right until fifty lashes had been administered, leaving her back raw and bleeding.

During the course of the punishment, another officer of the regiment named Davis went up to the adjutant and told him that the woman's soldier husband, watching his wife being publicly stripped and flogged, had fainted in the ranks. He begged that the man be allowed leave the parade and Trench answered that the man 'might go where he pleased', and 'did not care if the devil took him'. The flogging being done, the woman – still half naked and with blood still running from the weal's on her back, was drummed out of the barrack-yard to the tune of the 'rogue's march', the historical act of being dishonourably dismissed from military service. Because of this and other severe punishments awarded by Trench, he became known in the regiment as 'skin him alive'. The severity of this summary justice imposed upon a woman may be judged by the fact that a later act of 1846 ordered that the maximum number of lashes with the 'cat' to which a serving soldier could be sentenced was to be no more than fifty.

As if these punishments were not brutal enough, even more savage was the practice of administering two or more punishments to a woman at the same time, often in the case of rather more serious offences. On 25 June 1664, a woman in the Tangier colony was found guilty of incitement to mutiny. She was sentenced first to be gagged, a punishment commonly employed against drunken seamen in the Royal Navy. This penalty is not as innocuous as it sounds, as can be imagined from this description of its infliction from a naval medical officer:

> A piece of wood or iron, various in diameter and length, is introduced
> into the mouth, exactly in the way a bit is introduced into the mouth
> of a horse, so that a portion of it shall project from each side. It is
> retained in this position by means of a cord passed over the projecting
> extremities and behind the head.[7]

With this in place and therefore unable to speak or cry out, she was then to receive fifty lashes with a cat o' nine tails on her bare back – ten strokes to be administered at each of five different locations, thus ensuring that her punishment would be witnessed by as many people as possible. Finally, she was to be deported from the colony aboard the first available ship, again being whipped on her bare back as she was dragged tied behind a cart from the prison to the dockside.

Extraordinary as it may sound to modern ears, female camp followers, even the wives of serving soldiers, had no rights when it came to sharing the regiment's provisions. They were often left to fend for themselves and their behaviour in marauding and scavenging for food became notorious. Charles James in the *Military Companion* of 1803 wrote:

> It is notorious that, during a march, these unfortunate women were at the mercy of every innkeeper in the kingdom, and when they arrived in camp or barracks, they were left to provide for themselves without the least regard to common decency or good order.

Whether she was starving or not, the usual punishment was meted out to any woman caught stealing. During the Peninsular War in 1814, Lady Salisbury took the Duke of Wellington to task for the alleged severe flogging of 'ill-disciplined' female camp followers. His reply was typically phlegmatic:

> There was no order for punishing women, but there was certainly none for exempting women from punishment. It is well known that in all armies the women are at least as bad, if not worse, than the men as Plunderers, and the exemption of the Ladies from punishment would have encouraged plunder.

Commanders of sixty years earlier felt no such obligation to justify the penalties imposed on women for similar such offences. In 1745, during the War of the Austrian Succession, the wife of a soldier was convicted of petty larceny. General Pulteney watched the woman receiving her punishment, obviously with some ghoulish amusement given his subsequent description of the scene to the Duke of Cumberland:

> Her tail was turned up before the door of the house, where the robbery was committed, and the Drummer of the Regiment tickled her with a 100 very good lashes, since which time the ladies have behaved like angels. The sex is not the worse for correction.

The subsequent angelic behaviour of the ladies is hardly surprising – one hundred strokes of the cat o'nine tails would have left the buttocks and thighs of the culprit completely flayed. The severity of this sentence can be judged against that awarded in the American Army of 1776 for the severely regarded crime of desertion, was also one hundred lashes.[8]

Any army is restrained by its supply chain and camp followers could represent a significant drain on what were often limited resources. For this reason the number of women authorised to accompany their men could be severely limited. In 1775, General Edward Braddock limited these numbers to four or five in various companies under his command and ordered that 'only provisions of that number will be supplied'. Even these rations were not generous – half of a soldier's to each woman and a quarter to each child. Any woman found in the camp without authorisation was to be severely punished (i.e. flogged) for the first offence and suffer death if caught for a second time.[9]

General Braddock obviously included his own mistress in the list of authorised women. He was ambushed and killed near Fort Duquesne (modern Pittsburg) and she was captured by native Americans, stripped naked and repeatedly raped before being eaten!

Military records often indicate women receiving punishment for selling liquor to the troops on the march. The orders of the Duke of Cumberland in 1755 prohibited soldier's wives from selling 'gin or other Spiritous liquers' to the troops upon pain of severe punishment. These punishments could be very severe indeed. In 1746 while campaigning in Scotland, he ordered a number of disorderly women be stripped bare to the waist and given 200 strokes with the cat o' nine tails, and this at a time when four dozen lashes was considered a not inconsiderable punishment for men serving in His Majesties' Armed Services.

The Duke of Cumberland was not alone in trying to prevent the dealing in 'spiritous liquers'. The practice of buying and selling drink was a favourite one with female camp followers generally and not least with the women following the King's Own Regiment stationed in Boston during the queen's birthday celebrations of 1775: 'Many of them engaged in the profitable occupation of buying and selling rum and, although the practice was forbidden, and some were caught and whipped, the business flourished.'

During the eighteenth century, more and more demands were placed upon the British army to garrison the overseas possessions, from Gibraltar to the colonial plantations of America, from the West Indies to the new lands of Australia, wherever the troops went the 'army women' went with them. All camp followers came under the Articles of War 1722 for discipline and could be 'tried in Gibralter, Minorca or in any Place beyond the Seas, where there is no form of our Civil Judicature in Force'. This meant that they could, as in England, be flogged for offences such as drunkenness or plunder:

> Mrs Drake, belonging to the Artillery, Mrs Mitchal and Mrs Clark,
> were flogged thro' the camp for having and receiving stolen property

and receiving stolen goods from the plunderers. One of them was an honest Midwife who will be of great loss to the Garrison, if she is sent out as ordered, for we marry and breed faster than ever known in peaceable times.

The punishment to which these three ladies were sentenced decreed that: 'They are [to be] stripped to the waist and to receive upon their bare backs one dozen lashes from the cat o' nine tails, having at the same time a label appraising their crime pinned to their respective breasts'.[10]

Having been stripped to the waist, where the label was to be pinned is not immediately apparent! Posted to the American colonies in 1759, the 42nd Regiment of Foot was experiencing all the same problems with its camp followers. Death was the penalty for 'any woman stealing, purloining or wasting army provisions.' Any woman caught outside the boundaries of the camp without a Regimental pass was 'to be tyed up [sic] and given 50 lashes'.

Adulterous wives did not escape military justice. In Louisberg, Private Daniel Buckley was tried by courts martial for the murder of Sergeant John Gorman. The defendant admitted to the crime, but in mitigation pleaded that the sergeant had 'been keeping company with and debauching his wife'. He was duly sentenced to death, but later pardoned. His wife, Lydia Buckley, was sentenced to be 'drum'd out of the Fort at the Carts' Tail, duck'd and sent to Boston for trial by the civil magistrates', where she would most probably be punished with a further whipping.

In the colony of New Hampshire in 1705, a woman died after having been flogged on the orders of Lieutenant John Moody, who was subsequently tried at a court martial; Lieutenant Moody's answer to the affidavit against him was as follows:

Christian was a notorious thief and strumpet. I turned her out of the fort as being a danger to the soldiers. When she resisted, she was *whipped* to frighten, not to hurt her. On hearing the malicious rumour that this caused her death, demanded an enquiry. At a Court held by Commodore Bridge, Capt. Fairborn and the 3 Fishing Admirals I was completely cleared.[11]

It is not clear how the hapless woman was whipped merely to frighten her. Nevertheless, Lieutenant Moody was exonerated from any blame. Some commanders however, gained a reputation for a less severe disciplinary code, such as General Eyre Massey, responsible for the garrison at Halifax from 1775 to 1778: 'While other commanders regularly prescribed the use of the whip on army women, he seldom if ever threatened them with corporal punishment'.

The subjection of female camp followers to military discipline and corporal punishment, both official and unofficial, prevailed for centuries in the British Army.

THE VIOLENT ABUSE OF WOMEN

Even as late as the middle of the nineteenth century, Article 72 of the Special Report of the Indian Law Commissioners 1842 was able say: 'it may be very necessary to flog camp followers and the prevailing sentiments against the punishment of flogging may not be altogether reasonable'.

And this at a time when the judicially ordered flogging of women for common law offences had been proscribed in Britain for twenty-five years.

The savage treatment of women accompanying their husbands and lovers on military service at home and overseas during the seventeenth and eighteenth centuries may seem brutal in the extreme, but set against that meted out to women in civilian life, who could be legally beaten by their husbands or masters or publicly flogged by the law, it appears to be nothing more or less than of its time: 'An age which had scant regard or its soldiers, serving or discharged, could hardly be expected to be particularly solicitous about their dependents'.[12]

However, by 1870 times had changed and the brutality with which female camp followers had been punished had softened considerably; for attempting to stab another wife, using abusive language and creating a disturbance in the barracks at Portsmouth, a woman was sentenced merely to be 'turned out of barracks and struck off the strength of the Regiment'.[13]

Chapter 18

The Morality Police

Following the more liberal attitudes to public and private morality that had pertained during the reign of Charles II, a new regime of respectability began to take hold following the 'glorious revolution' of 1688. The ascent of William III and Mary to the English throne saw a proliferation of societies dedicated to the improvement of religious observance and public morality.

Baron de La Brède et de Montesquieu was a French judge, man of letters, and a political philosopher. After a visit to England in 1736 he declared that 'Je passe en France pour avoir peu de religion, en Angleterre pour en avoir trop' (I go to France to have little religion, in England to have too much). This may have been due in part to the efforts of organisations such as the Society for Promoting Christian Knowledge (founded in 1698) and the Society for the Propagation of the Gospel (incorporated under Royal Charter in 1701).

Apart from the need to improve religious observance, many felt that the law did not do enough to persecute those who offended against the new morality and setup their own vigilante organisations to remedy this perceived shortcoming. The most successful of these was the 'Society for the Reformation of Manners', founded in London in 1691 and whose branches quickly spread to towns and cities throughout the country as far north as Edinburgh, where the author Daniel Defoe was an enthusiastic member. (Author of *Robinson Crusoe* but also more applicably *Commentary on Conjugal Lewdness* 1727.)

'Manners' in the seventeenth century should be taken to mean 'morals', and unsurprisingly the society's espoused aims were the suppression and punishment of profanity, immorality, and other lewd activities in general, and of brothels and prostitution in particular. This inevitably meant that women generally became the principle objects of the society's attention, and those who would presently be regarded as 'sex workers' in particular.

The society was organised on four levels, in a structure which largely reflected the tiers of society in general. The highest level – the Society of Original Gentlemen was largely comprised of the society's founders; wealthy aristocrats, lawyers, judges and members of parliament, who directed the organisation and financed the prosecutions. The second level consisted largely of tradesmen whose responsibility it was to actively suppress vice and immorality. Level three was the Association of Constables, who would execute the raids on suspicious premises and make the resulting arrests. Finally, there came a network of informers (termed 'moral guardians') with two stewards in each parish, who would gather information and gossip relating to any alleged moral infractions and pass them up the line in order that the 'original gentlemen' could inform the local magistrate, thus enabling the guilty parties to be prosecuted and punished. The Society would either pay others to bring prosecutions, or bring prosecutions on its own account.

The first report from the Society was published in 1694 and stated that it was intended 'for the satisfaction of many who have been desirous to know what progress we have made in this reformation of manners'. Clearly there was now a section of the public who wanted to know what the reformers were achieving, among whom must have been those men whose financial contributions kept the Society in business. The report contained a 'Black Roll' that listed those convicted and punished during the preceding twelve months for the offences of keeping a bawdy house, cursing, being a night walker, or being a 'plyer' in a bawdy house, i.e. the list was comprised almost entirely of women. From a total of 313 prosecutions and convictions in this document, women punished specifically for night walking or plying their trade in or near bawdy houses accounted for more than 250 successful actions taken by the reformers.

By 1701 a sixth 'Black List' was able to report that 'Eight Hundred and Forty three Lewd and Scandalous Persons, who by the Endeavours of a Society for Promoting a Reformation of Manners [i.e. morals] in the City London and Suburbs thereof, have been legally Prosecuted and Convicted etc.' By 1706, the eleventh 'Black List' was able to name another 830 'Lewd and Scandalous Persons' whom the Society had been instrumental in prosecuting during the previous twelve months, and who as a result had been fined or whipped, and notes that these are in addition to those named on the previous ten lists or rolls; a total of 7,995 people – a list comprised overwhelmingly of women.

The list contained a key to identify the offence for which the individual had been prosecuted – five offences are listed; Bh = keeping a bawdy-house, W = a whore, Dh = keeping a disorderly house, Dp = a disorderly person, Pp = a pickpocket. An indication of the bias against women is evidenced by the disproportionate number of their gender who found themselves in the Bridewell. Of the 830 people convicted in the twelve months to Christmas 1705, only seventy-three were men – all convicted as disorderly persons. Of the 757 women, 561 were convicted as 'whores' and would have been stripped to the waist and whipped at the post in the Bridewell or flogged while being dragged through the streets behind a cart. This punishment was clearly not as effective a deterrent as the law expected it to be; sixty-seven of those women were convicted 'on divers occasions' in the previous twelve month period, often two or three times, but sometimes many more as in the case of one

Mary Sanford, who appears from the lists to have suffered the agony of the lash on no less than ten separate occasions!

Unsurprisingly, the use of informers (or 'thief-takers' as they were known) who gained financially from their services, eventually gave rise to significant public opposition. Additionally, critics of the system pointed out that the blacklists were comprised entirely of the disadvantaged, while the vices of the socially superior escaped prosecution altogether. As already shown in a previous chapter (see At the Mercy of the Mob) between 1780 and 1790 a group of aristocratic ladies known as 'Pharaoh's Daughters' kept gambling houses around Covent Garden in London. Their clubs became notorious for fleecing young army officers and other young men of their money, and so came to the attention of Lord Chief Justice Kenyon, who had threatened that he 'would pillory any person no matter their rank found guilty of gambling offences', so the public gleefully awaited the pillorying or whipping of their ladyships. However, the judge merely admonished and fined them and the only whipping Lady Buckinghamshire received was in a satirical cartoon by James Gillray.

This example demonstrated clearly the social divide that determined what offenders against public morality might expect from the law. The author Daniel Defoe succinctly described the anti-vice laws of the time as 'Cobweb Laws, in which the small Flies are catch'd, and the great ones break through.' For these reasons the number of prosecutions by the society declined sharply after 1725 and after 1738 the organisation completely disappears from the historical record.

However, the demise of the Society for the Reformation of Manners was not the end of the story for privately funded morality-policing. In 1757, a group of churchmen led by Justice John Fielding (half-brother of Henry Fielding, founder of the Bow Street Runners) formed a society to suppress Sabbath-breaking, and later widened its campaign to include swearing, gambling, and prostitution, all of which they began to prosecute in 1758. The society initially enjoyed great success and according to John Wesley, by August 1762 they had brought 9,596 people to trial. In the next seven months, 550 arrests were made for 'lewdness' (i.e. prostitution). However, this success was not to last; in 1763 a legal action charging assault and false imprisonment of a supposed brothel-keeper led to the award of substantial damages against the reformers. Even though one of the prosecution's witnesses was later found to be guilty of perjury, the action brought an end to the society's activities.

In the 1780s the 'Gordon Riots' as they were known, anti-Catholic protests in London against the Papists Act of 1778, had raised fears among the authorities of rising crime rates and social upheaval, or even worse still, revolution. In accordance with conventional thinking of the time, the cause of crime and disorder was directly attributable to widespread immorality and dissolution. The problems surrounding the prosecution of such offences had already been amply demonstrated in 1763, and was now made even more difficult by changes to the legal framework around such prosecutions, for example:

- Convicting women of prostitution simply on the basis of their reputation or hearsay, or the fact that they were arrested walking the streets at times and in places frequented by known prostitutes was deemed unacceptable.
- Charges of being 'loose, idle and disorderly' were unacceptable and required a specific form of misbehaviour to be identified and charged.
- Arrest warrants were required to specify the precise person to be apprehended. Constables could no longer be issued with general warrants authorising the arrest of individuals guilty of a range of illegal behaviours.

Nevertheless, at the instigation of William Wilberforce and others, King George III was persuaded in 1787 to issue a 'proclamation for the discouragement of vice' against drunkenness, gaming, profane swearing and cursing, lewdness, profanation of the Sabbath, 'or other dissolute, immoral, or disorderly practices'. However, some lessons had been learned and the 'Proclamation Society' as it became known relied less upon the lash and more upon persuading offenders to reform. Officials were encouraged to carry out their duties more rigorously but arrested offenders were to be discharged without punishment, unless their behaviour was 'outrageous and overt'. In common with its forebears, society's distrust of the process and legal challenges led to a transformation of the reformers' strategies and tactics; rather than prosecute prostitutes the society took up alternative strategies: inspecting prison conditions and setting up philanthropic societies, eventually transforming itself into the Society for Bettering the Condition of the Poor.

It is often said that those who do not know their history are doomed to repeat it, and such is the case with moral reformers. The Society for the Suppression of Vice was founded in 1802 and initially brought large numbers of prosecutions, although mainly, it must be said, for the profanation of the Sabbath rather than for lewd behaviour. As on many previous occasions, paid informers were employed to identify offenders and volunteer prosecutors were recruited to bring the accused to court. As before, this strategy attracted criticism from both the legal profession and the general public, and the prosecutors were forced to compromise in many cases and drop prosecutions if the accused promised to reform. And like its predecessor, the Society also engaged in a number of philanthropic activities from which the Guardian Society, founded in 1815, strove to reform prostitutes and 'fallen' under-age girls, rather than having them whipped. In 1825, the Society acknowledged the government's reluctance to prosecute prostitutes, given public and legal hostility to such prosecutions, but continued its other activities until its final demise in 1885.

Chapter 19

The 'Whipping Toms'

Throughout history women have been the victims of casual, low-level violence perpetrated by men involving pinching, slapping or groping, which are not in themselves serious physical assaults, but nevertheless are sexual in nature and often leave the victim feeling demeaned and humiliated. Samuel Pepys was not averse to meting out such treatment:

> Thence to White Hall, and there did hear Betty Michell was at this end of the towne, and so without breach of vowe did stay to endeavour to meet with her and carry her home; but she did not come, so I lost my whole afternoon. But pretty! how I took another pretty woman for her, taking her a clap on the breech [i.e. a slap on the buttocks], thinking verily it had been her.[1]

In the seventeenth and eighteenth centuries however, such physical assaults sometimes took a more serious turn, as in the strange case of the so-called 'whipping toms'. Over a period of thirty years across the turn of the seventeenth and eighteenth centuries, a bizarre series of attacks on women took place, mainly in London and the then nearby rural village of Hackney – now a London borough. 'Whipping Tom' was the nickname given to the attacker or attackers who would assault women walking home unaccompanied late at night.

The earliest properly documented instance of such assaults occurred in central London in 1681. A man (and the assailant is invariably male) would approach unaccompanied women in quiet alleyways and courtyards and, turning up their skirts and petticoats, spank them on the bare buttocks before fleeing into the night. The inability of the authorities to apprehend the offender (or offenders) gave rise to much complaining about the ineffectiveness of London's law enforcement to apprehend the criminals. Although there are no documented records of such assaults before 1681, a publication of that year makes reference to 'the Generation of that Whipping Tom, that about Nine years since proved such an Enemy to the Milk-wenches Bums', implying that a similar attacker (or attackers) with the same nickname had operated nearly a decade earlier in about 1672.

THE VIOLENT ABUSE OF WOMEN

A two-page bestselling broadsheet of 1681 described in some detail the assailants modus operandi, snappily entitled: *Whipping Tom Brought to Light and Exposed to View: in an Account of Several Late Adventures of the Pretended Whipping Spirit. Giving a Full Relation of Several Maids, Widows and Wives, &c. that Have Been by Him Used in a Most Barbarous and Shameful Manner in and about the City of London.*

The 'Whipping Tom' of 1681 would loiter in the dark in the small courtyards between Fleet Street, Strand and Holborn. Upon coming across an unaccompanied woman, he would grab her, pull up her skirts and petticoats, and slap her naked backside repeatedly (knickers or drawers not then being commonly worn) while shouting the word 'spanko' before running off into the night. Sometimes he used his bare hand to administer the beating, while upon other occasions he would employ a birch rod, the severity of its application leaving several of his victims with quite serious wounds. Given the complaints about the lack of effective policing in London, vigilante patrols were sometimes raised by the public in the affected areas. Women would carry 'penknives, sharp bodkins, scissors and the like', and the male vigilantes would dress in women's clothing and patrol the areas in which the attacker was known to operate. The broadsheet goes on to graphically describe his first assault:

> His first Adventure, as near as we can learn, was on a Servant Maid in New-street, who being sent out to look for her Master, as she was turning a Corner, perceived a Tall black Man standing up against the wall, as if he had been making water, but she had not passed far, but with great speed and violence seized her, and in a trice, laying her cross his knee, took up her Linnen, and lay'd so hard upon her Backside, as made her cry out most piteously for help, the which he no sooner perceiving to approach (as she declares) then he vanished.

It should be noted that, following the convention of the day, 'Tall black Man' in this context most likely refers to his clothing or hair colour, not his ethnicity.

The case engendered a series of lascivious broadsheets. In 1684 *Whipping Tom turn'd citizen* even recommended the tune to which it could be sung:

> Whipping-Tom turn'd citizen: or, The cracks terror being a true account of his many strange adventures; as likewise a relation of his whipping several wives, widdows, maids, bawds, cracks, &c. in Fleet-street, the strand, Holborn, Whetstones-Park, Fetter-Lane, New-Street, and other places. Together with the opinion that several

144

have given concerning him, and of the strange method he uses in
whipping them. Tune of, A figg for France.

A second attacker, also nicknamed 'Whipping Tom', was active between October
and December 1712 in the then rural village of Hackney. This attacker would
approach lone women in the countryside, and beat them on the buttocks with 'a Great
Rodd of Birch'. Around seventy such attacks were carried out before a haberdasher
from Holborn named Thomas Wallis together with an unnamed accomplice were
captured and confessed to the attacks. According to Wallis, he was 'resolved to
be Revenged on all the women he could come at after that manner, for the sake of
one Perjur'd Female, who had been Barbarously False to him'. He claimed that his
plan was to attack a hundred women before Christmas, cease the attacks during
the Twelve Days of Christmas, then resume the attacks in the new year. As usual,
the broadsheet writers were there, a rather more light-hearted version appearing in
1722 entitled: *The second part of Whipping-Tom or, a rod for a proud lady. Bundled
up in five feeling discourses, both serious and merry.*

What became of Wallis and his accomplice following their confession is not
known for certain as all the court records of their subsequent trial seem to have
been lost. However, a broadsheet published around 1740, entitled: *The tryal,
examination and conviction; of Thomas Wallis, vulgarly called Whipping Tom for
whipping and abusing Mary Sutten, Susanna Murrey, Ann Evans, Dorothy Webster,
and several others in and about London,* claimed that at his trial Wallis said that
'unless women be whipped out of their native pride and baseness, mankind will
become women's slaves' and it was alleged that he was sentenced to be whipped
weekly by two women in the Bridewell, but is probably later wishful thinking by
fetishists as there is no evidence that any such sentence was ever passed.

'Whipping John' of Islington

The Library of Congress in the USA is possessed of a strange etching dated 11 July
1748, of which little seems to be known. The monochrome illustration shows a
room in which a bare-bottomed woman with a pained expression on her face is held
horsed over the stooping back of a man while another woman holds up her skirts.
A second man, identified in the picture as 'Whipping John' wields a birch over
her exposed posterior, while a third man peeps in at the door, allegedly deriving
gratification from the scene, as the commentator opines that he ought be paying for
the pleasure. The accompanying verse indicates that the woman has made herself
thus available for the gratification of John's 'flogging whim' for which they should
both be ashamed.

Spring-Heeled Jacks

There is a strange codicil to the various seventeenth- and eighteenth-century legends of men who physically assault women in public places. Throughout almost the whole of the Victorian period from 1837 onwards, several locations in England, Scotland and Wales reported attacks by a male figure who disappeared after the assault by leaping over high walls, and towards the end of his manifestations in the first decade of the twentieth century, over whole buildings. Thus he became popularly known as 'spring-heeled Jack'. He would typically accost young women in the street and by way of some innocent pretence, gain their trust, only to then tear at their hair and clothing. When the journalists of the day attempted to track down victims or witnesses of reported crimes, they could find no one to interview.

Then in February 1838, a woman who had been the alleged victim of such an attack gave a detailed statement before magistrates 18-year-old Jane Alsop told how, on the evening of 20 February, a cloaked man had appeared at the door of her family home in Bearbinder Lane, near Bow in London. He requested that she bring a lantern to assist the police, who had apprehended 'Spring-heeled Jack' in the lane. She did as he requested, but the second she handed it to him he threw off his cloak to reveal what she described as 'a most hideous and frightful appearance, and vomited forth a quantity of blue and white flame from his mouth, and his eyes resembled red balls of fire … he wore a large helmet; and his dress, which appeared to fit him very tight, appeared to resemble white oil-skin.[2]

The figure set upon her with what she believed were metal claws, ripping at her skirts and bodice in an effort to tear her clothes from her body. She managed to get away from him and ran for her life but he pursued her to her front door, where he continued to rip at her clothes and tearing hair from her head. She was saved by her elder sister who pulled her inside the house and slammed the door. Less than a month later, close by in the district of Limehouse, one Lucy Scales was returning home with her sister when a gaunt looking man she described as being 'of gentlemanly appearance' stepped out of Green Dragon Alley and spat a ball of flame in her face. She collapsed and suffered a fit, laying helpless on the pavement, but on this occasion the attacker simply walked away without attempting to interfere further with her or her clothing.[3]

This strange figure continued to make further unsubstantiated appearances throughout the nineteenth century, often later found to be by pranksters, until his last reported sighting in Liverpool in 1904, after which he disappears from sight.

Postscript

The French have a saying: *plus ça change, plus c'est la même chose* – the more things change, the more they stay the same. Whipping Tom's successors are apparently alive and well, more widespread than ever and still operating in twenty-first century Britain:

- In September 2014 local Guildford newspapers reported that a man had been placed on the sex offenders' register for five years after slapping two teenage girls and another young woman on the bottom.
- In September 2015, the *Daily Telegraph* reported the court case of a 72-year-old church minister who used the Bible to justify spanking vulnerable women on their bare bottoms to 'instil discipline and drive out evil spirits'. Grown women were persuaded to strip naked so that he could spank them over his knee.
- In February 2016, a 46-year-old ex-army sergeant was convicted of sixteen offences following a trial at London's Southwark Crown Court. His campaign of sexual abuse began by spanking women on the bottom, leading the trial judge to comment: 'To slap a young woman on the bottom, whether over the clothes or not, is to invade their privacy and is to act towards them in a way that is demeaning and distressing to them.'
- In February 2017, local Brighton newspapers and the *Sun* reported that police were hunting 'a serial bottom slapper who has attacked 20 women' in the town, before escaping on a bicycle. However, a little time later the paper was able to report:

> a suspected sex attacker has been arrested over 24 bum-smacking assaults on women in 30 days. Police have received 22 reports from women stating they have been grabbed or touched from behind, or had sexual gestures made towards them by a man riding a bicycle. Twenty of these have been made since January 3 and the incidents were not isolated to a particular area within the city. Most of the offences happened during the hours of darkness ranging from early evening through to 3 a.m. Descriptions of the suspect and the bicycle he was believed to ride vary but many of the reports described him as white with tanned skin, aged between 20 and 30 years, of average build, with dark hair and wearing a hooded top with the hood pulled up.

Chapter 20

Growing Distaste & Abolition

Between the years 1735 and 1789, thirty-three women had been burned alive in England for one of two offences: coining – punished as High Treason, or matricide – punished as Petty Treason. The great majority of these, twenty-five, were women who had murdered their husbands. Three female servants were burned for murdering their mistresses, also punished as Petty Treason.

The last three such executions in London were moved from Tyburn where they had traditionally taken place, to a spot just outside Newgate prison in the city. The surrounding area contained a respectable business district and the residents there had already petitioned the Lord Mayor of London asking for executions to be carried out elsewhere, even before the first of these, that of Phoebe Harris, had taken place. Nevertheless, the execution went ahead as planned and it was reported in *The Times* that some residents became ill as a result of the inhalation of smoke from the burning body:

> When remission of burning was refused, the scene of inhumanity should have been changed; the consequences have been serious; several persons in the neighbourhood of Newgate lying ill, have been severely affected by the smoke which issued from the body of the unhappy female victim.[1]

The Times newspaper had also taken up the theme of public distaste and revulsion, highlighting the fact that women were punished in a more savage manner than men for the same offence:

> The execution of a woman for coining on Wednesday morning, reflects a scandal upon the law and was not only inhuman, but shamefully indelicate and shocking. Why should the law in this species of offence inflict a severer punishment upon a woman than a man. It is not an offence that she can perpetrate alone – in every such case the insistence of a man has been found the operating motive upon the woman; yet the man is but hanged, and the woman burned.[2]

Notwithstanding these public outcries, two more such executions of women were to take place at Newgate, Margaret Sullivan in 1788 and Catherine Murphy in 1789. The Sheriffs whose duty it was to officiate at such occasions were also becoming increasingly unhappy about attending public burnings. On 10 May 1790, the Sheriff of London in the person of Sir Benjamin Hammett MP moved a Bill in Parliament to abolish the practice. The whole ghastly and obscene process was brought to an end by the passing of the Treason Act in 1790[3] and replaced by hanging. (This Act was itself repealed when the death penalty for treason was abolished by the Crime and Disorder Act 1998.)

As early as 1696, there is evidence that there was a growing public distaste (at least among the more liberally minded in society) for the public humiliation and physical punishment of women. Although physical chastisement was still on the tariff, judges began to occasionally include the condition that it should be administered away from the lascivious public gaze, often in the prison yard or in the whipping room of the Bridewell: 'Mary Collins of Stoke Mandivile [*sic*], spinster, for stealing a smock from Mary Pickton. To be 'privately' whipped.[4]

'Grace Davies (alias Giles) Spinster of StClements, for stealing goods to the value of tuppence from Anne Lemon – to be privately whipped.'[5]

In spite of this, publicly administered corporal punishment of women continued to be ordered, and throughout the early part of the eighteenth century increased in frequency and severity for a range of offences (see 'Judicial Savagery'). Towards the end of the seventeenth century, Ned Ward, who had already given a graphic account of the punishments administered in the Bridewell, gave his incisive opinion of the nature and effect of this form of correction for women, especially given the sexually titillating overtones it carried:

> I only conceive that it makes many harlots but that it can in no measure reclaim 'em. I think it is a shameful indecency for a woman to expose her naked body to the sight of men and boys, as if it were designed rather to feast the eyes of the beholders than to correct vice, or reform manners, therefore I think it both more modest and more reasonable they should receive their punishment in the view of women only, and by the hand of their own sex ... their bodies are by nature more tender, and their constitutions more weak, we ought to show them more mercy, and not punish 'em with such dog-like usage, unless their crimes were capital.[6]

Towards the end of the eighteenth century, judges were increasingly liable to order only private whipping for women, although men were still liable to be publicly whipped:

Mary Weston (21) Margaret Beale (24) Sarah Hart (29) Mary Willis (26) William Figes (18) Ann Morris (21) Jane Brooks (29)

Mary Brundiff (30) Mary Rendall (24) Walter Malone (49)
Elizabeth Brown otherwise Lyons (30) Elizabeth Hart (30) Mary
Brown (49) Eliza Brown (19) were severally Convicted of Grand and
Petit Larceny And were then and there severally Ordered and Adjudged
to be Imprisoned and kept to hard Labour in the House of Correction
at Clerkenwell (to wit) the said Mary Weston Margaret Beale Sarah
Hart Mary Willis and William Figes for the space of twelve Calender
Months and the said Jane Barnes, Ann Morris, Jane Brooks, Mary
Brundiff, Mary Kendall, Walter Malone, Elizabeth Brown otherwise
Lyons, Elizabeth Hart, Mary Brown and Eliza Brown for the space of
Six Calander Months And the said Sarah Hart Mary Willis Elizabeth
Hart, Mary Brown and Eliza Brown were further ordered to be
privately whipped and the said William Figes to be publickly whipped.

Dated this Twenty ninth day of March in the year of our Lord
1783.

Reynolds. Clerk of the Session of Gaol Delivery for the County
of Middx.[7]

Likewise, as the eighteenth century wore on, some judges became more sensible
to the erotic connotations of the public stripping and flogging of women and even
when a public whipping was ordered, adjusted the sentence accordingly; on 27
October 1790 Maria Griffin was indicted for stealing goods worth two shillings
(10p) and sentenced 'to be publickly whipped, in the presence of women only',
although how this public punishment was to be arranged and who was do the
whipping is not immediately apparent.

Outside the legal system, the workhouses continued to administer corporal
punishment to inmates for infractions of the rules:

4th Jan 1797
Mary Preynald for embezzling bread, cheese, beef and candles, to be
publicly whipped in the hall before dinner next Wednesday. A frame
for whipping persons is to be immediately made on the plan of that
at the House of Correction at Montgomery.

8th Feb. 1797
Elizabeth Jones to be flogged the 1st Board Day after Mr Baxter
reports her fit for the operation, for absenting the house without
leave.[8]

At the same time, some individuals personally involved in the administration of
such occasions were beginning to express repugnance at the frequent imposition

of corporal punishment on women, as this later entry from the Montgomery and Pool workhouse minute book clearly shows:

9th Aug. 1797
Clerk reports opinion of full meeting of Directors that the Porter from the repugnancy which he hath to the executing corporal punishments, though in other respects a good servant should be permitted to employ J. Davies on Monty, or another proper person to do that part of his duty.

The writing was clearly on the wall as far as the public chastisement of women was concerned, as sentences from one day at the Old Bailey on 2 April 1800 illustrate, although by this date even some men are also sentenced to be privately whipped:

Confined two-years in the House of Correction, and whipped in the jail: John, alias George Jones.
Confined eighteen months in the House of Correction, and fined 1s: Ann Dennis, alias Susannah Drew, James Hawkins.
Confined twelve months in Newgate, and publicly whipped: George Martin.
Confined twelve months in Newgate, and privately whipped: Francis Wrangham, Ann Syree.
Confined twelve months in Newgate, and fined 1s: John Patman, Thomas Stretch.
Confined twelve months in the House of Correction, and fined 1s: William Davis, Catherine Rasseedy, Owen Collins, John Nicholson, Joseph Hewitt, Mary Parrott.
Confined six months in Newgate, and privately whipped: Richard Tucker.
Confined six months in the House of Correction, and privately whipped: William Brown, Mary Hamilton, William Tweed.
Confined six months in the House of Correction, and publicly whipped: Joseph Fitchett, William White, James Cavanaugh, John Speak.
Confined six months in Newgate, and find sureties for six months more: Catherine Dunn, Mary Dunlap, Ann Mincher, James Elton.
Confined six months in the House of Correction, and fined 1s: Ann Evans, James Pennyman, Thomas Long, William Dracott, Joseph Chadwick, William Bryant, Sarah Barton, Thomas Lawsoa, William Sangster, William Powell, George Mitchell, alias John, alias Richard Ashley, Thomas Holdham.

Confined three months in Newgate, and whipped 100 yards in St Martin's-le-Grand: Charles Spring.

Confined three months in Newgate, and privately whipped: John Hall.

Whipped 100 yards in Seething-lane: Samuel Shailer, William Halfpenny.

Privately whipped, and discharged: Elizabeth Clarke, John Smith.

(On the same day in the same court nineteen people were sentenced to death and eighteen to various terms of transportation)

Although there had been growing distaste among some enlightened members of the public for more than a century, the corporal punishment of women being viewed by spectators was still taking place well into the nineteenth century, as evidenced by this disapproving press report of the public flogging of a woman in Scotland:

Last Friday, a woman of the name of Grant, was flogged through the streets of Inverness, we understand for the third time, (once the previous week,) for intoxication and bad behaviour in the streets. No doubt example is necessary, and was here made with the best intention; yet public and repeated flagellation on the naked body of this woman, is revolting to our general ideas of decency and humanity; it is to be regretted, that some equally effectual punishment could not be fallen upon.

It was the strongest argument in effecting the excellent and salutary change in the discipline of our army, that a soldier once publicly flogged became callous to all future disgrace – all after hope of reclaiming him was lost, and he became only anxious to make his depravity less conspicuous, by enticing others to participate in it; how much more must this apply to a female?

There is something so repugnant to the usual sentiments of respect and delicacy, with which we are naturally inclined to consider even in the lowest of the sex, that we doubt whether such an exhibition is calculated to amend our morals: on the unfortunate object in question, (a young and handsome woman) the hardened indifference and audacity with which she bore and ridiculed the punishment, showed that it failed of that effect – so much indeed that, notwithstanding this third flagellation, we understand she returned from her 'banishment' the same evening. It may be well to consider the effect of familiarising the public to such sights; and whether hard labour and solitary confinement, would not be a more successful punishment.[9]

GROWING DISTASTE & ABOLITION

This particular press report came to the attention of the House of Commons, who added their disapproval, as reported in *The Times* newspaper on Tuesday 11 June 1817:

> General THORNTON moved for leave to bring in a bill to abolish the public whipping of women: he had been more especially led to this by an article in The Inverness Journal, which stated, that a woman, young and beautiful, had been whipped in the public streets – that she was in a state of intoxication – seemed quite lost to every sense of her situation, and shortly returned to her old courses. Spectacles such as this were not likely to improve public morals.

The law was amended to the effect that the public whipping of women was abolished, although they could still be flogged in private, 'judgement shall not be given or awarded against any female convicted of an offence that such female offender do suffer the punishment of being publicly whipped'.[10] However, General Thornton proposed to abolish it completely, by commuting the punishment of any whipping sentence on a woman to one of hard labour in a workhouse, for a period not exceeding three months. Abolition of whipping as a judicial punishment for all women eventually came via an Act of Parliament in 1820.[11]

Virtually the last criminal trial in England at which a female was sentenced to be whipped was heard at the Surrey Sessions on Tuesday 3 December 1822. *The Times* reported the case in detail next day:

> Matilda Dunn, a child described in the record as being under 10 years of age, was indicted for stealing 12 yards of printed cotton, the property of Mr Cornell, a linen draper, residing at Newington. The circumstances of this case have been fully detailed in our police reports. It appeared from the evidence, that on the 28th of October, the prisoner, accompanied by a younger sister, entered Mr Cornell's shop, and asked for a quarter of a yard of muslin. Whilst the shopman was engaged in serving her, she rolled up the cotton mentioned in the indictment, and thrust it into a basket which was carried by her sister. The action was observed, and she was apprehended. The prisoner, when called upon for her defence, said she knew nothing about the matter. The Jury immediately found the prisoner guilty, but recommended her to mercy.
>
> The prosecutor begged to add his recommendation to that of the jury. It would, he said, afford him great satisfaction if the prisoner could be placed in some benevolent institution, where she might, if possible, be reformed. He had made inquiries in the neighbourhood

in which the prisoner lived, from which he had been able to learn that the father of the prisoner was in confinement preparatory to being tried on a charge of receiving stolen goods. The child who was with the prisoner when she committed the theft was in the parish workhouse. The family consisted of five children and the father – the mother being dead. A brother of the prisoner was at present in Brixton gaol. Not one of the children had been taught to read or write.

THE CHAIRMAN (Mr Harrison) observed, that in one view he was glad to hear of the latter circumstance. Mr Cornell said the prisoner had been known to be in the practice of stealing in shops for the last two years. She had confessed that she had robbed him of a table-cloth about a fortnight before she committed the theft of which she had been convicted. He understood that she was 13 years of age.

THE CHAIRMAN said, he was convinced that the prisoner was an experienced thief as soon as he heard her declare that she knew nothing about the matter. Then addressing the prisoner, he said, 'Prisoner, you stand here a dreadful instance of the effects of vice generated by ignorance. It appears that your parents have totally neglected your education and left you destitute of instruction, except, indeed, for wicked purposes; for I have reason to believe that one of your parents has been the occasion of your being placed in your present unfortunate situation. Your case presents a great difficulty to the Court, which hardly knows how to deal with you for the best. I have, however, consulted with my brother magistrates, and we think that the most advisable course we can pursue is to direct you to be imprisoned for three months in the House of Correction at Brixton, there to be kept to hard labour, and to be twice during that period privately whipped.

The prisoner was of small stature: the expression of her countenance was a mixture of shrewdness and depravity seldom to be met with in so young a child. During the trial she maintained the most perfect indifference, but after the verdict was delivered she seemed to weep.

However, even leaving aside the obvious confusion regarding Matilda's true age, it was already too late to award a female defendant a sentence which included a whipping, either public or private, as a correspondent subsequently pointed out:

Sir, – In your report of the trial of Matilda Dunn, at the Quarter Sessions for the County of Surrey, contained in The Times of

Wednesday, the 4th inst., I observe that the Court passed the following sentence upon her, viz., 'To be imprisoned for three months in the House of Correction at Brixton; there to be kept to hard labour, and to be twice, during that period, privately whipped.' Now, Sir, upon referring to 'Gifford's English Lawyer,' I find that by the 1st Geo. IV, c.57, the punishment of public and private whipping of females is abolished, and instead thereof hard labour in the gaol or house of correction, for any time not exceeding six months, nor less than one, is substituted. Such being the case, and the act above cited not having been repealed by the Legislature, it is manifest that the Court exceeded their authority.

I am, Sir, your most obedient humble servant A.W.

Postscript

The judicial flogging of women in the United Kingdom, either publicly or privately, is a thing of the past; it was however to continue in the British colonies for some years. The 1829 returns for the gaols and workhouses of the island of Jamaica show that the lash was still being liberally and illegally applied to female backs, the colony of Jamaica apparently being particularly guilty in this regard: '26th January 1829. Janet Grant and Becky Gray – 1 month's hard labour plus 1 flogging. Betsy Clarke – a runaway. Workhouse – 1 month + 24 lashes.'[12]

Nearly a decade later, nothing much seems to have changed:

> the infraction of one of the most stringent provisions of Imperial law, namely, the prohibition to flog females. In defiance of this positive injunction, a legal quibble has been invented, by means of which under cover of prison discipline, females have frequently been, and may still be flogged for the commission of apprenticeship offences.[13]

The Parliamentary report went on to report detailed testimonies from thirty-four women who had been punished by a flogging with the cat o'nine tails. It drew unintentionally ironic comparisons with other colonies, including other parts of the West Indies, 'in the Bahamas for instance, [where] there had been hardly any flogging for some months'.

Appendix A

'How the Women went from Dover' 1662 – John Greenleaf Whittier

This poem by John Whittier graphically describes the infamous multiple public floggings of three Quaker women in Boston, in 1662.

The tossing spray of Cocheco's fall
Hardened to ice on its rocky wall,
As through Dover town in the chill, gray dawn,
Three women passed, at the cart-tail drawn!

Bared to the waist, for the north wind's grip
And keener sting of the constable's whip,
The blood that followed each hissing blow
Froze as it sprinkled the winter snow.

Priest and ruler, boy and maid
Followed the dismal cavalcade;
And from door and window, open thrown,
Looked and wondered gaffer and crone.

'God is our witness,' the victims cried,
'We suffer for Him who for all men died;
The wrong ye do has been done before,
We bear the stripes that the Master bore!

'And thou, O Richard Waldron, for whom
We hear the feet of a coming doom,
On thy cruel heart and thy hand of wrong
Vengeance is sure, though it tarry long.

HOW THE WOMEN WENT FROM DOVER

'In the light of the Lord, a flame we see
  Climb and kindle a proud roof-tree;
And beneath it an old man lying dead,
  With stains of blood on his hoary head.'

'Smite, Goodman Hate – Evil!-harder still!'
  The magistrate cried, 'lay on with a will!
Drive out of their bodies the Father of Lies,
  Who through them preaches and prophesies!'

So into the forest they held their way,
  By winding river and frost-rimmed bay,
Over wind-swept hills that felt the beat
  Of the winter sea at their icy feet.

The Indian hunter, searching his traps,
  Peered stealthily through the forest gaps ;
And the outlying settler shook his head,
  'They're witches going to jail,' he said.

At last a meeting-house came in view;
  A blast on his horn the constable blew;
And the boys of Hampton cried up and down
'The Quakers have come !' to the wondering town.

From barn and woodpile the goodman came;
  The goodwife quitted her quilting frame,
With her child at her breast ; and, hobbling slow,
  The grandam followed to see the show.

Once more the torturing whip was swung,
  Once more keen lashes the bare flesh stung.
'Oh, spare! they are bleeding !' a little maid cried,
  And covered her face the sight to hide.

A murmur ran round the crowd: 'Good folks,'
Quoth the constable, busy counting the strokes,
  'No pity to wretches like these is due,
They have beaten the gospel black and blue !'

THE VIOLENT ABUSE OF WOMEN

Then a pallid woman, in wild-eyed fear,
With her wooden noggin of milk drew near.
    'Drink, poor hearts!' a rude hand smote
Her draught away from a parching throat.

'Take heed,' one whispered, 'they'll take your cow
For fines, as they took your horse and plough,
    And the bed from under you.' 'Even so,'
She said;'they are cruel as death, I know.'

Then on they passed, in the waning day,
Through Seabrook woods, a weariful way ;
    By great salt meadows and sand-hills bare,
And glimpses of blue sea here and there.

By the meeting-house in Salisbury town,
The sufferers stood, in the red sundown
    Bare for the lash! O pitying Night,
Drop swift thy curtain and hide the sight!

With shame in his eye and wrath on his lip
The Salisbury constable dropped his whip.
    'This warrant means murder foul and red;
Cursed is he who serves it,' he said.

'Show me the order, and meanwhile strike
A blow to your peril!' said Justice Pike.
    Of all the rulers the land possessed,
Wisest and boldest was he and best.

He scoffed at witchcraft; the priest he met
As man meets man; his feet he set
    Beyond his dark age, standing upright,
Soul-free, with his face to the morning light.

He read the warrant: 'These convey
From our precincts; at every town on the way
    Give each ten lashes.' 'God judge the brute!
I tread his order under my foot!

HOW THE WOMEN WENT FROM DOVER

'Cut loose these poor ones and let them go;
Come what will of it, all men shall know
No warrant is good, though backed by the Crown,
For whipping women in Salisbury town!'

The hearts of the villagers, half released
From creed of terror and rule of priest,
By a primal instinct owned the right
Of human pity in law's despite.

For ruth and chivalry only slept,
His Saxon manhood the yeoman kept;
Quicker or slower, the same blood ran
In the Cavalier and the Puritan.

The Quakers sank on their knees in praise
And thanks. A last, low sunset blaze
Flashed out from under a cloud, and shed
A golden glory on each bowed head.

The tale is one of an evil time,
When souls were fettered and thought was crime,
And heresy's whisper above its breath
Meant shameful scouring and bonds and death!

What marvel, that hunted and sorely tried,
Even woman rebuked and prophesied,
And soft words rarely answered back
The grim persuasion of whip and rack!

If her cry from the whipping-post and jail
Pierced sharp as the Kenite's[1] driven nail,
O woman, at ease in these happier days,
Forbear to judge of thy sister's ways!

How much thy beautiful life may owe
To her faith and courage thou canst not know,
Nor how from the paths of thy calm retreat
She smoothed the thorns with her bleeding feet.

Appendix B

'The Ducking Stool' 1780 – Benjamin West

This poem by Benjamin West was included in a collection of his 'Miscellaneous Poems, Translations and Imitations' published in 1780. It included a footnote indicated *: 'To the honour of the fair-sex in that neighbourhood, this machine has been taken down (as useless) several years'. West clearly didn't write the ode; the entry includes a note which shows it to be a much older piece: 'This piece (which has been written near sixty years), has been transmitted to the author by a friend, who assures him he has great reason to think it has never been printed. This, he hopes, will be a sufficient apology for admitting it into his miscellany.'

> Of all the wholesome acts we find
> Made for the use of womankind,
> There's none so useful as that law,
> which keeps their restless tongues in awe;
> For those curst evils, loud as thunder,
> Let loose would rend the world asunder.
> Of all the plagues on earth, we hold
> There's not a greater than a scold,
> Nor can the wisest mortal show,
> The method how to tame a shrew;
> Nor threats, nor promises avail
> Be kind, or cross, they're sure to rail;
>
> And if to blows or stripes you fly,
> That's but a useless remedy,
> For like the cobbler in the play,
> The more you beat, the more you may.
> There's yet a thing, but none of these
> Will yet their furious rage appease

'THE DUCKING STOOL' 1780 – BENJAMIN WEST

Though other methods can't prevail
This never yet was known to fail.

There stands, my friend, in yonder pool
An engine, called a 'Ducking Stool'
By legal power commanded down,
The joy, and terror of the town;
If jarring females kindle strife,
Give language foul, or lug the coif;
If noisy dames should once begin,
To drive the house with horrid din;
Away we cry, you'll grace the Stool,
We'll teach you how your tongue to rule.

The fair offender fills the seat
In sullen pomp, profoundly great,
Till some kind hand assists the Dame,
To take the fury off her flame;
Down in the deep the Stool descends
But here, at first, we miss our ends
She mounts again and rages more,
Than ever vixen did before.
So throwing water on the fire
Will make it burn but up the higher;
If so, my friend pray let her take
A second turn into the lake
And rather than your patient loose
Time and again repeat the dose;
No brawling wives, no furious wenches,
No fire so hot but water quenches.

In Prior's skilful lines we see
For these another recipe,
A certain lady, we are told,
(A lady too, and yet a scold)
Was very much relieved you'll say
By water, yet a different way
'Twas this, when'er the storm began
The patient tipped the harmless can,
A mouthful of the same she'd take,

161

THE VIOLENT ABUSE OF WOMEN

Sure not to scold, if not to speak,
At length the water all was gone,
The fits as bad as e're came on.

With R—y* wives it is not so,
Water we'll have what'er we do,
If this small pool our expectation fails,
The boundless Avon shall supply their tails.

Appendix C

Trial of Eleanor Beare 1732 – Sentenced to be Pilloried & Imprisoned

This is the full transcript of Eleanor Beare's trial as reported in *The Gentleman's Magazine* Vol. 2, August 1732, and which included a description of the first day of her punishment in the pillory. Today, a trial for these serious charges would occupy weeks of the court's time whereas this trial seems to have taken less than an hour, an indication of the summary justice dispensed to women by the eighteenth century courts. Examination of witnesses breaks almost every rule of modern legal process; the acceptance of 'heresay' evidence, character assassination, lack of cross examination etc.

Eleanor's escape from the pillory before the expiry of her allotted time was apparently possible due to the instrument being in a poor state of repair, rather than from any humane motives.

Indicted for the first time
Eleanor Merriman, now the Wife of Ebenezer Beare, indicted for a Misdemeanor, in endeavouring to persuade Nicholas Wilson to poison his Wife, and for giving him Poison for that End.

Indicted a second time
By the Name of Eleanor Beare, for a Misdemeanor, in destroying the Foetus in the Womb of Grace Belfort, by putting an iron Instrument up into her Body, and thereby causing her to miscarry.

Indicted a third time
For destroying the Foetus in the Womb of a certain Woman, to the Jury unknown, by putting an iron Instrument up her Body, or by giving her something to make her miscarry.

Pleaded Not Guilty.
Counsel for the King – Gentlemen of the Jury, you have heard the Indictment read, and I must observe to you, that the Crime for which the Prisoner stands indicted,

is an Offense of the highest Nature, next to Murder itself; it is the Instigation of a Man to kill his Wife, in the most secret Manner, in order to keep it from the Eyes of the World, and thereby to escape the Punishment due to such a Crime, by giving her Poison in Drink, of such a Nature, as should not work suddenly but my degrees, and thereby to kill her without any Suspicion of Murder; and it is owing to the good Providence of God, that the Man did not give his Wife the Poison, for if he had, and she had died, the Prisoner would have been tryed for the Murder.

Call Nicholas Wilson.

Court – Do you know the Prisoner? N Wilson – Yes

Court – How long? N Wilson – It is about 3 Years since I unfortunately met with the Prisoner at a Publick House at Wirksworth; after some Conversation, she told me I was young, and could not take my Liberty for fear of having Uneasiness with my Wife, but if I would be ruled by her, she would put me in a way to be rid of it. I ask'd her how? She said she would give me something to give my Wife in her Drink which would do her Job. I told her that we should both be hang'd. She said I need not fear that, for it would not kill her suddenly but by degrees, and that it would never be suspected. In a few Days I met with the Prisoner again, and she gave me something in a Paper to give my Wife in her Drink, and told me it would quickly do her Job. I took the Paper and buried it, and went Home and told my Wife what had pass'd between me and the Prisoner; and she desired me to keep out of her Company; and I have never seen her since, till now I see her at the Bar.

Prisoner – Did not you hire one Mary Tecmans to poison your Wife; and did not you receive some Poison (if it was Poison) from her, and afterwards send for me, and tell me the Stuff you had from Mary Tecmans would do no Good?

Evidence. [N Wilson] – No, I had the Stuff from you and no other, and I buried it as above.

Call John Wilson.

Court – What have you to say to the Prisoner?

J. Wilson – Since she was in Prison she sent for me, and told me she had something against my Brother which would touch his life, and desired he would keep out of the Way at the Assizes.

Counsel – Your Lordship will observe, that the Prisoner fearing Nicholas Wilson might be an Evidence against her, had that Contrivance to send him out of the Way.

Call Hannah Wilson.

H. Wilson – My Husband told me he had received something from the Prisoner, which she bid him give me in some Drink, and it would shut me quickly.

To the Second Indictment.

Counsel – Gentlemen, You have heard the Indictment read, and may observe, that the Misdemeanor for which the Prisoner stands indicted, is of a most shocking Nature; to destroy the Fruit in the Womb carries something in it so contrary to the natural Tenderness of the Female Sex, that I am amazed how ever any Woman should arrive at such a degree of Impiety and Cruelty, as to attempt it in such a manner as the Prisoner has done, it has really something so shocking in it, that I cannot well display the Nature of the Crime to you, but must leave it to the Evidence: It is cruel and barbarous to the last degree.

Call Grace Belford.

Grace Belford – I lived with the Prisoner as a Servant about ten Days, but was not hired, and I was off and on with her about fourteen Weeks: When I had been with her a few Days there came Company into the House, and made me drink Ale and Brandy (which I was not used to drink) and it overcame me; my Mistress sent me into the Stable to give Hay to some Horses, but I was not capable of doing it, so laid me down in the Stable; and three came to me one Christopher, a young Man that was drinking in the House, and after some Time I feared I was with Child by Christopher; upon that, my Mistress asked me if I was with Child, I told her I thought I was; Then she said if I could get 30 shillings from Christopher, she would clear me from the Child, without giving me Physick. A little Time after, some Company gave me Cyder and Brandy, my Mistress and I were both full of Liquor, and when the Company was gone, we could scarce get up the Stairs, but we did not get up; then I laid me on the Bed, and my Mistress brought a kind of Instrument, I took it to be like an Iron Skewer, and she put it up into my Body a great Way, and hurt me.

Court – What followed upon that?

Evidence. [Belford] – Some Blood came from me.

Court – Did you miscarry after that?

Evidence. [Belford] – The next Day after I went to Allestree, where I had a Miscarriage.

Court – What did the Prisoner do after this?

Evidence. [Belford] – She told me that the Job was done. I then lodged two or three Nights with one Ann Moseley (now Ann Oldknowles) and coming one Morning to see the Prisoner, I called for a Mug of Ale and drink it, and told her I was going Home; then came in John Clark, and on the Prisoner's saying I was going home, he said he would give me a Glass of Wine to help me forward, which accordingly he did, out of a Bottle he had in his Pocket, then I took my Leave of him; and when I was a little Way out of Town, I fell down at a Style, and was not well, I lay a little while, then got up, and went to Nottingham that Night.

Call Ann Oldknowles.

Court – Do you know of any Thing of Grace Belford having a Miscarriage?

Evidence. [Ann Oldknowles] – I know nothing, but when she lay with me, I saw all the Symptoms of Miscarriage on the Bed where she lay.

Call John Clark.

Court – Do you know the Prisoner?

Clark – Yes, I have frequented her House.

Court – Did you ever hear her say anything that she had used Means to make a Woman with Child miscarry, by putting any kind of Instrument up their Bodies, or by giving them anything to take inwardly?

Clark – Yes, I have.

Court – Have you seen her Instrument for that Purpose, or have you seen her use any Means to make any Woman with Child miscarry?

Clark – No, but I have heard her say she had done it, and that she then had under her one Hannish ——, whose other Name I know not.

Court – Have you heard her say she had been sent for these wicked Practices, or had any Reward for causing any one to miscarry?

Clark – I heard her say she had been once sent for to Nottingham, and, as I remember, she said she had five Pounds for the Journey.

Prisoner – Did not you say you never heard me say anything of using any Means to cause Miscarriage in any Person, or saw me use any Means for that End?

Clark – No, I said I never saw you do anything that Way, but had heard you say you had done it. Would you have me forswear myself?

Prisoner – No, but I would have you speak the Truth.

Clark – I do.

Then the Prisoner called several Persons to speak in her Behalf, but only two appeared, and they only gave her Friends a reputable Character, and said the Prisoner had had a good Education, but they knew nothing of the latter Part of her Life.

Mr Mayor – The Prisoner at the Bar has a very bad Character, and I have had frequent Complaints against her for keeping a disorderly House. Many Evidences were ready in Court to have proved the Facts she stood charg'd with in the third Indictment; but his Lordship observing that the second Indictment was proved so plainly, he thought there was no Necessity for going upon the third.

His Lordship summed up the Evidence in a very moving Speech to the Jury, wherein he said, he never met with a Case so barbarous and unnatural.

The Jury, after a short Consultation, brought the Prisoner in Guilty of both Indictments, and she received Sentence to stand on the Pillory, the Two next Market-Days, and to suffer dole Imprisonment for Three Years.

Derby, August 18, 1732. This Day Eleanor Beare, pursuant to her Sentence, stood for the first Time in the Pillory in the Marketplace; to which Place she was attended by several of the Sheriff's Officers; notwithstanding which, the Populace, to show their Resentment of the horrible Crimes wherein she has been charged, and the little Remorse she had shown since her Commitment, gave her no Quarter, but threw such quantities of Eggs, Turnips, Ect. that it was thought she would hardly have escap'd with her Life: She disengaged herself from the Pillory before her the Time of her standing was expired, and jump'd among the Crowd, whence she was with Difficulty carried back to Prison.

Appendix D

Trial of Elizabeth Cammell 1783 – Sentenced to be Severely Whipped & Hard Labour

This is the full transcript of the trial of Elizabeth Cammell, tried at the Old Bailey on 4 June 1783 for theft and grand larceny. The trial probably took less than an hour. Found guilty, she was sentenced to be severely whipped and then to be confined to hard labour for six months in the house of correction. A sentence of 'severe whipping' meant exactly that; eye witnesses to the severe whippings of Mary Hamilton in 1746 described how her back was so scarified by 'so many lashes' as to be completely flayed without an inch of skin remaining.

ELIZABETH CAMMELL was indicted for feloniously stealing, on the 16th day of May last, one silk handkerchief, value 12d. one canvas bag, value 1d. thirty-two pieces of gold coin of this realm called guineas, value 33 l. 12 s. and one shilling, value 12d. the property of Thomas Hunt.

THOMAS HUNT sworn.
I am a drover from Gloucester, on the 16th of last month, I lost a silk handkerchief and thirty-two guineas, and one shilling, I had been in Smithfield with a drove of cattle, and that was the money for them, which was my master's; it was in a yellow canvas bag; I met the prisoner in St Giles's next door to the Royal Oak: I went in there to have a pint of beer, and the prisoner was there, and drank two pints; it was then between ten and eleven: I went out, and the prisoner followed me, I went up to Oxford-market, and there had another pint of beer, she followed me, I stopped there sometime, and she followed me back to the house where I was at first; I could not get away from her, she pulled me into a passage next door to the Royal Oak, and robbed my pocket of the bag and thirty two guineas.

Court. Had you any criminal conversation with her? – *No, my Lord.*

What did you suffer her to attend you all the way? – *I could not get her away, she would follow me.*

167

Court. Could not you have resisted and prevented it if you had thought proper? – *I could not get the money out of her hand: This was about three in the morning.*

Court. Was you so long with this woman, and yet have no criminal conversation? – *I know nothing more then I tell you.*

But you was in liquor? – *No.*

What could you have been doing for four or five hours? – *That is all that I know about it.*

You had more than one pint? – *We had two pints at the first house, and one more at the other.*

Was you in a private room with her at Oxford-market? – *No, in a public room.*

Was any other company there? – *Yes.*

What public house, was it in Oxford-market? – *I cannot tell that.*

Which way did you go up the market? – *We turned to the right from Oxford-road.*

Court. Did you make no resistance? – *All that laid in my power, but I could not get the money, I called the watchman, and he came to my assistance, he took her up and shook her, and one guinea dropped out of her bosom, and another guinea was found in her pocket, and my handkerchief; the rest and the bag was never found; a woman came on her side.*

PRISONER'S DEFENCE.
He asked me to drink part of two pints of beer, I went up stairs with him, he said he had no money, and he gave me his handkerchief and some half-pence, a woman went out of the room, he pulled off his shoes, and I pulled off my stays, and we went to bed.

Court to Prosecutor. Is there any truth in all this? – *No.*

Jury. Did you ever give her this purse of yours? – *I told her I was going to Smithfield, I never took my purse out, I was as sober as I am this minute.*

You are sure you never went up stairs? – *No.*

Did you never kiss her all these five hours? – *I never touched her only setting by her.*

DENNIS M'CARTY sworn.

The prosecutor called out to me in Lawrence-lane, High-street, St Giles's, next door to the Royal Oak, that the prisoner had robbed him.

Court. What kind of character has the Royal Oak? – *There is a parcel of loose women there, the prosecutor said, the prisoner had pulled him in, and taken the handkerchief off his neck, and robbed him of almost 70 l. I took her, shook her, and one guinea dropped from her, and the other guinea I took out of her pocket, she was stretched down; the man was over her, I would not let her go at all; I would not believe he had so much money in his pocket, and he pulled out ten guineas and a 50 l. bank note out of his pocket; (The prosecutor deposes to the handkerchief, there was no person near me all the night but this girl.)*

Prisoner. *I was laying down, and the man was kicking me violently, and it was me that called out watch; I have no witnesses.*

Verdict: Guilty

Sentence: Let her have a severe whipping and be confined to hard labour six months in the house of correction.

Tried by the first Middlesex Jury before Mr Baron PERRYN.

Appendix E

Tariff of Corporal Punishments – Female Apprentices in Jamaica – 1858

Nearly forty years after the corporal punishment of women was made illegal in England, and despite a highly critical Parliamentary Report in 1838, the 'female apprentices' in the colony of Jamaica were still liable to be punished by whipping with a cat o'nine tails. This report followed numbers of reports of women in the colony being flogged;

Jamaica ss., St Catherine – Mary Ann Smith, apprentice to Turnbull's Pen, in the parish of St Catherine, being duly sworn, maketh oath and saith, that about the middle of last year she was sentenced by Mr Special Justice Moresby to punishment on the tread-mill in the house of correction of this parish, and that while undergoing the aforesaid punishment she was flogged with a cat on the legs by the driver thereof. Deponent further declares, that another woman was at the same time similarly punished by flogging.

Sworn before me, this seventeenth June 1838   Mary Ann Smith
(signed) Geo. Ousley Higgins   her X mark

This tariff was published on 10 February 1858 in *The British Emancipator*, a campaigning bi-monthly periodical of the period.

Offence	Punishment
Absence for 2 days in a fortnight	20 lashes
Refusing or neglecting labour	20 lashes
Willful negligence or damage to property	20 lashes
Drunkenness – 1st offence	20 lashes
Frivolous complaint	20 lashes
Absence for 3 successive days	30 lashes
Wandering without leave	30 lashes
Absence for 1 week	39 lashes
Insolence	39 lashes
Keeping firearms or gunpowder	39 lashes

TARIFF OF CORPORAL PUNISHMENTS

Insubordination	39 lashes
Drunkenness – 2nd offence	40 lashes
Endangering property by careless use of fire	50 lashes
Ill using of cattle	50 lashes
Injuring or destroying property	50 lashes
Combines resistance	50 lashes
Riotous assembly	50 lashes
Indolence/neglect/improper performance of work	50 lashes
Inferior misdemeanours	50 lashes

(It is worth noting that an act of Parliament in 1846 ordered that the maximum number of lashes with the 'cat o' nine tails' to which a serving soldier in the British army could be sentenced was to be no more than fifty.)

Appendix F

Seventeenth & Eighteenth Century Slang – Women's Bodies, Characters & Professions

This period coined a huge vocabulary of derogatory words specifically relating to women. Most of the terms are highly insulting and the majority relate to prostitution or a woman's allegedly dubious or unsavoury reputation. Although a word might relate specifically to a prostitute, it could and was used pejoratively against any woman by way of an insult. Given a little thought many are self-explanatory, however many more are of obscure origin and (perhaps fortunately) very few have survived into modern times. The list does not claim to be exhaustive.

Definitions are from a number of sources, including:
Dictionary of Canting & Thieving Tongue, Nathan Bailey 1736
Dictionary of the Vulgar Tongue, Francis Grose 1811
The Universal Etymological English Dictionary N. Bailey 1737
Many are quoted in *Words Like Daggers* Kirilka Stavrega. University of Nebraska 2015

ABBESS (also LADY ABBESS) – a mistress of a brothel who procured women for prostitution
ACADEMICIAN – a whore
APE LEADER – an old maid (it was commonly said that when she died she would be leading apes to hell for having neglected to increase and multiply the human race)
APPLE-DUMPLING SHOP – a woman's bosom, especially a substantial one
ARCH DOXEY – female leader of a gang of thieves or gypsies
ATHANASIAN WENCH – a girl who will do anything to oblige a man
AUNT – a procuress (see also ABBESS, MACKEREL, MOTHER)
AUTEM MORT – a woman with several children hired to elicit charitable donations
BAGGAGE – any woman, especially of perceived low morals
BARBER'S CHAIR – 'she is as common as a barber's chair'
BAWDY BASKETS – door to door sellers who mainly steal for a living

BAT – a low whore

BLEACHED MOTT – good looking woman/blond woman

BLOWEN – mistress of a thief or a woman cohabiting outside marriage

BLOWER – a whore

BOB TAIL – a lewd woman

BRIM (or BRIMSTONE) – an impudent lewd woman, a harridan

BUNDLE TAIL – a short fat woman

BUSHELL BUBBY – a full-breasted woman.

BUTTOCK – a whore

BUTTOCK & FILE – a thieving whore

CAMBRIDGE FORTUNE – a woman of no substance

CASE VROW (see also 'FROE') – prostitute attached to a particular whore-house

CAT – a whore

CLEAVE – a wanton woman

CLOVEN – woman who falsely claims to be a virgin

CLUCK(S) – a woman's propensity to playful conversation with men

COOLER – a woman generally

COMFORTABLE IMPORTANCE – a wife

CONVENIENCY/ CONVENIENT – a mistress, a woman with a regular man, a kept woman

COVENT GARDEN NUN – a whore

CRACK (CRACKISH) – a whore (whorish)

CURTEZAN – a whore (from the French 'courtisane' and/or from the obsolete Italian 'cortigiana' = female courtier)

DASHER – showy harlot (modern parlance 'to cut a dash' = put on a show)

DELLS – young women prone to venery but still virgins (Old English = young wench)

DIMBER MORT – a pretty woman

DIRTYHEELS – a whore

DOLLY – a drab, slattern, useless woman

DOXIE – a female beggar (prossibly from the Dutch 'docke' = doll)

DRAB (also DIRTY DRAB) – a whore or a slut

DRIGGLE-DRAGGLE – an untidy woman

DRAGGLETAIL – a whore

DRURY LANE VESTAL – a whore (London theatreland and then centre of the sex trade – the harlot of William Hogarth's *A Harlot's Progress* practiced her profession in Drury Lane, as did many others)

EVE'S CUSTOM HOUSE – a woman's private parts

EWE – a very beautiful woman

FAIR ROEBUCK – a good looking woman in her prime

FEN – a whore

FILTH – a whore

FLAP – a whore

FLASH PIECE OF MUTTON – older beautiful woman

FLIRT – any woman

FLORENCE – a tousled unkempt woman

FRIGATE (also FRIGATE WELL-RIGGED) – a well dressed and/or genteel woman

FROE – any sexual partner; wife, mistress or whore (from the Dutch 'Vrowe')

FUSSOCK – a lazy fat woman.

FUSTILUGS (also FUSTY LUGGS) – a dirty slattern, a nasty woman

GAME PULLET – a young whore

GENTRY MORT – a gentlewoman, a lady

GIGGLER – a wanton woman

GIMCRACK – a well set-up woman (Middle English 'gibecrake' = a cheap and showy ornament)

GILL – a whore

GILL-FLURT (FLIRT?) – a sluttish housewife

GUN POWDER – an old woman

HARLOT – a whore

HARRIDAN – a shrew or noisy old woman (from French: 'Haridelle' – worn out old horse)

HAT – a prostitutes private parts (i.e. they are frequently felt!)

HATCHET-FACE(D) – hard faced woman

HELL CAT – a very lewd woman

HEDGE-CREEPER – a whore, presumably a rural one

HIGH-FLYERS – impudent, forward women

HIGHTY-TIGHTY – a rude posing girl (survives in modern parlance as 'hoity-toity'?)

HOPPER-ARSED – large bottomed woman

HORSE GODMOTHER – a large, masculine woman

JADE – a bad tempered/disreputable woman (probably from French = an old/worn-out horse)

JILT – a deceiving woman (perhaps ancestor of modern 'jilted'?)

KINCHIN MOTT – under-age prostitute

LACED MUTTON – a whore or a particular woman

LADY BIRDS – light lewd women (perhaps ancestor of modern 'bird' = young woman)

LEFT-HANDED WIFE – a mistress.

LIGHT FRIGATE (also LIGHT CRUISER) – a whore

LOAD OF MISCHIEF – a wife

LONG MEG – a very tall woman

MACKEREL – a bawd (female brothel keeper)

MADAM RAN – a whore

MISS – a whore of quality (also any kept woman)

MISTRESS PRINCUM (also PRANCIUM) – a stiff, over-nice or precise woman

SEVENTEENTH & EIGHTEENTH CENTURY SLANG

Mob – a wench or harlot

Moll (also Mollisher) – a whore or woman in general

Mopsie (also Mopsey) – a dowdy or homely woman

Mort(s) – all women generally

Mother (see also Abbess, Aunt, mackerel) – a bawd (female brothel keeper)

Mott – a whore

Natural – (see also Convenient, Peculiar) a woman with a regular man, a kept woman

Naughty-pack – a whore

Peculiar – a mistress, a woman with a regular man, a kept woman

Pennycunt – a cheap whore

Pintle-merchant – a whore (probably from Old English pintel = penis)

Piper's wife – a whore

Platter-Faced – plain looking woman

Poisoned – the condition of a pregnant woman

Public ledger – a whore (i.e. anyone can make an entry)

Prime Article – a good looking young woman

Punk – a whore of small stature

Pure (also Purest-Pure) – a top mistress or very fine woman

Queere Doxy (also Queere Mort) – shabby/dirty/drab/sexually infected woman

Receiver General – a whore

Rum Blowen – whore kept by a particular man/beautiful woman

Rum Dell (also Doxy, Dutchess, Mort) – a very handsome woman

Scab – a sorry worthless woman (also a male scoundrel)

Screw – a whore

Short-Heeled Wench (i.e. a woman prone to falling on her back!) – a whore or any woman of low moral standards

Slut – a whore or any woman of low morals

Squirrel (tailed) – a whore

Squirt – a whore

Stale Maid – a dying woman

Stammel (also Strammel) – a brawny or lusty woman

Strumpet – a whore or any woman of easy virtue

Sue Pouch – a hostess or landlady

Tail (squirrel) – a whore

Tallow-breeched – woman having a large bottom

Thornback – an old maid

Tib – a young girl

Trapes (also Traipes) – a slatternly woman (First recorded as 'traipse' late seventeenth century)

Tart Dame – sharp, quick, witty or pert woman

THE VIOLENT ABUSE OF WOMEN

TRIGRY MATE – an idle female companion

TROT – a poor old woman

TRUG – an ordinary sorry looking woman (late Middle English denoting a basin)

TRULL – a whore also a Tinker's woman (from the German 'Trulle' = prostitute)

VAN NECK – a woman with large breasts

VIRAGO – a masculine woman (from the Latin word 'vir', meaning 'man' hence 'virile')

WAGTAIL – a lewd woman

WASP – whore infected with a disease (i.e. a sting in the tail)

WENCH – young usually subservient or servant girl

WHITHER-GO-YE (also WHITHER D'YE GO) – a wife

WIFE IN WATER COLOURS – a mistress

WYCH – a witch

XANTHIPPE – a scolding or shrewish wife (after the wife of Socrates)

Epithets commonly employed in conjunction with many of the pejorative verbs:
Base; Common, Arrant; Strong; Tempting; Palsie-headed; Curtailed (i.e. Cart-Tailed; has been whipped at the cart's tail, a common punishment for prostitutes); Impudent; Dirty; Drunken; Copper-nosed (i.e. has lost own nose due to venereal disease and has a false one) Pissabed; Scurvy; Rascal; Stinking; Platter-faced; Filthy

Appendix G

Women Burned at the Stake 1721–1789

All of these women were burned at the stake as punishment of a crime for which a man would simply have been hanged. This is because the murder of a 'superior' such as a husband or master, the forging (counterfeiting) of money or the clipping of gold or silver coins (coining) were classed as 'Petty Treason' if committed by a woman. There are three teenagers and one woman of eighty among those so executed. At least fourteen of these women had male co-defendant(s) in their case who were hanged at the same time as the women were burned, in the case of Phoebe Harris – six, and Catherine Murphy, no less than seven.

Name:	Date Executed:	Location:	Crime:
Barbara Spenser	5 July 1721	Tyburn, London	Counterfeiting
Catherine Hayes*	9 May 1726	Tyburn, London	Murder of Husband
Elizabeth Wright	19 December 1733	Tyburn, London	Coining
Mary Haycock }			
Elizabeth Tracey } 3 executed	2 October 1734	Tyburn, London	Coining
Catherine Bougle}			
Margaret Onion	8 August 1735	Chelmsford	Murder of Husband
Mary Fawson (aged 19)	8 August 1735	Northampton	Murder of Husband
Ann Mudd	25 June 1737	Tyburn, London	Murder of Husband
Mary Bird	1 July 1737	Ely	Murder of Husband
Mary Grote (or Troke) (aged 16)	18 March 1738	Winchester	Murder of Mistress
Ann Goodson*	12 April 1738	Guildford	Murder of Husband
Susannah Broom (aged 67)	21 December 1738	Tyburn, London	Murder of Husband
Elizabeth Moreton	10 August 1744	Evesham	Murder of Husband
Mary Johnson	? April 1747	Lincoln	Murder of Husband
Amy Hutchinson*	7 November 1749	Ely	Murder of Husband
Elizabeth Packard	?/?/ 1750	Exeter	Murder of Husband
Ann Whale (aged 21)	8 August 1752	Horsham	Murder of Husband
Ann Williams*	13 April 1753	Over, Gloucestershire	Murder of Husband

Susannah Bruford (aged 19)	3 September 1753	Wells	Murder of Husband
Mary Ellah	28 March 1757	York	Murder of Husband
Alice Davis*	31 March 1758	Tyburn, London	Coining
Mary Larny*	2 October 1758	Tyburn, London	Coining
Mary Hilton (or Hutton)	6 April 1762	Lancaster	Murder of Husband
Margaret Beddingfield*	8 April 1763	Ipswich	Murder of Husband
Mary Heald	23 April 1763	Chester	Murder of Husband
Mary Saunders	21 March 1764	Monmouth	Murder of Mistress
Mary Norwood	8 April 1765	Ilchester, Somerset	Murder of Husband
Ann Sowerby	10 August 1767	York	Murder of Husband
Susannah Lott*	21 July 1769	Maidstone	Murder of Husband
Mary Hilton	6 April 1772	Lancaster Moor	Murder of Husband
Elizabeth Herring	13 September 1773	Tyburn, London	Murder of Husband
Margaret Ryan	18 March 1776	Maidstone	Murder of Husband
Elizabeth Boardingham*	30 March 1776	York	Murder of Husband
Ann Cruttenden (aged 80)	8 August 1776	Horsham	Murder of Husband
Isabella Condon*	27 October 1779	Tyburn, London	Coining
Rebecca Downing	29 July 1782	Exeter	Murder of Master
Mary Bailey*	8 March 1784	Winchester	Murder of Husband
Phoebe Harris*	21 June 1786	Newgate, London	Coining
Margaret Sullivan*	25 June 1788	Newgate, London	Coining
Catherine Murphy* (alias Christian Bowman)	18 March 1789	Newgate, London	Coining

*Woman had one or more male co-defendants who were hanged.

Appendix H

A Woman's Tyburn 'Hanging Day'

What did a public hanging at Tyburn involve and what could the unfortunate condemned expect? Through the eighteenth century there were up to eight 'hanging days' a year, when up to 200,000 people would turn out to watch either the procession from the prison to the gallows (along what is now Oxford Street) or the actual executions. The gallows at Tyburn consisted of three tall uprights joined at the top with beams in the form of a triangle. Usually three carts would arrive, each containing up to eight condemned prisoners, and they would arrange themselves so that each cart stood under a separate beam.

A woman to be put to death would be transferred from the court to Newgate prison, to await the next 'hanging day'. If she was lucky, the Recorder of London would include her in his report to the king and Privy Council with a recommendation for mercy, perhaps because she had shown herself to be pregnant. If her sentence was commuted to transportation, she would eventually be transferred to one of the prison ships lying at Gravesend, otherwise she would find herself in the 'condemned hold' to await her fate.

She would have access to the 'Ordinary' or prison chaplin, and she would attend Sunday services, where condemned criminals had a special area in the centre of the chapel, surrounded by a high partition so that they could not be seen by or communicate with the other prisoners.

When the fateful day arrived she would be brought to the Press Yard of Newgate where the noose was placed around her neck and her arms tied to the sides of her body. She and her fellow prisoners would be lifted into the cart where each of them had a coffin upon which to sit and in which they were destined to spend eternity. Thus assembled, the procession of carts, accompanied by the prison Chaplin, the hangman and his assistants and a guard of 'javelin men', would set out on its two and a half mile journey to the gallows. The journey included several stops along the way; first at the church of St Sepulchre where the bell would be tolled and the priest would extort the prisoners: 'You that are condemned to die, repent with lamentable tears; ask mercy of the Lord for the salvation of your souls.' Relatives and friends of the condemned might present them with nosegays of flowers as the priest addressed the onlookers: 'All good people, pray heartily unto God for these poor sinners who are now going to their death, for whom the great bell tolls.' Further halts were made at two public houses along the way, thought most likely to be the 'Bowl Inn' at St Giles and the 'Mason's Arms' in Seymour Place, where the prisoners, presumably released from their bonds, would be allowed to drink what was sometimes quite a large quantity of alcohol in order to provide some respite from the horror that awaited them.

Around three hours after they had left Newgate, the procession would arrive at Tyburn around noon, where a boisterous crowd of thousands of spectators awaited them. The hapless woman's cart would be backed under one of the three beams of the gallows and the hangman would throw the uncoiled end of her rope up to one of his assistants balanced precariously astride on the beam above. They would pull the rope taut and tie it securely off. The priest would say his last prayers with the prisoners and get down from the cart. If the woman had been able to purchase one, or had been given one by friends, the hangman would pull a night cap over her face before tightening the noose.

Everything in readiness, the City Marshall would signal the drivers and the horses would be whipped away, leaving the prisoners dangling by their necks in mid-air. A great cheer would go up as the prisoners writhed in agony, twisting and turning with their legs paddling in empty space, a dance referred to in the macabre humour of the time, as the 'Tyburn Jig'. It might take several minutes before the merciful end to their suffering came, and the friends and relatives (and sometimes the hangman and his assistants if they had been adequately bribed) might hang on the legs of the sufferers, in order to hasten the moment of release. The bodies would be left hanging for up to thirty minutes before the relatives could claim them for burial, or they could be removed by the surgeon's men if their sentence had included dissection.

Appendix I

Benefit of Clergy

Through the mechanism of benefit of clergy, many defendants found guilty of certain felonies were spared the death penalty and given a lesser punishment. Dating back to the middle ages, benefit of clergy was originally a right accorded to the church, allowing it to punish its own members should they be convicted of a crime. In this instance the court did not prescribe any punishment for the defendant and instead handed him over to church officials.

Since it was difficult to prove who was affiliated with the church, convicts who claimed benefit of clergy were required to read a passage from the Bible. Judges usually chose verses from the 51st Psalm, which was termed the 'neck verse', since it saved many people from hanging.

As literacy became more common outside the church, the practice gradually developed of permitting all men convicted of allowable felonies to be permitted benefit of clergy if they could read the 'neck verse'. This test was a flexible one, and judges could be lenient or strict in their choice of text and level of literacy required, depending on whether they wished to impose the sentence in a specific case, or not.

It was not until 1623 that women found guilty of the theft of goods less than ten shillings in value were also allowed benefit of clergy, and it was even later in 1691 that women were granted the privilege on the same terms as men.

Benefit of clergy remained for some offences, however, until the reforms of the criminal laws, and dramatic reduction in the number of capital statutes in the 1820s. It was abolished in 1827.[1]

Appendix J

Relative Value of Money

There are many references throughout this work to the wages paid to servants, the price of goods purchased or the fines levied in the courts of law and by any modern standard these seem to be extraordinarily low. In 1663, Samuel Pepys complained that due to a shortage in the market, he was obliged to pay wages of £4 per year in order to hire a cook maid. This was not exceptional; during the two centuries covered by this work wages for women could range from £4 and £8 for a housemaid, and up to £15 per annum for a skilled housekeeper. Higher up the social scale a footman could expect to earn £8 per year, and a coachman between £12 and £26 (although servants would also have received their board and lodging from their employer).

However, the purchasing power of monetary units was much higher in the period covered by this work, during which both wages and prices remained relatively stable. There are many different formulae for calculating the relative value of money between then and now and the results they achieve often vary widely. Simply multiplying historic values by some form of retail price index can be misleading; the relative cost of many commodities, including labour, has changed dramatically as supply and demand is now very different. For example, the eighteenth-century First Lord of the Treasury earned £4,000 per annum against a coachman's £26, a factor of almost 154 times as much. In the first quarter of the twenty-first century, the minimum legal wage equates to approximately £15,000 per annum against that of a Cabinet Minster earning £135,000, a factor of only nine times as much.

A more useful illustration of relative values can perhaps be made by comparing how much the seventeenth-century individual needed to spend on essentials, against the same measure for a twenty-first century British citizen. An early statistician Gregory King (1648–1712) compiled a work entitled *Natural and Political Observations upon the State and Conditions of England 1696* which gives a weekly cost of food per individual of 1s 3¾d (nearly 16d), equivalent to slightly less than the modern 7p. This weekly sum is further broken down into bread 3½d; meat and fish 4¼d; Dairy produce 2d; Beer 4d; vegetables, fruit, salt, pickles and other groceries 2d. All this adds up to an annual housekeeping bill for food of less than £4, which makes the wages of Pepys's maid seem much less miserly!

However, King's figures take no account of items whose status has changed over the intervening period and which demonstrate the danger in simply applying indexes; a chicken, a relatively cheap foodstuff in the twenty-first century, cost up to 1s 4d in 1634[1] equivalent to more than a week's housekeeping in his 1696 study, or the £55 spent weekly by a family on food and non alcoholic drink in 2016.[2]

Bibliography

de la Bédoyère, Guy, *Particular Friends – The Correspondence of Samuel Pepys & John Evelyn* Boydell Press 1997

Blaugdone, Barbara, *An Account of the Travels, Sufferings & Persecutions of Barbara Blaugdone* 'TS' Shoreditch 1691

Blodgett, Harriet, *Centuries of Female Days* Alan Sutton 1989

Boswell, James, *London Journal 1762-63* Heinemann 1950

Burford, E.J., *Wits, Wenchers and Wantons – London's Low Life* Hale 1986

Buxton, Antony, *Domestic Culture in Early Modern England* The Boydell Press 2015

Burford & Shulman, *Of Bridles & Burnings* St Martin's Press 1992

Camden, Carroll, *The Elizabethan Woman 1540-1640* Cleaver-Hume Press 1952

Crawford, Patricia, *Women in Early Modern England* Clarendon Press 1998

Dabhoiwala, Faramerz, *The Origins of Sex* OUP USA 2012

Donagan, Barbara, *War in England 1642-1649* OUP 2008

Eriksson, Brigitte, 'A Lesbian Execution in Germany 1721' *Journal of Homosexuality* Vol.6 1981 1-2

Evelyn, John, *Fumifugium or The Smoake of London 1661* Ashmolean Museum, Oxford (Reprint) 1930

Fox, Vivian C. 'Historical Perspectives on Violence against Women' *Journal of International Women's Studies'* Vol.4 Bridgewater State University November 2002

Hardy, William & Reckitt, Geoffrey (eds.) *County of Buckinghamshire Session Records. 1694-1712* Aylesbury County Council 1939

Harris, Tim, *Restoration – Charles II and his Kingdoms* Alan Lane 2002

Henri, Edwin J. *Kiss of the Whip* Walton Press 1961

Hughes, Robert *The Fatal Shore* Collins Harvill 1987

Kenyon, Olga *Women's Voices* Constable 1995

Lamb, Jeremy *So Idle a Rogue* Allison & Busby 1993

Latham, R&L *A Pepys Anthology* Unwin Hyman 1987

Laurence, Anne *Women in England 1500-1760* Weidenfeld & Nicolson 1994

Linnan, Fergus *London – The Wicked City: A Thousand Years of Prostitution and Vice* Robson Books 2003

BIBLIOGRAPHY

Latham & Matthews *The Diary of Samuel Pepys. 11 volumes* G.Bell & Sons 1971–76

Lonsdale, R (ed.) *Eighteenth Century Women Poets* Oxford University Press 1989

Malay, Dr Jessica *The Case of Mistress Mary Hampson* Stanford University Press 2014

Mendelson, Sara & Crawford, Patricia *Women in Early Modern England* Clarendon Press 1998

Mendelson, Sara & Moore, Wendy *Wedlock: The True Story of the Disastrous Marriage & Remarkable Divorce of Mary Eleanor Bowes, Countess of Strathmore* Crown 2009

Mortimer, Ian *The Time Traveller's Guide to Restoration Britain* Bodley Head 2017

Norton, Rictor (ed.) *Early Eighteenth-Century Newspaper Reports (A Sourcebook)* April 2002

Norton, Rictor (ed.) *Homosexuality in Eighteenth-Century England (A Sourcebook)* December 2003

Paulson, Ronald *Hogarth's Harlot: Sacred Parody in Enlightenment England* John Hopkins UP 2003

Philip, Neil *Working Girls – An Illustrated History of the Oldest Profession.* Bloomsbury Pub. Ltd. 1991

Reinhard, Wilhelm *Nell in Bridewell (Lenchen im Zuchthause)* Luxor Press 1967

Robbins, Rossel Hope *Encyclopedia of Witchcraft & Demonology* Crown Publishers NY 1959

Shevelow, Kathryn *Charlotte* Henry Holt & Co 2005

Stavreva, Kirilka *Words Like Daggers* University of Nebraska 2015

Stone, Lawrence *Road to Divorce* OUP 1990

Weekly, Ernest *An Etymological Dictionary of Modern English* Dover Publications NY Inc. 1967

Williams, Noel St John *Judy O'Grady & the Colonel's Lady* Brassey's Defence Pub. 1988

Van Yelyr, Prof. R.G. *The Whip and the Rod* Longmans Green 1941

Notes

Introduction

1. Letter to Samuel Pepys from John Evelyn dated 29 July 1685
2. *Centuries of Female Days* Harriet Blodgett, Alan Sutton 1989
3. *Discourse of the Sovereign Power* Rev. Dr George Hickes 1642–1715
4. *The Schole House of Women* attrib. Edward Gosynhill 1541
5. *England as Seen by Foreigners in the Days of Elizabeth & James the First* William B.Rye 1865

Chapter 1 – Domestic Violence

1. *Marriage in seventeenth century England: The Woman's Story* Alice Brabcová. University of West Bohemia
2. *The Whip & the Rod* Professor R.G. Van Yelyr 1941
3. *Origin and Growth of the Moral Instinct* Alexander Sutherland 1898
4. *Regulation on Domestic Violence in Seventeenth Century Moldavia & Walachia.* Cosmind Ariesco, University of Iasi, Romania
5. *A Plain & Compendious Relation of the Case of Mrs Mary Hampson* 1682
6. *Justice in Eighteenth-century Hackney: The Justicing Notebook of Henry Norris and the Hackney Petty Sessions Book* London Record Society 1991
7. *Stripping, Whipping and Pumping, Or, the Five Mad Shavers of Drury Lane* John Taylor Printed by J.O., London 1638
8. Middlesex County Records Sessions Book 472 February 1690. Originally published by Middlesex County Record Society, London, 1905
9. Sessions Book 649 May 1707. Originally published by Middlesex County Record Society, London, 1905
10. Quoted in *Old Time Punishments* William Andrews. London 1890
11. National Archive – Middlesex County Records Session Book 472, February 1690

Chapter 2 – Sexual Abuse

1. Chapbooks were small booklets, cheap to make and to buy. They provided simple reading matter and were commonplace across the country from the seventeenth to the nineteenth century.(British Library)

2. *Women in England 1500–1760* Anne Laurence, Weidenfeld & Nicolson 1994
3. Letter to Samuel Pepys from John Evelyn, dated 29 July 1685
4. *Women in the World of Pepys - Plague, Fire & Revolution* Laura Gowing, Thames & Hudson 2015
5. *Women in Early Modern England* Mendelson & Crawford, Clarendon Press 1998
6. *Rape in England 1600–1800* Rebecca Frances King, Durham Thesis, Durham University 1998
7. *Sexual Underworlds of the Enlightenment* Antony E. Simpson, Manchester University Press, 1987
8. The average income of a male servant at this time was about £2.25p per annum, so the damages awarded to Agnes Griffin would probably have kept her fed for a month.
9. weaponsandwarfare.com/2015/09/20/mercenaries-in-the-english-civil-wars
10. 27PROAssi 45/21/2/44B
11. *War in England 1642-1649* Barbara Donagan Oxford University Press 2008
12. *The Civil Wars: A Military History of England, Scotland, and Ireland, 1638-1660* Charles Carlton, Oxford University Press 1998
13. *Rape & Resistance: Women & Consent in Seventeenth Century Legal & Political Thought* Prof. Julia Rudolf. Cambridge University Press 2000
14. In modern times, the term 'age of consent' refers to the age at which a girl or boy can legally consent to sexual intercourse, whereas in the period that is the subject of this book the term referred only to the age at which one could consent to marriage. The reason for this is that, until relatively recent times, sex outside marriage was an offence in law regardless of age.

Chapter 3 – Libel & Slander

1. Nothing has changed in the subsequent three centuries – one online twenty-first century slang dictionary lists 205 generally derogatory terms for women.
2. *The Smoake of London* John Evelyn 1661
3. *London Journal* James Boswell 1762–63

Chapter 4 – Abduction & Clandestine Marriage

1. *History of the Fleet Marriages* John Southerden Burn 1846
2. www.oldbaileyonline.org

Chapter 5 – The Smart of the Lash

1. Old Bailey Proceedings 11 December 1678
2. Caption under a portrait of King Edward VI in the chapel of the palace
3. In 1866, the Howard League for Penal Reform was founded in his honour

4. Middlesex Sessions: Sessions Papers – Justices' Working Documents. June 1761
5. *The Hesperides & Noble Numbers* Robert Herrick 1591–1674
6. Bridewell Royal Hospital: Minutes of the Court of Governors 8th September 1699
7. *Lenchen im Zuchthause* Wilhelm Reinhard, Germany 1840
8. County of Middlesex. Calendar To the Sessions Records: New Series, Volume 4, 1616-18. Originally published by Clerk of the Peace, London, 1941
9. Middlesex County Records. Calendar of Sessions Books 1689-1709. Originally published by Middlesex County Record Society, London, 1905
10. Middlesex Sessions: Sessions Papers – Justices' Working Documents February 1715
11. Minute Books of the General Prison Committee, Bridewell Royal Hospital 1792–1802
12. Buckinghamshire Session Records – Epiphany Session 1708–09
13. Bridewell Calender – Buckinghamshire Quarter Sessions Book vol.7 1709
14. Buckinghamshire Session Records – Epiphany Session 1708–09
15. *From England's Bridewell to America's Brides* – Alice Meyer - Nebraska University, Thesis 2015
16. Bridewell Royal Hospital: Minute Books of the General Prison Committee 8th May 1799
17. Buckinghamshire Session Records 1694-1707)
18. Historical Collections of Private Passages of State: Volume 3, 1639–40. Originally published by D. Browne, London, 1721
19. The British Gazetteer January 1725
20. Appleby Indictment Book 1791
21. Lawrence M. Friedman 'History of American Law' 1973

Chapter 6 – Burned Alive

1. James Oldham, 'On Pleading the Belly: A History of the Jury of Matrons' Criminal Justice. History 6, 1985
2. Gregory J. Durston – Wicked Ladies: Provincial Women, Crime and the Eighteenth-Century English Justice System. Cambridge Scholars Publishing 2013
3. Middlesex County Records: Volume 3 1625–67. Originally published by Middlesex County Record Society, London, 1888

Chapter 7 – An Exiled World

1. The actual number could well be even higher as some of the records are acknowledged to be defective.
2. Letter from Michael Hayes to his sister Mary 2 November 1802, ML, Sydney

3. Report of Ernest Augustus Slade 1837. Quoted in 'The Fatal Shore' Robert Hughes, Collins Harvill 1987
4. www.janesoceania.com/australia_convicts
5. Tasmanian Archive Historical Office, AC480/1/1
6. Historical Records of NSW Volume 2 Appendix E. p779-80
7. trove.nla.gov.au/newspaper/article/71623595
8. Accounts & Papers relevant to the Abolition of Slavery – Sagwan Press 2016

Chapter 8 – At the Mercy of the Mob

1. Rarer forms of the pillory trap the fingers in a wooden block, using an L-shaped hole to keep the knuckle bent inside the block, was often used by ecclesiastical courts for punishing minor offences such as sleeping in church.
2. Crime, Punishment, and Reform in Europe' Ed. Mary Anne Nichols & Louis A. Knafla, Praeger 2003
3. Ronald Paulson – Hogarth's Harlot: Sacred Parody in Enlightenment England. Johns Hopkins University Press 2003
4. St James's Chronicle 29–31 October 1761

Chapter 9 – Locked in the Cage

1. Burford & Shulman 'Of Bridles & Burning' St Martin's Press 1992
2. 'Cuckynge' is derived from the Old English word for defecation – originally the victim would have remained on the 'cuckynge-stool' for many hours, probably needing to utilise the large hole in the centre with which the device was usually furnished

Chapter 10 – Hot Iron and Cold Steel

1. www.oldbaileyonline.org

Chapter 11 – Hanged by the 'Bloody Code'

1. 'Treatise on the Law, Privileges, Proceedings and Usage of Parliament' Charles Knight & Co 1844
2. 'Wicked Ladies – Provincial Women, Crime & the Eighteenth Century Justice System' Gregory J. Durston. Cambridge Scholars Publishing 2013
3. 'The Devil's Children: A History of Childhood and Murder' Loretta Loach. Icon Books 2011

Chapter 12 – Male Impersonators & Female Actors

1. London Chronicle 7 February 1760
2. Fog's Weekly Journal – 15 October 1737

3. Francis Grose 1731?-1791 – Antiquities of England & Wales
4. Quoted in 'A Lesbian History of Britain, Love and Sex between Women since 1500' Rebecca Jennings – Greenwood World Publishing 2007
5. Brigitte Eriksson – 'A Lesbian Execution in Germany 1721: The Trial Records' – 1985
6. Rictor Norton. (Ed.) Homosexuality in Eighteenth-Century England: A Sourcebook. 2003
7. Tim Hitchcock – 'English Sexualities, 1700-1800' Macmillan Press, 1997.
8. Ten pounds would have bought you a horse in 1620
9. Claudia Durst Johnson. 'Church and Stage: The Theatre as Target of Religious Condemnation in Nineteenth Century America' 2007

Chapter 13 – Seen but not Heard

1. James Boswell 'The Life of Samuel Johnson' 1791
2. Ralph Gardiner 'England's grievance discovered in relation to the coal-trade … The tyrannical oppression of those magistrates, their charters and grants, the several tryals, depositions, and judgements obtained against them' 1655
3. 'The Lamb's Defense against Lyes' – Dorothy Waugh 1656. Quoted in 'Renaissance Woman – A Source Book' Kate Aughterson (ed.) 2003
4. 'Newes from Scotland, Declaring the Damnable Life of Dr. Fian, a Notable Sorcerer', pamphlet published in 1591
5. Records of the Town of East-Hampton, 1639–80
6. John Winthrop 1587-1649 – History of New England
7. Parish of Montgomery & Pool Workhouse Officer's Reports Book

Chapter 14 – Gracing the Stool

1. Quoted in 'A Pepysian Garland' – Hyder E. Rollins. Harvard University Press 1971
2. 'Commentaries on the Laws of England' Sir William Blackstone, Clarendon Press, Oxford, 1765–69
3. Quoted in 'Atheneum or Spirit of the English Magazine' Apr – Oct 1817. Boston
4. 'Mémoires et Observations faites par un Voyageur en Angleterre'- Francis Misson 1698
5. London Journal 27th December 1729
6. The Gentleman's Magazine and Historical Chronicle, 1687 Volume 223
7. William Waller Hening (Ed) 'The Statutes at Large; Being a Collection of all the Laws of Virginia from the First Session of the Legislature, in the Year 1619' R. & W. & G. Bartow New York, 1823
8. The American Historical Record Vol.1 Chase & Town 1872

9. Alice Morse Earle 'Curious Punishments of Bygone Days' Herbert S. Stone 1846
10. State of New Jersey v. Marion Palendrano, Superior Court of New Jersey, Law Division (Criminal) 13 July 1972.

Chapter 15 – Religious Belief: Persecution & Punishment

1. 'An Account of the Travels, Sufferings & Persecutions of Barbara Blaugdone, Given as a Testimony of the Lord's Power, and for the Encouragement of Friends' 1691
2. Richard & Mary Overton 'The Commoner Complaint; or, A Dreadful Warning from Newgate' 1647
3. Larry Joseph Kreitzer – 'Seditious Sectaryes – The Baptist Conventiclers of Oxford 1641-1691' Paternoster Press 2006
4. 'The Friend' Quaker periodical December 1846
5. 'The First New Persecution' London 1654. Quoted in Kate Peters 'Print Culture & Early Quakers' Cambridge University Press 2005
6. An Abstract of the Sufferings of the People called Quakers 1733
7. 'The Friend' Quaker periodical December 1846
8. William Sewell 'The History of the Rise, Increase and Progress of the Christian People called Quakers' 1834
9. William Sewell 'The History of the Rise, Increase and Progress of the Christian People called Quakers' 1834
10. Prof. R.G. Van Yelyr 'The Whip & the Rod' Gerald G. Swan 1941
11. William Sewell 'The History of the Rise, Increase and Progress of the Christian People called Quakers' 1834

Chapter 16 – Suffer a Witch

1. Pamphlet 'Newes from Scotland, Declaring the Damnable Life of Dr Fian, a Notable Sorcerer' 1591 and was subsequently published in King James's dissertation on contemporary necromancy titled '*Daemonologie*' in 1597.

Chapter 17 – Military Wives & Camp Followers

1. 'The King's Own (4th Foot) -The Story of a Regiment' Colonel Cowper, O.U.P 1939
2. 'Living History' – 2nd Battalion 95th Rifles
3. 'The Tangier Papers of Samuel Pepys' 1935 Volume LXXIII E. Chappell
4. Grose – 'Military Antiquities' 1786
5. Lacourcière 1968, p. 239
6. Louis Fréchette, 'Une Relique – La Corriveau', Almanach du Peuple 1913
7. Scott Claver – 'Under the Lash, A History of Corporal Punishment in the British Armed Forces' Torchstream Books 1954

8. Charles P. Neimeyer 'America Goes to War: A Social History of the Continental Army' New York University Press, 1996
9. General Edward Braddock's Orderly Books 1755 Pub. 1878 – MOD Library
10. Jack Russell – 'Gibraltar Besieged'. Heinemann 1965
11. Calendar of State Papers Colonial, America and West Indies: Volume 23, 1706–1708. HM Stationery Office 1916
12. R.E. Scouler, 'Armies of Queen Anne' Oxford Clarendon Press 1966
13. 82nd Regiment of Foot – Punishment Book for Barrack Women 1866-1891

Chapter 19 – The 'Whipping Toms'

1. Diary of Samuel Pepys 1 October 1666
2. *Morning Chronicle* 22 February 1838
3. *Morning Post* 7 March 1838

Chapter 20 – Growing Distaste & Abolition

1. *The Times* 24 June 1788
2. *The Times* 23 June 1786
3. 30 Geo 3 c 48
4. Buckinghamshire Session Records–Epiphany Session 1701-2
5. Truro Quarter Sessions 1759
6. *The London Spy* periodical Ned Ward 1698–1703
7. Old Bailey Sessions Papers – Justices' Working Documents 1783
8. Montgomery and Pool Workhouse Minute Book 1797
9. *Inverness Journal* 14 March 1817
10. 57 Geo.3 c.75
11. 1 Geo. IV. c. 57
12. Returns for the Island of Jamaica Gaols & Workhouses – Despatch from the Earl of Belmore to the Rt.Hon. George Murray 1 December 1829
13. Parliamentary Report 1838: Negro Apprenticeships in the British Colonies

Appendix A – How the Women went from Dover

1. The tribe from which the father-in-law of Moses was a member and which lived in the area between southern Palestine and the mountains of Sinai.

Appendix I – Benefit of Clergy

1. www.oldbaileyonline.org

Appendix J – Relative Value of Money

1. Sara Paston-Williams 'The Art of Dining' 1993
2. Family spending in the UK: financial year ending March 2016, ONS

Index